Towards a History of
Archaeology

Towards a History of Archaeology

*Being the papers read at the first
Conference on the History of Archaeology
in Aarhus, 29 August – 2 September 1978*

EDITED BY

GLYN DANIEL

THAMES AND HUDSON

To the memory of Ole Klindt-Jensen

**Printed and bound in Great Britain by
William Clowes (Beccles) Limited, Beccles and London**

Contents

Preface
GLYN DANIEL

My dear friend, Professor Ole Klindt-Jensen, who died suddenly on 13 June 1980, and I had many interests in common and not least was the history of archaeology. We both believed, as Professor Robin Collingwood did, that no issue in archaeology should be studied without discussing its history. And many years ago we thought of having a Conference on the History of Archaeology, and this did indeed happen in Aarhus from 29 August to 2 September 1978. The idea of such a Conference had occurred independently to Klindt-Jensen and myself, and we were both very happy to be the organizers and co-chairmen, and to find that the Conference was sponsored by our own Universities in Denmark and England. The meeting in Denmark coincided with the 50th anniversary celebrations of the University of Aarhus, and our Conference was one of the many special symposia organized in Aarhus for that anniversary occasion. The Conference having been a success we then decided that a second Conference should be held somewhere else, possibly in Cambridge, but no date has yet been fixed.

It seemed essential to keep such a Conference to a small membership and some people who were invited were unable to be present; some others submitted papers which they were not able to give personally, namely Chakrabarti, Gathercole and Kristiansen.

The Conference ended with a resumé by Professor Stuart Piggott and he has now re-written what he said in the light of the text of the chapters.

We realized that a first Conference of this kind could be no more than a tentative, and exploratory, exercise. We did not expect a definitive history of archaeology to appear from our deliberations. But a great deal of interest did emerge and this is why we are delighted that Thames and Hudson, whose record of publishing archaeological and art historical books is outstanding, were happy to issue this book. We have deliberately called it *Towards a History of Archaeology*, and this is what it is. But we have no doubt that some of the papers which now form our chapters will be integral parts of any future full history of archaeology.

In 1976, at the Nice Conference of Prehistoric and Protohistoric Sciences, there was passed a resolution saying that the history of archaeology was not being properly studied or recognized. This was true. Since the Nice Conference the Executive Committee of the International Union of Prehistoric and Protohistoric Sciences met in Berlin in October of 1978 and set up a Commission on *L'Histoire de l'Archéologie Préhistorique et Protohistorique* with myself as President, Professor Gordon Willey as Vice-President, and Dr Bø Gräslund of Uppsala as Secretary. The other members of the Commission are Dr Andrzej Abramowicz from Lodz in Poland, Professor Dr Karl Böhner from the Römisch-Germanisches Zentralmuseum in Mainz, Dr Leo Klejn from Leningrad, Professor Sigfried De Laet from Ghent, Professor Klindt-Jensen from Aarhus, Professor Massimo Pallottino from Rome, Professor Carl-Fredrik Meinander from Helsinki and Professor Ignacio Bernal from Mexico.

It was agreed that the papers from the Aarhus Conference should be edited by Professor Klindt-Jensen and myself, but now that he is no longer with us I have edited the book with the help and skilled assistance of Eric Peters, of Thames and Hudson, who has already edited between eighty and ninety volumes of the 'Ancient Peoples and Places' series to which Klindt-Jensen contributed the volume *Denmark*.

When the new 'World of Archaeology' series came into existence Thames and Hudson and I were able to persuade Klindt-Jensen to write *A history of Scandinavian archaeology*, and this book has been widely acclaimed in Europe and America.

All of us who were at the 1978 Aarhus Conference and have written our chapters for this book deeply regret Ole Klindt-Jensen's death and wish to dedicate this book to his memory.

I
Introduction: The necessity for an historical approach to Archaeology

GLYN DANIEL

University of Cambridge, England

When I was invited by Lord Horder to contribute a volume on archaeology to the Duckworth Hundred Years series I found that little had been written on the history of the subject. There was A. Michaelis's *Die archäologischen Entdeckungen des neunzehnten Jahrhunderts* first published in Leipzig in 1906 (and two years later in English under the title of *A century of Archaeological Discoveries*); Friedrich von Oppeln-Bronikowski's *Die archäologischen Entdeckungen im 20 Jahrhundert* (Berlin, 1931) took the story on another thirty years but both Michaelis and von Oppeln-Bronikowski were mainly concerned with classical archaeology.

H.J.E. Peake devoted his Huxley Memorial Lecture to the Royal Anthropological Institute for 1940 to a survey of the development of prehistoric archaeology, and his extended publication of this lecture under the title of 'The Study of Prehistoric Archaeology' is a model presentation of the subject and a landmark in the history of archaeology. I was fortunate, forty years ago, to have many helpful discussions with Peake, as also with Sir John Myres. Both men were keenly interested in the development of archaeology and had themselves lived through exciting and formative years. Myres's own Huxley Memorial Lecture for 1933 was entitled *The Cretan Labyrinth: a Retrospect of Aegean Research* and it was in this lecture he said that when he learnt of Schliemann's death it seemed to him that 'the spring had gone out of the year'.

It is sad that neither Peake nor Myres wrote their autobiographies. We can see so much of the history of archaeology through the autobiographical back-looking of archaeologists and much valued books such as Flinders Petrie's *Seventy Years in Archaeology*, Margaret Murray's *My First Hundred Years*, Sir Mortimer Wheeler's *Still Digging*, Sir Leonard Woolley's *Spadework*, Sir Max Mallowan's *Mallowan's Memoirs*, and O.G.S. Crawford's *Said and Done*, to mention a few. What a pity we do not have comparable memoirs from Sir John Evans, General Pitt-Rivers, Worsaae Montelius, the Abbé Breuil, Cartailhac, Gabriel de Mortillet and many another. We hope this Conference will encourage some of us to set down our personal views about archaeology and archaeologists in our time.

When we go back to the history of antiquarianism and archaeology in our own countries we all have our heroes, our founder fathers of a faith which has become well established and world-wide. In Italy it would be Michael Mercati (1541-93), Superintendent of the Vatican Botanical Gardens and adviser to Pope Clement VIII, who insisted that primitive stone implements were man-made and not supernatural. His *Metallotheca*, though not published until 1717, influenced writers particularly in France.

In Scandinavia our father figures are Ole Worm, Olaf Verelius, Thomsen and Worsaae; in Holland, Reuvens; in my own country Camden, Aubrey, Lhwyd and Stukeley.

William Camden (1551-1623) was Headmaster of Westminister School in London. He travelled extensively in **Britain**, studying its visible antiquities, and produced in 1586, when he was thirty-five, his *Britannia*, the first general guide to the antiquities of Britain. It contained an illustration – the first illustration in any British archaeological work, and the remarkable observation about cropmarks, over three hundred years before air photography: 'But now age has eras'd the very tracks of it; and to teach us that Cities dye as well as men, it is at this day a corn-field, wherein when the corn is grown up, one may observe the draughts of streets crossing one another for where they have gone the corn is thinner.' This was written in 1586. The *Britannia* went through many editions: the latest was Gough's of 1789. What other archaeological book has been reproduced and revised for two hundred years?

Camden wrote in Latin: his fine words were translated into English by Dr Philemon Holland in 1657. These are words from the Preface to the Reader: 'Some there are which wholle contemne and avile this study of Antiquities as a back-looking curiositie, whose authority as I do not utterly vilefie, so I do not overprice their judgement ... in the study of Antiquity (which is always accompanied with dignity and hath a certain resemblance with eternity) there is sweet food of the mind well befitting such as are of honest and noble disposition.'

Camden's back-looking curiosity was the curiosity that has made us all archaeologists. But now, we are involved in a second backward-looking curiosity. We are looking back on our predecessors from Mercati, Ole Worm, and Camden onwards. Why should we bother to do this? Is it merely an amusing and sentimental exercise in past history, like collecting pictures of Copenhagen and French megaliths in 1800?

Not at all: the history of archaeology needs studying not only as an interesting and exciting story in itself, an account of the development of one of the newest humanistic disciplines in the historical sciences, but because without an historical perspective we can at the present day forget, at our peril, or even repeat, past errors. There is one main issue that I want to discuss, namely, false archaeology.

Of False Archaeology there are three main kinds: first, the creation of fakes and forgeries, secondly, the creation of false archaeological theories for political ends – the false prehistory of Nazi Germany and Fascist Italy, for example, and the chauvinism that lay behind the acceptance of Glozel in France and the Minnesota Stone in America. And thirdly, the creation of false archaeologies for financial and personal promotional gains by people like Bellamy, Velikovsky, von Däniken and most recently in America, Professor Barry Fell.

I will confine myself to the first of these three: the fakes and forgeries. When I was an undergraduate student in Cambridge, reading archaeology under Miles Burkitt and Ellis Minns, we were told nothing about fakes: indeed nothing about the seamier side of archaeology at all. Miles Burkitt never mentioned forgeries, although the Cambridge Museum had a case full of the splendid work of Flint Jack – that great nineteenth-century forger Edward Simpson who, when once asked 'Have you any of your specimens in the British Museum?' replied 'Yes and jolly good things they are.' And Ellis Minns, then Disney Professor of Archaeology, in his long and boring lectures on Scythians and South Russia, never mentioned the Tiara of Saitaphernes. The Tiara is an object lesson to us all; and so to come nearer to our present home in Aarhus, is the very strange affair of the turkeys at Schleswig. Most of you will remember that when the wall paintings in Schleswig Cathedral were being restored it was discovered to the surprise of everyone (except the man who had painted them) that there were representations of turkeys. As far as I know no one queried these turkeys at the time or approached the problem historically. They concentrated on the interpretation of these paintings and tried to explain why there should be turkeys in medieval paintings in what was then Denmark in pre-Columbian times, and they got to the answer – ethnologists and anthropologists and archaeologists are very good at this – the completely wrong answer: namely that turkeys were not introduced from America into Europe in post-Columbian times but must have been introduced by the first Europeans to visit America, namely, the Vikings, and what more natural than there should be turkeys displayed in Schleswig: in the homeland of the Vikings? This was all nonsense, and was not revealed until the trial of Dietrich Fey for the Lübeck forgeries, when he confessed that he had invented the Schleswig turkeys. Now here was a simple case when the history of the site should have been studied. Did no one look at photographs of the walls before restoration started? Apparently no one did.

We in England were electrified when, in 1952, three very distinguished and highly reputed scholars: Le Gros Clark, Weiner, and Kenneth Oakley revealed convincingly that the alleged ancient remains from Piltdown, which had been canonized as *Eanthropus dawsoni*, were fakes. The problem of the association of a human calvarium with a chimpanzee jaw, which had worried people for so long, was resolved.

All hocus-pocus. Now there are three things that the historian of archaeology must reflect upon here. First, that nobody studied the discovery of the remains in detail: indeed we still do not know where Piltdown II was found or alleged to have been found. Gross carelessness. If there is a serious car accident, all details are recorded. The details of the finding of the Piltdown remains are negligible. Secondly, no one was prepared to discount the chauvinist element in all this. Smith Woodward, the main scientist in the British Museum (Natural History) concerned with the whole affair, wrote a popular book about it all called *The First Englishman*. Here is the nub of the matter. Early man had been found in Java and Heidelberg: here at last was an even earlier man from England. Bravo! and while you were shouting bravo and waving the Union Jack you forgot your critical standards.

But my third point is the really important one. In the nineteenth century a Frenchman and an Englishman had shown that by the analysis of the fluorine content of bones, apparently of the same age and apparently deposited simultaneously in the same level, it could be shown whether they were in fact contemporaneous. Now this technique could have been used on the Piltdown remains in the 1912-14 period (apart from the fact that some thought the remains were virtually sacred – the earliest Englishman – and could not be violated by dirty scientific hands), but no one knew about the fluorine test. They had all forgotten about it, if indeed they ever knew about it. Kenneth Oakley himself only discovered it in the middle of the 1939-45 war. But if there had been an adequate history of scientific techniques in physical anthropology available in the early years of this century we would not have had to go through the nonsense of Piltdown Man, which I regard as one of the most embarrassing and distressing incidents in British Archaeology. What is fantastic, looking back on the whole affair, is that nobody at any time referred to the Moulin Quignon jaw. Why not? Because they did not know about it. The archaeologists and anthropologists who were studying the Piltdown remains in 1912 were historically ignorant. At least some of them ought to have thought back to Boucher de Perthes: but no, science is new, it is what we find and do now – the past is the past. This is why the study of the history of archaeology is so valuable: the past is what we make it and we made it hideously wrongly at Moulin Quignon and Piltdown – and may do so again.

There are two sites in France which constantly distress me, so much so that no French archaeologist except Mademoiselle de Saint-Mathurin and Pierre-Roland Giot mention them in my hearing. They are Rouffignac and Glozel. Rouffignac with its hundreds of mammoths was discovered in 1956 by Nougier and Robert and announced triumphantly at the Congrès Préhistorique de France in Poitiers on 20 July of that year. It had been authenticated by Abbé Breuil and was accepted and acclaimed. Now Breuil was an old man with failing eyesight when he spent a few hours at Rouffignac: I do not hold it against him that he had visited the site many years before, spent a whole day there with a friend looking for insects but saw nothing. Nor do I hold it against him that, like all great prehistorians, he had made mistakes before. With Sollas in 1912 he authenticated as Palaeolithic art paintings on the wall of the Bacon Hole cave in South Wales which we know to be random daubings made by workmen in 1898. This 'discovery' was claimed at the time to be sensational, the first Palaeolithic art in Britain. A historical examination of the site would have revealed the nature of the paintings, yet neither Sollas nor Breuil thought of doing this: they relied entirely on their subjective judgements. This is surely what the history of archaeology teaches one not to do; examine all the possible, if disputed, facts first and then make your personal judgement. The Bacon Hole painting is very interesting: as I have said – cynically – before, it is the only accurately dated Palaeolithic cave-art and the date is AD 1898. Yet even today, writers do not go through the records: they pick up the article by Sollas and Breuil in *The Times* and insist that there is Palaeolithic cave art in Britain.

Breuil did not find it possible to have any rational conversation with me about Rouffignac; he realized I was in no way a specialist in Palaeolithic studies but never appreciated that every site has its history and that I was becoming a specialist in the history of Rouffignac, and embarrassingly so to those who like, unfortunately, Breuil, accepted it as authentic. One of the great values of studying the history of archaeology is to realize that it is not a simple straightforward record of discovery; it is a record of discovery mixed with false assumptions and forgery and the refusal of established archaeologists to regard their work historically. This Conference will have achieved one thing if it teaches us all that the past, as set out in books and papers at the moment, is only the past as it seemed to be in the late seventies; it may bear no relation to the past as it was, and certainly not to the past as set out by Lubbock in 1865 or Childe in 1925. Camden in the elegant words of Philemon Holland's translation called our study the 'back-looking curiositie'. This is true: we are curious about the past of man, and more particularly the past of man before written history. But we must also be curious about ourselves: why do we study the prehistoric past and why do we think it relevant to modern thought? In my view the long perspective of prehistory is one of the most surprising pieces of knowledge which has been added to us in the last hundred years, and the beginnings of man keep on going further back into the distant years between two and two-and-a-half million years. But also what do we make of the shortness of the historic record? The life and religion of Egypt and Sumeria began five thousand years ago: Christianity, Buddhism, and Islam are much younger. By studying how we have learnt about our own past, we may expose, if not answer, some vital issues about the name and nature of man himself.

II
Archaeology and Ethnography in Denmark: early studies

OLE KLINDT-JENSEN

University of Aarhus, Denmark

The idea of comparing early ancestors with contemporary primitive peoples was conceived independently at various times. Pliny, who knew the Germani at first hand, was aware of this when he wrote: 'For among the ancients the most sublime expression of victory was that the vanquished held out a plant; with this they gave the land, the very burial place, a custom which I know still persists among the Germani' [1] His contemporary, Tacitus, even warns against the Germanic tribes as they were still living an unspoilt and valiant life like the ancient Romans and therefore could be a real danger to any degenerate people.

In Britain many centuries later descriptions of the natives in the far-off colonies were printed and primitive objects like stone arrowheads acquired; these were compared with arrowheads found in the soil in Britain and at the same time painted Indians recalled the Britons of Caesar's age, bluepainted, long-haired and dangerous. [2]

In Denmark, too, antiquaries were struck by the resemblance between objects acquired from their colonies or other far-off areas and antiquities from their own country. As a matter of fact it began with a description of the Royal Danish Collection of antiquities, coins, ethnographic objects, etc.

The splendid catalogue was first edited by Professor Jacobæus in 1696, but it was not until the *Supplementum* came out in 1699 that Danish antiquities could be set against the ethnographic evidence, making it possible to deduce the use to which these objects had been put. In this volume the editor was anonymous. [3]

The second edition of the *Royal Danish Kunstkammer* of 1710 contains literally the same texts on the subject, and now we have the name of the author, J. Laverentzen, head of the Royal printing office. [4]

Born 1648, Laverentzen went to a grammar school, but did not adopt an academic career. In his younger years he was attached to the central financial administration and to the Kunstkammer.

Known as a clever numismatist, he assisted Professor Jacobæus in compiling the first edition of the Kunstkammer catalogue. As Jacobæus had the privilege of re-editing the catalogue, it is understandable that Laverentzen published the *Supplement* discreetly. The

Royal collection had taken over Ole Worm's Museum from the family and acquired more antiquities and ethnographic objects.

From Iceland Worm had obtained an interesting object of black stone, found lodged in the blubber of a large sea mammal. It had a hole in one end and Laverentzen, who knew of harpoons used by the natives of Greenland, had no difficulty in recognizing it as the head of a missile. Through the hole a cord presumably had been threaded.

Moreover Laverentzen knew contemporary descriptions of savages such as were contained in the book by the Frenchman Père Louis Hennepin on Louisiana.[5] Even if Hennepin's observations were not up to modern anthropological standards, he made some interesting points, and these were used by Laverentzen in his research, such as this: 'Avant que les Européans fussent dans l'Amérique, les Sauvages se servoient, & toutes les Nations de la Louisiane se servent encore aujourd'huy, de pots de terre, au lieu de chaudières, de pierres aigues n'ayant point de hache ny de couteaux. Quand ils veulent faire quelque plat, ecuelles ou cuillières; ils accomodent le bois avec leurs haches de pierre; Ils la creusent avec des charbons de feu & les raclent ensuitte avec des dents de Castors pour les polir.'

Hennepin goes on to explain the use of stone axes and how trees could be hollowed by burning.

It is interesting that Laverentzen compared this account of primitive life with the remains from Danish antiquity. He interpreted a large number of Danish artifacts, describing them as axes, daggers and so forth, identifications which he based on comparable objects from Greenland and America. He divided them into two main groups, stone and metal, avoiding terms such as 'thunderstones' and the like employed by many of his fellow antiquaries. He maintained that the poems of Hesiod and Lucretius provided evidence for a chronological evolutionary process, which fitted in with his ideas.

In the course of time Laverentzen's sober observations were virtually forgotten. He was, however, read and cited by later Swedish and German scholars, who were influenced by his ideas and who in due course came to be regarded as pioneers themselves. Moreover, the source material remained in the collections, and in the nineteenth century C.J. Thomsen made use of it to build up an ethnographical museum. Recognizing the importance of such objects as counterparts to Danish antiquities, he put some shafted axes in the showcases beside the Danish exemplars, in order the better to make his point. Also in a paper published in 1832 he mentions traces of wear on the artifacts, which gives evidence of their use. 'Experience shows that related conditions and particularly a related cultural level bring about related implements to obtain necessary goods'. When discussing the Danish flint types he remarks that the arrow points were triangular in section: 'The arrow points of the savage North American Indians are quite like these.'

In his *Ledetraad til Nordisk Oldkyndighed,* 1836 (Guide book on Scandinavian Antiquity) he worked out more analogies, and at the same time his correspondence shows that he recognized the work of the learned Scanian antiquarian Professor Nilsson, who published an interpretation of Stone Age people as fishermen.

From an unexpected quarter, however, came new evidence. It was a paper published in 1839, [6] by the keen scientist P.V.Lund, who lived at Lagoa Santa, a quiet little Brazilian village north of Rio de Janeiro. Lund described the use of stone axes in that part of the world. As a young man he had to go to a warm climate as a cure for tuberculosis but he soon became involved in extensive zoological investigations. In Brazil he met a roving Norwegian who told him about great numbers of caves containing bones that were to be found in Minas Gerais. They went there together, this odd partnership of scrupulous scientist and notorious adventurer, and between 1835 and 1844 Lund – helped by his Norwegian companion – excavated some 800 caves. In one of these caves he found thirty human skeletons of a recognizable type lying together with the remains of animals long extinct; other finds included stone axes. Lund sent a rich collection to the University Zoological Museum as well as to the Society, of which he had meanwhile become a member.

In the report published in *Annaler for nordisk Oldkyndighed* Lund gave details of some polished stone axes sent to the Society and described the technique used by the savages of South America.

The common form of the axe is oblong, rather flat with an edge at each end. The Indians look for a hard but strong tree stem, which at one end is split in the form of a cross. In this opening the stone is put in an oblique position and fastened by a *cipó* (a twining plant).

'The savage is not able to fell a tree with such an axe. He proceeds in the following manner to obtain his aim: using the axe he cuts a cavity in the side of the tree. Here he puts embers which are kept glowing by blowing until they are reduced to ashes. These are then removed, and the charred part of the cavity is cut away with the axe. The cavity is again filled with embers, and the aforementioned procedure is repeated until the whole tree is burnt through, which will take less time than one would imagine. It is of importance to the savage and costs less energy than to fell the whole tree with a cutting implement. Is the felled tree intended to be a canoe, the bark is first removed with the stone axe, and when the tree is dry the upward part is covered by embers for its whole length, and the hollowing is made in the same way as the aforementioned burning.'

This description was skilfully adapted by the young Worsaae when some few years later, in 1843, he wrote his book *Danmarks Oldtid,* which was translated into English and published in 1849. The words in Lund's text can easily be recognized in this description of Stone Age life in Denmark (p. 13):

'The most ancient inhabitants, or as we may term them, the aborigines, would have made but little progress, had they attempted to fell a large and full-grown tree with nothing more than so imperfect an instrument as the stone hatchet. They doubtless pursued the same method as the savages of our days, who when about to fell a tree with stone hatchets, avail themselves also of the assistance of fire, in the following manner. In the first place some of the bark is peeled off, by means of the hatchet, from the tree which is to be felled. In the opening thus made coals are placed, which are fanned till they are consumed. By this means a portion of the stem is charred, which is then hewn away with the hatchet, and fresh coals are continuously added until the tree is burned through. In our peat bogs old stems of trees have been found which appear to have been thus felled by stone hatchets with the aid of fire.

'It can scarcely be doubted that their boats must have been of a very simple kind. From several relics which have been dug out we may conclude that the aborigines in the usual manner of the savage nations, charred the stem of the tree close to the summit only and then hollowed it out by means of fire till it acquired its equilibrium on the water. For this use the instruments which have been termed hollow chisels were most probably destined.'

It may be questioned whether the tropical conditions bear comparison with North European Stone Age conditions. As a matter of fact flint axes in Denmark are very efficient for cutting a tree, almost like iron axes, as Sehested of Broholm demonstrated by his practical experiments some few years later.

Inspired by Worsaae and a number of other continental archaeologists of note, Sir John Lubbock (later Lord Avebury) visited Denmark in the eighteen-sixties in order to collect material for what was to become a classic work, *Prehistoric Times*. The book aroused keen interest in Scandinavia and was translated into Danish in 1874 under the title *Mennesket i den forhistoriske Tid*. Among the illustrations, which added greatly to the book's popularity, was a picture of life at a kitchen midden with people engaged in many different activities, some of whom are shown hollowing out a canoe by means of hot coals. Others are fishing in the water just outside the settlement. W.J. Dreyer, in his *The Antiquity of Scandinavia* (1899), later borrowed this motif and it became a favourite illustration in numerous popular books, on account of the idyllic flavour of the original Danish version. There was, it must be admitted, a tendency to make prehistoric life appear romantic, which also coloured Dreyer's portrayal of the Bronze Age. Whilst the ornaments and objects faithfully reproduce well-known actual finds, the people seem to be behaving as if they were taken from a novel with a setting of contented country life around 1900; in the round hut (looking like a house urn) the young men and women are happily chattering.

This attitude is in clear contrast to the accounts of primitive existence provided by Victorian travellers and explorers. Lubbock knew them too well to give his interpretation a saccharine flavour. Men like Captain Gray are cited, and this leads on to considerations of morality:

the reader should realize how privileged his life is compared with that of the savage. The Australian aborigine, said Gray, adored whale blubber, even if it were in a stinking condition. Lubbock would seem to be quite justified in stressing the more civilized customs of Western society; it shocked him to see an attractive young girl creep out of the belly of a rotting whale.

The Victorians saw the life of contemporary primitive peoples as hard and unhappy, but felt it could, unlike that of prehistoric man, be ameliorated by introducing them to science and the arts, so overcoming illiteracy and its attendant vices and opening up for them a rewarding future. This model differs in several respects from the Danish one, coloured as it is by nationalistic ideas. The temptation to fill the void that surrounds antiquities has always been strong, and it is only natural that when fleshing out an obscure period one gives something of oneself, one's ideals and fantasies.

In the 1920s the body of a young girl who had lived in the Bronze Age, clad in a skirt made of cords and a smart jacket, was found in an oak coffin at Egtved and attracted a great deal of attention. Now, it would be tempting to show off a modern Danish girl wearing a replica of such Bronze Age attire but it would not be very helpful. For it is evident that a girl of the 1920s represents a certain type, trim and athletic, whereas by 1950 she had changed significantly: she has now a sophisticated, sexy look. Such models tell us more about changing fashions in the twentieth century than about Early Bronze Age styles.

Another aspect of the case is that when ethnographic parallels are taken into consideration the viewpoint again changes. As there are some present-day primitive tribes whose women wear string skirts, an anthropologist has pointed out that the Egtved girl, like these latter-day relatives of hers, may have had a bare midriff,[7] a suggestion that has astonished other scholars. This has led to lively argument, but as a matter of fact we have very little evidence to decide how Bronze Age women wore their garments.

It is clear that ethnography, which has often been brought closer to archaeology by displays in museums, has influenced the way finds are interpreted. It is worth nothing, too, how it has added to our understanding by providing a more realistic picture of the various models that have been used by archaeologists. In Denmark a strong tradition grew up during the period between the days of the early researchers and the present century, inspired by personalities such as Gudmund Hatt and Kai Birket Smith, who were at one and the same time ethnographers and archaeologists. This tradition has been carried on to good effect by their successors. However, our widening knowledge should not lead scholars into the error of too closely relating facts and theories pertaining to two separate fields of study. Comparisons are always rewarding but we should not deduce too much from them, for identity is rarely encountered.

BIBLIOGRAPHICAL REFERENCES

1   *Naturalis historia* XXII: 8.

2   B. Orme in A.C. RENFREW (ed.), *The Explanation of Culture Change: Models in Prehistory*, 1973: 487.

3   *Auctarium rariarum, quae Museo regio per triennium Hauniae accesserunt, ubioribus illustrata commentariis*, 1699.

4   *Museum Regium seu Catalogus Rerum naturalium, quam artificialium, Quae in Basilica bibliothecae Havniae asservantur, ab Obligero Jacobaeo quondam describtus, Nuncvero magna ex parte auction Johanne Lauerentzen, Hauniae*, 1710.

5   L. HENNEPIN, *Déscription de la Louisiane*, Paris 1683: II, 86.

6   *Annaler for Nordisk Oldkyndighed*, 1838-39: 153-61.

7   H. HARALD HANSEN, *Aarbøger for nordisk Oldkyndighed og Historie*, 1949: 222 (last exchange of views in *Aarbøger* 1952).

III
A social history of Danish Archaeology (1805-1975)

KRISTIAN KRISTIANSEN

Ancient Monuments Directorate Copenhagen, Denmark

Today an historical consciousness is taken for granted. Owing to industrialization and the global expansion of capitalism changes are taking place more and more rapidly, a state of affairs that has become an inescapable part of man's perception of the world, and thus has come to seem 'natural'. We tend to forget that this is historically a unique situation, and are therefore too easily led to regard both historical and archaeological research as the outcome of a 'natural' development. But there is indeed a difference, rather of kind than of degree, between a historical consciousness *per se* and the establishment of an archaeological science with a body of institutional rules and regulations, museums to implement them, university departments to develop and teach new knowledge and scientific periodicals to communicate it. How did all this actually come about, and why did it reach its present level? To answer such questions satisfactorily we need to make an analysis of the functioning of archaeology in society, transcending the limits of traditional archaeological history and setting it in a wider social and political framework. In this way alone can we arrive at a better understanding of the expansion of archaeology during the last 150 years (Daniel, 1975), not only in western Europe, but also in most of the developed or developing countries of today; and such an understanding is probably the best precondition for formulating the future goals of archaeology. This argument I shall try to elucidate by presenting a general survey of social and political dimensions in the development of Danish archaeology from 1805 to 1975 in the hope that it may stimulate further research in other areas. But first a few introductory remarks.

The development of archaeology, it should be noted, was dependent upon two overall factors, the most important of which was perhaps the agrarian reforms of the later eighteenth century, including the conversion of strip holdings into compact holdings and the complete break-up of the traditional agricultural system, which had remained largely unchanged since the Middle Ages. Vast areas which had served as common land and pastures are now tilled, agricultural techniques improved, especially in the nineteenth century, and as a result many thousands of barrows were levelled and wet areas drained (Kristiansen

1974).[1] These activities, which accelerated during the nineteenth century, brought to light an increasing number of archaeological finds, especially hoards and graves, which in the decades around 1800 were for the most part destroyed. This was one of the cogent arguments for the foundation of the *Royal Commission for the Preservation of Northern Antiquities* in 1807 (Hermansen 1931), and a direct precondition for archaeological work throughout most of the nineteenth century. It was not until the second half of that century that systematic excavations were first undertaken, and 1937 before a general conservation law was passed; it took a further four years for an archaeological institute to be established. So the rapid economic development of Denmark, and Western Europe, from the late eighteenth century onwards and the resulting transformation of the cultural landscape, led to the uncovering of archaeological remains in quantities unparalled in history, thereby laying the necessary foundation for later scientific research (Kristiansen 1974, Fig. 1).[2]

The second factor was the development and subsequent consolidation of nationalism throughout Europe during the nineteenth century. Shaped by the philosophy of Enlightenment, which claimed equal rights and sovereignty for the people – politically manifested in the American Constitution and the French Revolution – these ideas soon found a stabilizing counterpart in the ideology of the national State, representing and defending the cultural and historical heritage of its people. It was this latter mixture of enlightenment and nationalism that formed the background for R. Nyerup's proposal for a 'National Museum' in Denmark in 1806, inspired by similar French initiatives. In scope it was completely different from those, mostly private, 'collections of rarities and antiquities' which had played a popular role in the cultural life of the European aristocracy since the Renaissance, as well as including a few highly educated and wealthy people like Ole Worm (Klindt-Jensen 1975, 14 ff). I therefore propose to deal, not specifically with the theme 'archaeology and nationalism', as the relationship between them remained well established throughout the period, but rather with the various social and political paths taken by archaeology. Important questions to be asked are: how was archaeology used? – by whom? – and for what ends? To help us answer them several sources are at our disposal:

1 The ledgers of the National Museum illustrate the communication structure between it and the finders, which gradually changes.
2 The channels of communication between archaeologists and the public through popular archaeological books, journals, newspapers, etc., which may also reveal important information.
3 The active groups of museum founders and the member lists of archaeological-historical societies, where some very concrete information concerning these questions is to be found.

How archaeology appealed to different social groups, at different times and for different political reasons, I shall now attempt to show, using a few illustrative examples from the three above-mentioned categories of sources.

1805-1850

A sequence of diverse dramatic events in the years shortly after 1800 forms an interesting prelude to the national and cultural streams in which archaeology was to become immersed. The chronological framework is represented by the battle between the Danish and the British fleets in 1801, which resulted in the final defeat of the former with the bombardment of Copenhagen in 1807. In the intervening period three minor events took place:

1 In 1802 the two famous gold horns from Gallehus were stolen and melted down, which aroused a public outcry.
2 In 1805 Adam Oehlenschläger wrote his famous poem, 'The Golden Horns', in which they became a symbol of lost glory. This and other poems that followed shortly after gave rise to a new romantic movement in literature whose motifs were frequently taken from prehistory and early history.
3 Finally, early in 1807, a 'National Museum' and a Royal Commission for the Preservation of Northern Antiquities were established.

Together these events set the scene for new directions in economic and political life and in the cultural climate. A period of economic setbacks that lasted a couple of decades ensured and slowed down the agrarian reforms: politically the absolutism of the monarch (Frederik VI) was strengthened and several political writers emigrated or were expelled (Vibak 1964). Against this background the relationship between archaeology and romanticism, closely interwoven as they were (Klindt-Jensen, 1975, 58 ff), took on an interesting aspect. Who was promoting archaeology and at whom was their campaign directed?

The successful work of the Commission was subject to the official subvention of the King, reflected in the prefix 'Royal'. This meant the support of the administration, which became decisive for the growth of archaeology in its early stage. [3] The King, for his part, took a purely pragmatic line, hoping to benefit from the potential nationalism that resided in the glorious past. [4] This was most clearly reflected, however, in the new wave of romantic literature, which glorified (and mystified) not only the past in general, but especially the system of feudalism; most romantic novelists were likewise declared supporters of the 'old system' and against parliamentarianism (Kristensen 1942a, 209 ff). [5] The archaeologists mostly restricted themselves to a few programmatic statements. Thus the importance of prehistoric monuments was interpreted by Thorlacius, a member of the Commission, in 1809 as follows: 'They remind us about the heroic deeds of the Scandinavian, they speak loud about his strength and giant force, they offer a rich opportunity to compare the past and the present.' (Thorlacius 1809, 68). Later, in 1843, Worsaae was both more historical, and more sophisticated, when stating that: 'It is inconceivable that a nation which cares about itself and its independence could rest content without reflecting on its past' (trl. Klindt-Jensen 1975, 70). And he continues: 'It must of necessity direct its attention to bygone times, with a view to enquiring to what original stock it belongs... For it is not until these facts are thoroughly understood, that the people acquire a clear perception of their own character, that they are in a situation to defend their independence with energy, and to labour with success at the progressive development, and thus to promote the honour and well-being, of their country' (Worsaae 1849, Introduction). It should be stressed, however, that this ideological bias did not to any significant degree penetrate archaeological research, which at that time was mainly concerned with the objects. Thomsen's mercantilist 'rationalism' was an important element in the development of a tradition of empirical research; a 'cultural history' was still lacking, and Worsaae's first moves were actually to defend archaeology against misuses and misinterpretations of its material as relics of historical and national myths, and later to establish a specific archaeological framework for interpretations and explanations (Klindt-Jensen 1975, 68 ff; Kristiansen 1978). As he wrote in his fragment of autobiography: 'Just as conservative as I was in politics, so was I liberal, nearly radical, in science' (Worsaae 1934, 93).

Another feature of archaeology at this early stage was that it quite clearly appealed to a very narrow segment of society, as did the literature of romanticism. From subscription lists we know that primary readers of the latter numbered less than a thousand people out of a population of approximately one million, and this small group comprised mainly government officials, army officers and academics (Kristiansen, 1942a, 20 ff) – the administrative, military and cultural upholders of absolutism. And the same goes for both members of the 'Committee' and subscribers to its periodical *Antikvariske Annaler* (since 1812), later superseded by *Nordisk Tidsskrift for Oldkyndighed* (from 1832), *Annaler for nordisk Oldkyndighed* (from 1836) and '*Aarbøger for Nordisk Oldkyndighed*' (from 1866) (Ørsnes 1966). The three last-named were published by the Royal Society of Northern Antiquaries, founded in 1825 to familiarize the public with the old Nordic sagas (Steen Jensen 1975), and from 1832 included archaeology, which thenceforth benefited from the remarkable international success of the Society (Worsaae 1875). In the member list for 1830[6] high-ranking army officers were clearly dominant (nearly 25%), followed by the mostly provincial bourgeoisie (typically merchants, pharmacists and the headmaster of the grammar school), academics (professors) (both 15-20%), and then in equal numbers (10-15%) the landed nobility, senior officials (mostly provincial) and clergy. Throughout the 1830s and 1840s the membership increased significantly for all these groups, but there were also some resignations. By 1844 the clergy had become dominant (nearly 25%), together with the mostly provincial, state officials (county prefects, mayors, district bailiffs), followed by high-ranking army officers (c. 15%) and then in equal numbers (10-15%) the landed nobility, the provincial bourgeoisie and university professors. Relatively, however, compared to their total number, the representation among the landed nobility/officers (very often the same group) is quite impressive. The petit bourgeois and farmers are not represented (apart from a few who owned large farms, the so-called propriéteurs), whilst industrial capitalists had scarcely yet featured in the Danish economy, just as a dominant and differentiated bourgeoisie was still lacking, owing to the prolonged rule of absolutism and the retarded economic development.

The picture presented here is confirmed by the ledgers of the National Museum, which inform us that it was regional and local government officials, especially the county prefects and the clergy, who established and maintained contacts between finders of artifacts and the museum, supported by the landed nobility.[7] Among the finders, mostly smallholders and farm labourers, the payment of rewards was decisive for the survival income of this social group, which during most of the nineteenth century often lived close to starvation (Engberg 1973; Riismøller 1971).

Thus the attitudes of the finders, the very few archaeologists and their primary audience (the 200-300 members of the Society) were governed by very varied motives. It should be noted, however, that several attempts were made to close the gap. In 1818, 1837, 1840 and 1844 efforts were made to establish small official archaeological collections in the provincial centres, but without success (Kjær 1974, 116ff). More successful were the publications of Thomsen and Worsaae. As early as 1831 the Royal Society of Northern Antiquaries had distributed a small pamphlet about the Nordic antiquities to all schoolteachers (Petersen 1938, 29), describing how to excavate and handle archaeological finds. Later, in 1836, 5,000 copies of Thomsen's book *Guide to Northern Archaeology* (as the English translation of 1848 was titled) were printed,[8] and Worsaae's book of 1843 (published in English in 1849 under the title *The Primeval Antiquities of Denmark*) immediately sold 5,200 copies, a remarkable number compared to even the more popular literature of that time. It was printed and distributed by The Society for the Proper Use of the Liberty of the Press, a name indicating that its members mainly belonged to the more established groups in society. As Thomsen observed in his commendation of Worsaae's manuscript: 'From the subscription lists it is clear that although the Society is widely distributed, only very few among its members belong to the common people' (Worsaae 1934, 233).[9] Both administratively and ideologically, archaeology remained an integrated part of absolutism during this period. But new social and political movements among the 'common people' and the rising bourgeoisie, which had originated in the 1830s, were soon to reform this framework (Skovmand 1964, 127-213).

1850-1900

a) 1850-1875. By now the scene has changed, both politically and economically. Absolutism has been replaced by parliamentarianism and a constitution in 1849, and the political power is held by the bourgeoisie (Skovmand 1964). Both farming and commerce are developing rapidly and the wars against Germany in 1848 and 1864, finally resulting in the loss of southern Jutland (and Schleswig-Holstein), arouse a wave of patriotic fervour. In archaeology the work of Worsaae and his colleagues establishes the first rough chronological and historical framework for a real prehistory, just as co-operation between archaeology, zoology and geology succeeds in demonstrating the first traces of a hunting subsistence in Denmark (Klindt-Jensen 1975, 68 ff) which together with similar French discoveries (Eggers 1959, 54 ff) and the works of Darwin and the early ethnographers revolutionize the traditional views on Man's origin and historical development. In literature the new age is reflected in the breakthrough of naturalism. In archaeology two trends are discernible, one dominated by national history, e.g. manifested in excavations of national monuments, the other adopting a more evolutionary and economic perspective, based on cooperation with the natural sciences. The latter, however, was soon to be overshadowed by the former for both scientific and (indirectly) political reasons.

Archaeology during this period was expanding. Between the two wars with Germany five provincial museums came into being under very similar conditions.[10] All members of the private founding committees had a solid background in the bourgeoisie of the now rapidly growing provincial towns, and in all cases the leading personality was an academic from the natural sciences (zoology, botany, geology), which is interesting considering the importance of these sciences for archaeology at that time. This is the progressive bourgeoisie, to be distinguished from the more wealthy, though not always politically motivated, early capitalists, who at the same time began to found art museums. In the founding committees we find that academics predominated (mostly grammar school teachers, then lawyers, army officers and county prefects), though businessmen too were represented, especially pharmacists and merchants – 'the best men in town', as the committee in Viborg claimed (Kjær 1974 and 1979). The aims of these museums which, though primarily archaeological, also included bourgeois culture, were twofold: to rescue archaeological material from destruction through agriculture, by spreading the knowledge of archaeology among the local population of farmers and peasant, and in so doing making them aware of their national and historical significance. This was regarded by several of the committee members as an important factor in the decentralization process after the abolition of absolutism and the subsequent development of the new parliamentarianism (Forchhammer 1866). It should be noted that at the same time the first 'folk' high schools for farmers and peasants were founded with similar aims.[11] The peasantry had begun to organize itself politically and culturally, developing a cultural identity with a strong historical perspective, stressing its own potential role in future development, representing the 'people' (Zerlang 1977, 273 ff).

At this time archaeology was gaining in popularity as a national science, supported by the active interest in it taken by King Frederik VII (Klindt-Jensen 1975, 82f). Privately conducted excavations and private collections became wide-spread among the bourgeoisie, as did trade in antiquities,[12] a development that increased rapidly in the last few decades of the nineteenth century. Among the nobility it became popular to establish small private museums, among which that of F. Sehested at Broholm on Fuen is one of the best known (Neergárd 1933; Oxenvad 1974). Archaeology had now become established as an important national science, as is evidenced by excavations of national monuments and by politically directed work at the border area with Germany.[13] These new trends in the spread of archaeology are also discernible in the member lists of the Royal Society of Northern Antiquaries. By 1866 the landed nobility had gained in relative importance at the expense of army officers – both together still making up nearly 30% of the members. Also the ranks of high officials, and especially the clergy, were now being reduced, whereas university professors still maintained their position. There was a rapid increase of the bourgeoisie, now making up about 25% or more, principally academic teachers at grammar schools, doctors and lawyers, but a lack of industrial capitalists. The decrease in the number of clergy, compared to other academic disciplines, reflects a general displacement within the academic structure, later to become much more pronounced (Kristensen 1942b, 145f); from now on the clergy were, at an increasing rate, becoming involved in religious movements at the expense of their former rather strong engagements in secular matters (Skovmand 1964, 395ff). In general the groups here mentioned were fairly well balanced against each other, showing a gradual change compared to the 1840s which, however, was soon to accelerate. It should be noticed that farmers and teachers were absent. The strict criteria for achieving membership of the Society conflicted with the cultural and historical traditions that were now being developed at the 'folk' high schools (Zerlang 1977, 246ff and 262ff). The only (but important) feature they had in common was the stressing of Nordic and national history as opposed to classical culture. These social and political differences were soon to be reflected in the expansion of archaeology.

b) 1875-1900. This period is characterized by serious political conflicts between farmers/peasants and nobility/bourgeoisie, leading to a government crisis with provisional laws between 1885 and 1894. It is also the active organizing period of the farmers at nearly all levels – politically, culturally (the still expanding 'folk' high schools) and economically (the development of a national network of co-operative organizations: dairies, butcheries, shops, etc.). The period also represents the final integration of Denmark into the capitalist world economy. Archaeologically the Worsaae era, with its rather flexible archaeological-historical framework, regionalization and overall perspective, comes to an end (Klindt-Jensen 1975, 68ff), and new avenues are introduced by Sophus Müller (from 1892 as director). Systematic excavations, classifications and publications of finds become the main objectives,[14] soon creating a basis for elaborate chronological systems and detailed culture-historical accounts. As a response to that the series of monographs *Nordiske Fortidsminder*, was initiated in 1889, and from 1873 onwards all parishes (some 2000) were visited and their monuments recorded (Worsaae 1877 and 1879). The publication of Müller's culture-historical synthesis, *Vor Oldtid*, in 1897 (translated into German in 1898) for the first time established a solid and detailed basis for popularization. Also the rapidly expanding newspapers became an important new medium, where the archaeologist and journalist Vilhelm Boye in particular was active, writing accounts of new finds and publishing a series of name lists of people who had barrows on their land protected. (All these articles are bound together in several books in Department One of the National Museum in Copenhagen.)

Between 1875 and 1900, nine provincial museums were founded[15] and most of them after 1887 – during the provisional years (1885-1894). They follow the lines of the earlier museums, but with important additions, later to become more pronounced. Besides being archaeological, collections of relics of folk culture became a prominent feature, most clearly at Herning, established to preserve the cultural and natural history of the heathlands in Jutland. In the founding committees the provincial town bourgeois were in a majority. Doctors and veterinarians, having close contact with the farmers and peasants, now play an important role, apart from becoming private collectors. These tendencies are also reflected in the member lists of the Society of Northern Antiquaries, where the number of Danish members now increases considerably at the expense of foreign members, to become much more pronounced after the turn of the century. This reflects the growing importance of the bourgeoisie. During the 1880s and 1890s they gain an absolute majority of more than 50%; as before, they comprise, on the one hand, merchants, directors, pharmacists and

the like, and on the other hand the now dominant academic bourgeoisie – doctors, veterinarians, grammar school teachers, engineers,
architects and so forth. University professors still hold their own,
whereas the nobility/high-ranking officers are much reduced in numbers (10-15%). [16] Most significant, however, is the falling off among
State officials (less than 5%) and clergy (less than 3%). The petit
bourgeois, as well as industrial capitalists, are only very modestly
represented.

Meanwhile new groups were beginning to occupy themselves with
archaeology, most importantly the school teachers, who played an
active role in historical and archaeological research from 1880 onwards (Olrik 1913). These activities may be regarded as a natural
extension of the cultural impact of the 'folk' high schools. [17] Also
farmers themselves were participating more and more. These trends
are reflected in the ledgers of the National Museum where teachers,
veterinarians and farmers play an increasing role as reporters, while
the regional and local government officials, including the clergy, are
disappearing. Neither farmers nor teachers, however, were members
of the Society that from now on may be said to represent progressively
an alliance between the bourgeoisie and archaeology, a point which
Sophus Müller makes when he writes: 'Rather than aristocratically
trace its ancestry back to the Middle Ages, the study of prehistoric
archaeology prefers to regard itself as a child of modern times, civi-
cally born in the dawn of the century of liberty.' (Müller 1896, 702).
These contradictory aspects of the archaeological milieu were un-
folded in the subsequent period. Their archaeological origin was
Müller's centralized and monopolizing policy, whereas their social
origin was the strong ties between archaeology and bourgeois culture;
this made it virtually impossible to reconcile the diverse social and
political trends which now transformed Danish society (Dybdahl
1965). [18] The first of these aspects (the scientific) was exemplified by
the policy against the provincial museums, whose activities were
regulated and legislated according to the wishes of the National
Museum, which forbad all excavations not supervised by the National
Museum at a time when any private person was free to undertake his
own excavations (Larsen 1935). The second aspect was evidenced by
Müller's hard fights with private entrepreneurs, who found a good
market, especially as museums now were eager to make purchases as a
compensation for excavations (although this procedure was also
abandoned by the National Museum). In Jutland a group of farm
workers and smallholders engaged in systematic 'robbing' excavations
of several thousand barrows during the 1890s (Quist 1975). The whole
sad business reflected the wide social and economic differences in
society, the lower classes supplying wealthy collectors and museums
with archaeological finds, partly as a result of the restrictive policy of
the National Museum (Thorsen 1979). This was not realized by

Sophus Müller, who, in a popular book about the National Museum, dubbed the former 'dangerous enemies' (the proletarian robbers/suppliers) and the latter 'devoted friends' (the wealthy collectors/buyers) (Müller 1907, 44ff). Very effectively Müller was able to use the threats presented by 'robbing' excavations, and agricultural activities, when mobilizing public opinion (Thorsen 1979), resulting in rather impressive appropriations during the 1890s, which became the basis of systematic excavation campaigns in Jutland (Klindt-Jensen 1975, 94; Eggers 1959, 79f).

   This was the situation at the turn of the century when farmers and peasants came into political power and had their cultural and historical traditions liberated in an outburst of activities, including the founding of numerous museums.

1900-1960

a) 1900-1930. Between 1900 and 1930 there followed a period of economic progress and prosperity, dominated by the organizational efficiency and increasing productivity of the farmers, in whose hands also resided the political power most of the time. Local museums largely owed their rapid expansion to the organizational experience of farmers/peasants and the propagation of a historical ideology during the second half of the nineteenth century through the 'folk' high schools, now reflected in the influence of schoolteachers in the founding committees of the many new museums. In the late 1930s, when a list of leading committee members of the culture-historical museums was published (Jensen and Møller 1939), the schoolteachers still played an important role, whereas farmers were only modestly represented[19] — perhaps owing to the agrarian crisis. The well-to-do provincial middle class (lawyers, doctors, merchants, etc.) exercised most power, followed by the lower middle class (shopkeepers, bank assistants, carpenters, etc.) — all in all a rather representative segment of the provincial bougeoisie as a whole, as opposed to the Royal Society of Northern Antiquaries which was now wholly dominated by the upper middle classes and where both nobility and high-ranking army officers were reduced to about 5%, while State officials had nearly disappeared. In the years shortly before and after 1900 a great many private collections of former senior officials, army officers and big landowners, founded between 1850 and 1890, were bought by the National Museum – often for substantial sums. In the Royal Society the traditional, well established bourgeois (directors, judges of the supreme court, merchants, etc.) and the more numerous academic bourgeois (doctors, architects, engineers, etc.) now made up about 65% of the members, whilst the proportion of university professors/lecturers increased to nearly 20%. Clergy, farmers, school teachers, the petit bourgeois and industrial capitalists were only sporadically represented (1-2%). Also, typically, 75% of the members were settled in Copenhagen and its suburbs. In 1866 the provinces had been represented by 45%, but as early as 1879 this had decreased to 25% – that is, before the founding of the majority of the provincial museums and the local historical societies. Thus the centralization of archaeology was both a scientific and socio-geographical phenomenon to which the many new museums and historical societies founded after 1900 were a natural response. Most of the many new museums concentrated on 'folk culture', supplemented by an archaeological exhibition, unlike the early provincial museums. This wave of historical interest was also reflected in the rapid expansion of historical societies between 1902 and 1928, when every county had one. To the fore were the same group of farmers, teachers and members of the provincial middle class which formed the founding committees of the local museums, but perhaps with a stronger academic representation (Hvidtfeldt 1949-52), and their activities were stimulated both by the many new museums and by the foundation of regional historical archives. Most of them also published a periodical for their members, which, around 1970, still amounted to some 30,000 for the country as a whole (Jversen 1968).

Thus an appropriate term for the decades after 1900 would seem to be 'the culture-historical era'. Never before had so many people been so involved in history in its broadest sense. Culture-history penetrated society – in literature, in national songs, in school books (Skovmand 1975) and was actively pursued in museums and historical societies all over the country. The scope of historical research had been widened to embrace 'the people' — their historical traditions, institutions and material conditions. Already in the 1860s there were systematic collections of folk tales, local dialects, and in the 1870s the idea of folk museums, displaying the reconstructions of interiors of houses, materialized in both Sweden and Denmark with the aim of preserving the tradition and the material relics of the now vanishing farmer and his folk culture (Rasmussen 1966). Among the provincial bourgeoisie it became popular to dress in folk costumes (Witt 1977, 11) and peasant dwellings and countrysides became popular motifs in pictorial art. These trends had, by the turn of the century, matured and a new culture-historical research tradition been established whose focus was increasingly local. The general evolutionary and diffusionist trends of the nineteenth century (Thomsen; Worsaae) had first been replaced by national culture-history (Müller) and now regional and local history on all levels became a main objective. In archaeology these developments were reflected in new types of settlement studies (la Cour 1927; Hatt 1949), including place names (Clausen 1916) and prehistoric roads (Müller 1904). It is also reflected in the formation of numerous private collections among farmers and schoolteachers who had earlier sold either to the landed nobility or to antique dealers. Now the farmer had become a collector himself and soon many a farm displayed its own small collection, a feature still in evidence in many places today. Between 1900 and 1930 many of these collections were offered to the National Museum which normally referred them to the provincial museums.

The extension of archaeological activities through the new local museums was not supported by the National Museum. Its director (until 1921), Sophus Müller, tried to keep control through an alliance with the early provincial museums (Arbøger, 1912) which likewise felt threatened. Official letters were sent to all clergy and school teachers, behind the backs of the provincial museums, with requests to communicate directly with the National Museum in the event of archaeological discoveries. This centralized policy, rooted in the scientific demands of a small élite, was clearly in opposition to the popular local support which archaeology itself had evoked and threatened to isolate archaeological research from the broad historical trends just as described, and from the general public. But it also, quite typically, reflected an alliance between what had now become 'the establishment' in culture-historical research – the National Museum, the Society of Northern Antiquities and the early provincial museums – against the new developments, reflected in the wave of local museums and historical societies. By preserving and studying the traditions and material relics of 'folk culture' the latter demonstrated the economic and political progress of these groups, aspects which should not be underestimated. But at the same time the culture-historical approach tended to isolate research based on material, geographical or other criteria, preventing general trends from becoming apparent as no theoretical perspective served to unify the evidence. Static reconstructions and historical descriptions were the main objectives, in history as well as in archaeology.

b) 1930-1960. This period sees a shift of balance in the economy between agriculture and industry, also manifested politically by the leadership of the social democrats most of the time. In general the social and cultural trends of the previous period continue, but basic structural changes are introduced prior to 1960. A new generation of archaeologists, headed by Johannes Brøndsted, come into power, initiated by a 'palace revolution' at the National Museum in 1932-33.[20] From now on popularization and protection[21] become the main objectives, combined with new types of research. As a foretaste of the new developments the National Museum started to issue a popular yearbook *Fra Nationalmuseets Arbejdsmark* in 1928, and in the 1930s fresh displays were arranged (Klindt-Jensen 1975, Fig. 119/120). New popular books were written, culminating in 1938-40 with Brøndsted's impressive three-volume *Danmarks Oldtid*, which achieved a wide distribution.[22] Therkel Mathiassen initiated a new type of research – regional settlement surveys (e.g. Mathiassen 1948 and 1959), often in

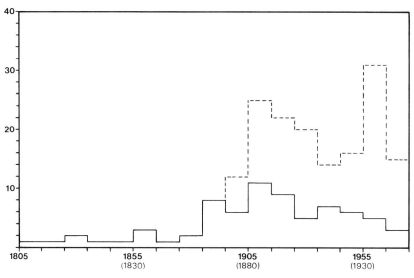

The frequency of private collections in the National Museum, plotted against the year of acquisition (continuous line). In brackets is the date of their foundation, on average 25 years earlier. The broken line shows the frequency of applications/inspections concerning private collections the Museum did not wish to acquire.

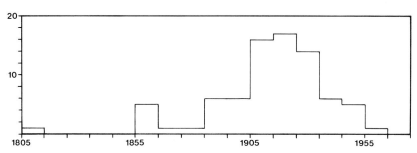

The frequency of culture-historical museums with an archaeological collection (see also Appendix) plotted against the date of their foundation.

collaboration with non-professionals – and a new active type of amateur came on the scene, scouring the fields for sites. This change in the composition of private collections, now mainly consisting of settlement material, was due in part to the new protection law of 1937, forbidding all private excavations, and partly to the new trends in archaeological research. But the stabilization of agriculture, which had yielded most earlier grave and hoard finds (Kristiansen 1974) was also an important factor, and from 1950 onwards the wide-spread use of tractors, leading to deeper ploughing, greatly increased the number of settlement sites uncovered. Many of these amateurs were recruited from among farmworkers, nurserymen, schoolboys, etc – and sometimes their collections later turned into small private museums of a very local nature, especially after 1950, reaching a peak between 1955 and 1964.

In general the founding of culture-historical museums with archaeological collections ceased after 1935; now most provincial centres, and even several small towns have their own museum. Along with this stabilization joint political and organizational procedures were laid down through the work of *DKM* (the Society of Danish Cultural Historical Museums, founded in 1929) and in 1958 new laws redefined their framework (Betænkning No. 152), opening up fresh possibilities through state subvention on a much larger scale than before, a development that accelerated throughout the 1960s and 1970s (Rasmussen 1979, Ch. IV). Also university departments for prehistoric archaeology were formed in 1941 in Copenhagen and in 1950 in Aarhus. An archaeological society for Jutland, Jysk arkæologisk Selskab (Jutland Archaeological Society) and a periodical, *Kuml*, were founded in 1950 as a counter-balance to the Royal Society of Northern Antiquities, whose members were mostly citizens of Copenhagen. Both societies increased their membership throughout the 1950s; it is now some 2,000. It should be mentioned, however, that new types of museums (non-archaeological) have been founded throughout recent years as well, most of them specialized, e.g. technical, musical, photographic history, others based on specific regional or local phenomena (Ørsnes 1978, Fig. 2).

1960-1975

The period after 1960 was characterized by big structural changes in Danish society which also materially affected archaeology. The stabilization of archaeological activities among amateurs and in the archaeological and historical societies led to the founding of archaeological clubs throughout the country, co-operating with museums, and often publishing a small periodical for their members, numbering 100-200 on average. The founding of smaller local historical societies and archives too has increased rapidly in recent years (Warthoe-Hansen 1978). Along with this development 'passive interest' has grown very significantly, reflected in mounting sales of archaeological books, more and more visitors to the museums and much coverage by newspapers, radio and television (Danmarks statistik 1979). The popular archaeological journal *Skalk*, published six times a year, typically reflects this development, an outcome of the very marked social and economic displacements in society which from the late 'fifties on greatly augmented the well educated middle class. From a modest beginning in 1957 the number of annual subscribers to *Skalk* rose to over 60,000 in the 1960s. This popularization process, for which archaeologists have been mainly responsible, now seems to have reached a preliminary climax. Rather typically – and this applies also to the culture-historical framework – the earlier works of Brøndsted and Glob have been reprinted, but gradually the impact of the 'new archaeology' and a growing politico-scientific consciousness is beginning to make itself felt among the younger generation. This is most clearly reflected in the very successful annual, interdisciplinary exhibitions of the National Museum in Brede, north of Copenhagen; these have focused on ecological, social and political problems in both prehistoric and historic perspective, reflected in themes like the history of food production, dress, medical care and health, sport, the position of women in society, etc. As a result of this growing 'passive' interest, and as part of a decentralization policy, the State and the regional authorities have gradually taken over the economic responsibilities of most culture-historical museums, a development that was initiated by the 1958 legislation and further stimulated by a radical government report in 1969 (Betænkning No. 517) which stressed the importance of cultural information in modern society. It was followed by new and more comprehensive laws, the latest in 1977 (Betænkning No. 728) that redefined the organizational structure of the museums within a regional framework. This has led to a remarkable expansion of museum activities through increased professionalization (appendix), reflected in new exhibitions, many new buildings and a flourishing debate about aims and means (e.g. in *Stof*, and Witt 1978). Also revisions of the protection laws in 1969 (Betænkning No. 461), which obliged State and communal authorities to finance excavations of monuments before their destruction, have increased archaeological activities significantly (Nielsen 1964 and 1971) and led to the formation of an autonomous department responsible for rescue excavations and the administration of the protection law (the Administration of Ancient Monuments and Sites, Ministry of Environment). Thus archaeological research has become increasingly differentiated and decentralized, but regulated by central legislations and carried out by professional archaeologists.

Summary and conclusions

Economic development in Denmark took a different course from the rest of Western Europe and strongly influenced the growth of archaeology. Agriculture here became the economic basis, resulting in a delayed development of social and political differentiation; at the same time, since agricultural reforms occurred only a few decades before the establishment of archaeological research, the growth of archaeology became closely linked with agricultural advances. It was not until the second half of the nineteenth century that capitalism and the middle classes developed (transport, trade and communication), heavily dependent on agricultural expansion, and not until the twentieth century that industrialization became a dominant feature of Danish society, including the growing political influence of the working classes. The way in which archaeology gradually penetrated

Danish society, perhaps to a degree unparalleled in other countries, was largely the result of this specific combination of economic, social and political factors. In that process we may distinguish between a *primary* and a *secondary* audience. The emergence of a primary audience (active interest) is linked with the foundation of museums and the closely connected work of collectors and amateurs, beginning in the 1850s and culminating some time between 1880 and 1930, although amateurs remain of great importance. The emergence of a large secondary audience (passive interest) is a later development, connected with the impact of the museums, but especially with the gradually increasing popularization process through books and newspapers. Despite its early beginnings (Thomsen and Worsaae) it was not until the publication of Sophus Müller's *Vor Oldtid* in 1897 that a basis for a more widespread popularization became established. This was furthered by the works of Brøndsted, especially after the publication of *Danmarks Oldtid* in 1938-40 and is reflected in the steady success of *Skalk*, with about one in every 100 Danes as subscriber. (The total population of Denmark is around five million.)

It seems probable that the process of expanding the secondary audience has now reached an optimum. The situation at the present time is shown in the table below:

ARCHAEOLOGISTS	PRIMARY AUDIENCE	SECONDARY AUDIENCE
Permanently employed:	Archaeological	Subscribers to *Skalk: c.*50,000
50 + temporarily employed: *c.*30	societies and clubs: *c.*2,500	Museum visitors: *c.*1 million (in 1975)

A summary of my observations so far, arranged in a chronological and developmental sequence, follows:

1 1805-1850. The beginnings of archaeology

Archaeology is established as a discipline, officially subvented by the King. Collecting and ordering takes first place, administratively supported by regional and local government officials. Interpretations of national and historical myths determine the utilization of its material, mostly by non-archaeologists. No significant popular support.

2 1850-1900. Archaeology is established and expands

A general archaeological prehistory is developed in close co-operation with the natural sciences, revolutionizing the traditional perception of Man's history. Archaeology begins to expand, supported by the progressively more politically and economically influential bourgeoisie, who play a major role in the setting-up of the first provincial museums (archaeology and bourgeois culture) and also by the nobility, who found large private collections. Archaeology becomes a national discipline and the annual accession of new finds reaches its climax.

3   1900-1960. *Consolidation*

Culture-history – the historical and cultural life of the people on all levels – penetrates the relevant sciences and popularizations become widespread. A detailed national and regional prehistory is developed, based on refined archaeological methods (systematic excavations and typology) and now representative archaeological material (burials and hoards). The economically and also politically dominant farmers/peasants and their cultural allies, the teachers, are the main founders of the many new local 'folk museums' throughout the country while becoming private collectors too, along with the still active provincial bourgeoisie. The rising political power of the working classes and, perhaps more important, the economic crisis and the war, gradually slow down this development, which however is compensated for by a growth of the secondary audience.

4   1960-   *Changes and new developments*

Expanded and professionalized popularization of traditional culture-historical type, e.g. *Skalk*, intended to meet the demands of the rapidly growing middle class, increases the secondary audience significantly. Archaeological work is regionally and locally intensified and professionalized; new exhibitions are mounted and new museums built. At the same time new scientific techniques and new theoretical perspectives, inspired by the natural and social sciences, change the scope of archaeology. The consequences of these still on-going developments belong to the future. But they are ultimately determined by the keen awareness among archaeologists of the direction their research within a wider social and scientific framework must take, now that they are dominating research on most of those levels that were formerly occupied by non-professionals during the expansion and integration of archaeology in Danish society.

I have tried to demonstrate how the history of archaeology in Denmark is closely interwoven with economic, social and political history. Having realized this, we may go one step farther, by turning aside from historical details to take a closer look at general points of similarity. A definite pattern then emerges. Thus, if we consider the different groups mainly responsible for archaeological and historical activities at certain times, it turns out that such periods of activity (the founding of archaeological-historical societies, museums, private collections, etc.) run parallel to periods of economic and political consolidation – often following a period of economic and political mobilization. This is true of the bourgeoisie, whose mobilization during the 1830s and 1840s, leading to their political victory in 1848, was followed by increased cultural and historical activities from 1850 onwards. This, in turn, was the mobilization period of farmers and peasants, which, after their political victory in 1901, was followed by a wave of historical and cultural activities, e.g. the 'folk' museums. Also the founding of the Royal Commission for the Preservation of Northern Antiquities and the National Museum came on top of the economic development initiated by the agrarian reforms in 1780s, supported by officials and academics of the great reform period, now facing national and political dangers. And the reason why archaeology failed to expand regionally until the 1850s was due to the economic crisis that ensued in 1813, and the subsequent delayed development of the bourgeoisie as a dominant class.

These general trends suggest that cultural and historical activities indirectly (sometimes also very directly) reflected a wish, perhaps rather a need, to legitimize political and economic positions for which national history provided a powerful ideological framework, making possible an identification of the dominant groups with the cultural heritage of the nation and the 'people'. Its ultimate effect was to change the focus of society from internal to external contradictions, stressing national identity and solidarity as a precondition for progress and sovereignty. Therefore it is hardly surprising that the working classes never took advantage of archaeology, their ideology being rooted in the theories of Marxism; whereas the industrial capitalists were oriented towards art and classical culture. Both groups were international but their internationalism rested on different premises. Today the development of new scientific perspectives, including Marxism, is shifting the scope of archaeology from reconstruction to explanation, from historical peculiarities to systematic and evolutionary regularities, from national archaeology to world archaeology. In many ways this may be said to represent an adjustment to political and economic developments characterized by supranational fusions of various types, by a world economy and by ecological problems on a global scale. This changed attitude towards archaeology poses new scientific challenges comparable to those of the mid-nineteenth century, but it also changes – or adds new possibilities to – the functions of archaeology in society. It follows from this that the importance of archaeological history extends far beyond the teaching of students about the scientific development of the discipline, and must be placed in a wider social context, owing to the simple fact that the evidence of the cultural sciences contributes to the formation of the conceptual framework of Man from which the decisions of tomorrow are taken.[23] The study of archaeological history should therefore be part of a constant and conscious concern with the place and the utilization of our science in society.

APPENDIX

REGIONAL AND LOCAL MUSEUMS IN DENMARK SINCE 1850
WITH CULTURE-HISTORICAL COLLECTIONS, INCLUDING
PREHISTORY.

Museums based on reconstructions and experiments are excluded, as are
private museums (mostly collections of flints) without an official museum
committee. Existing special-purpose museums are marked with an asterisk

LOCALITY OF MUSEUM (Centres in bold type)	FOUNDING YEAR Jutland	Islands	PROFESSIONAL ARCHAEOLOGIST (S) since
Ribe	1855		
Odense		1860	1940
Viborg	1861		1960
Aarhus	1861		1950
Aalborg	1863		1936
Randers	1872		1962
Maribo		1879	1979
Haderslev	1887		1936
Aabenraa	1887		
Hjørring	1889		1959
Kolding	1890		
Herning	1892		1971
Rønne		1893	
Køge		1896	1971
Vejle	1899		1979
Rudkøbing		1900	1946
Nykøbing Mors	1901		1975
Thisted	1903		1971
Silkeborg	1903		1971
Horsens	1906		
Steenstrup		1907	
Sønderborg	1908		
Skive	1908		
Ringkøbing	1908		1972
Kalundborg		1908	
Svendborg		1908	
Nykøbing Sjælland		1909	
Ebeltoft	1909		
Holbæk		1910	1979
Tranebjerg		1910	
Hobro	1910		
Glud	1911		
Skanderborg	1912		
Varde	1912		1978
Stege		1913	
Nykøbing Falster		1913	

Sorø		1915	
Vordingborg		1915	1976
Næstved		1917	
Grenå	1917		
Holstebro	1917		1972
Sæby	1919		
Middelfart		1919	1978
Bogense		1920	
Aars	1920		
Stevns		1921	
Mariager	1922		
Ringe		1922	
Grindsted	1923		
Tønder	1923		
Them	1924		
Haderup	1924		
Reersø		1926	
Odder	1927		
Brande	1928		
Struer	1929		
Skjern	1929		
Try	1929		
Roskilde		1929	
Gilleleje		1929	
Marstal		1929	
Søllerød		1930	
Randbøl	1930		
Fredericia	1930		
Klosterlund	1933		
Faarevejle		1934	
Løgstør	1935		
Orø		1936	
Esbjerg	1936		1969
Mjesing	1937		
Høve		1938	
Helsingør		1944	
Frederikshavn	1946		
Fur	1953		
Hinge	1953		
Værløse		1953	
Ølgod	1954		
Otterup		1958	
*Aarhus (Viking settlement)	1967		
*Roskilde (Viking ships)			
*Vestervig (Early Iron Age settlement)	1975		
Vamdrup	1975		
Strandby	1976		

ACKNOWLEDGMENTS

During my research, the archives and the library of Department One of the National Museum in Copenhagen have been sources of information to which I constantly returned, and my thanks go to all the staff for their hospitality and friendliness throughout the years. In preparing this paper the 'Private Collections' section of the archive was put at my disposal, as well as the records of earlier meetings of the Royal Commission for the Preservation of Northern Antiquities from 1807 to 1834, stored in Department Two. I was allowed to consult member lists of the Royal Society of Northern Antiquaries, which have been published regularly since its inception in 1825. I am specially indebted to Birgitte Kjær, of the Old Town Museum in Aarhus, who permitted me to read her Ph. D thesis 'The Foundation of the first provincial Museums in Denmark in the Middle of the 19th Century', from which I benefited greatly (Kjær 1974). My thanks also go to Holger Rasmussen, of Department Three of the National Museum, for giving me access, before publication, to his manuscript about the history of Danish museums (Rasmussen 1979), and the same applies to Sven Thorsen, of the Administration of Ancient Monuments and Sites (Thorsen 1979), and Jørgen Street-Jensen, of the university library in Aarhus (Street-Jensen 1979). Finally, it gives me special pleasure to express my gratitude to Ole Klindt-Jensen (posthumously, alas) and Peder Mortensen, both of the University of Aarhus, who always aided my research in every possible way, officially and personally, since my early student years.

NOTES

1   A more comprehensive description of this development and its implications for archaeology will appear in a forthcoming book titled *The Representativity of Archaeological Remains from Danish Prehistory* in the series 'Studies in Scandinavian Prehistory and early History', vol. 2.

2   The lack of comparative archaeological material was probably one of the main reasons why archaeology did not develop scientifically during the time between the Renaissance and 1800-1850, despite the efforts of men like Ole Worm, Ole Pontoppidan and others (Klindt-Jensen 1975, 14-45). A case in point is Worsaae's description of how he was led to his first interpretation of the hoards of the Bronze Age when re-arranging the collections of the National Museum, re-establishing the 'closed finds' which had formerly been split up for the greater part (Worsaae 1866: 314). Apparently rather similar conditions were leading Hildebrand and Montelius to their discovery of the principles of typology in Stockholm (Almgren 1965).

3   The Commission was allowed to use the royal seal on letters, and was exempted from paying postage – an important consideration in view of the extent of their correspondence (see also note 8).

4   Frederik VI did not show any serious interest in archaeology, as opposed to his successors, Christian VIII and Frederik VII, who were both active as archaeologists, especially the latter (Klindt-Jensen 1975: 82 f). The royal prestige of archaeology was demonstrated when in 1838 the Czarevitch (later Emperor Alexander II) visited the King at Christiansborg, where the museum was at that time housed. On that occasion several new rooms were added to the exhibition in order to impress the prince (Hindenberg 1859, 70 f). In 1845 Czar Nicholas I was presented with one of the 'lures' from the Bronze Age (now in Leningrad's Hermitage Museum).

5   This goes also for the archaeologists C.J. Thomsen and J.J.A. Worsaae, most explicitly in Worsaae's case. Thomsen's social and cultural background was the age of mercantilism and rationalism and his approach to archaeology reflected this. A 'natural' precondition was economic independence. Worsaae, on the contrary, the son of a senior regional official but without independent means, had gained his position directly through the intervention of the King, who inaugurated a special chair for him in 1847. Since then archaeological research has featured in the State budget, and the archaeologists have been State officials (for a comprehensive account on these economic aspects, see Street-Jensen 1979)

6   The inconsistencies in social terminology and the lack of precise definitions of e.g. 'bourgeoisie middle class' are due to difficulties arising from historical changes in such terminology, from imprecise or unspecific terminology (e.g. titular appellations very common

in the early and middle part of the nineteenth century) – problems which I am not in a position to solve satisfactorily at the present time. For these reasons a more precise quantative analysis of social categories had to be abandoned and replaced by general trends based on statistics from 1830, 1844, 1866, 1887, 1897 and 1931. The stated figures should therefore be regarded as no more than approximations.

7 Throughout this period farmers and peasants had to visit the county office twice a year to pay taxes, a splendid opportunity for an archaeologically interested official – or his son – to establish contact, as described by Worsaae in his memoirs (Worsaae 1934).

8 Already the Commission had adopted the practice of sending copies of the *Annaler* to interested finders of antiquities and to influential persons throughout the country – just as they had already in 1807 written to all pastors asking for information about archaeological monuments which was quickly analysed and published (Thorlacius 1809). The large print-run of Thomsen's book, however, was used as a systematic publicity campaign, in the same way as had the small pamphlet a few years earlier and free copies were widely distributed e.g. to the landed nobility with a plea to distribute copies to their tenants and farm bailiffs. These extensive and expensive campaigns were undoubtedly decisive in widening contacts with all parts of the country, reflected in the rapidly increasing number of finds sent to the museum (Kristiansen 1974, Fig. 1). The economic basis of the campaigns was the increasing wealth of the Royal Society of Northern Antiquaries (Worsaae 1875) who now took over the work of the Commission, which was dissolved in 1849.

9 A remarkable exception to this pattern were the first publications of the sagas in cheap, translated versions (Danish, Icelandic and Latin), which in their homeland, Iceland, were subscribed to by 770 persons (2% of the total population), most of them farmers and ordinary people (Steen Jensen 1975, 13). From other sources we know, however, that the ordinary people in Denmark at that time, mostly farmers and peasants, hardly read any other literature than the Bible and perhaps an almanac (Kristensen 1942a, 19 ff and 1942b, 171 ff).

10 The foundation of the Flensborg museum in 1852, directed by Engelhardt who had settled there to become a schoolteacher, was an outcome of the border conflicts with Germany. In 1859 Engelhardt had started excavations at Nydam and the sensational finds, including the boat, were in the last days of the war shipped to Denmark marked 'unknown destination'. Immediately after the war this resulted in a political wrangle which continued until the secret hiding-place of the finds was at last betrayed when a very impressive reward was offered by the German government (Orsnes 1969).

11 Most of the 'folk' high schools were founded between 1864 and 1870 and soon one in three of each year's prospective young farmers passed through these schools, entirely based on lectures/discussions and without examinations. Thus they represented an important cultural addition to the strictly educational agricultural schools, while representing a unique Danish contribution to the history of education.

12 On Fuen, at his estate Elvedgård, Vedel Simonsen, one of the oldest collectors and members of the committee since 1810, wrote to his old friend and former committee member, Professor Werlauf, in 1852 complaining about the many collectors who were now appearing everywhere. Although he employed four assistants to travel around Fuen, the yields were, he claims, becoming lower: 'because it now becomes a positive mania to collect antiquities, as not only the 'white Doctor' (a well-known and rather controversial figure of the day, who earned his nickname through habitually riding on a white horse and calling himself 'Doctor') travels from house to house, but also the King through his officers buys everything for his collection; added to that come English emissaries and Hamburger-Jews who buy indiscriminately, and finally Count Ahlefeld, the chamberlains Holsteen, Blixen, Wind, 'war adviser' [krigeråd] Theil, ... establish private collections so that one outbids the other.' (Wad 1916, 267). It should be mentioned, however, that until his death in 1858 Vedel Simonsen every year handed over 500 objects to the museum in Copenhagen. From Jutland, too, we hear about foreign antiquity buyers. Feddersen, on the committee of the Viborg museum, writes that the many antiquities uncovered by the construction of the railroad to Viborg in 1865 mainly went to collectors in England. 'Along the tracks the countryside was for several miles roamed by buyers of antiquities for those collectors, and the competition was so brisk that prices for even simpler tools rose considerably; but this only stimulated the demand further and many a worker spent his working day digging in barrows in the hope of finding antiquities.' (Rasmussen 1979, note 4).

13 Note the impressive number of kings and

other royalty, in the founder lists, compared e.g. to the 1830s, indicating the rapidly growing European importance of national archaeology – and the international success of the Society, as seen in the foreign member lists.

14   There was a general advance in many sciences at this time. Thus in 1882 the University was reorganized and divided into separate disciplines along the lines of the German model which was then spreading throughout Europe, reflecting both the growth of learning and the need for more diverse and specialized knowledge to meet the requirements of an increasing economic and social diversification of society.

15   In 1861, 1866, 1889 and 1899 regional historical-topographical periodicals were introduced on Fuen, in Central Jutland and on Zealand (Hvidtfeldt 1949-52).

16   Among the large number of army officers after the German wars were over many were employed in other official work. Not untypically, two of the very active assistants at the National Museum were officers – Captain A.P. Madsen and Lieutenant Daniel Bruun – the latter only for a short period.

17   In addition a specific branch of literature, the so-called 'School-teacher literature' originated from this background (Zerlang 1977,   ).

18   It should be noted that women were not allowed as members of the Royal Society of Northern Antiquaries until 1951.

19   Farmers in particular were culturally active in the more than a thousand local youth associations throughout the country, centred around the village hall. Their activities were closely related to the impact of the 'folk' high schools.

20   As part of newly introduced legislation concerning the protection of the environment all prehistoric monuments were protected by law in 1937, and during the following twenty years recorded and classified according to the degree of protection. Approximately 78,000 monuments, mostly barrows, were recorded and of these 24,000 fully protected (Mathiassen 1938 and 1957).

22   As a concrete example of the popular support the National Museum enjoyed, a national subscription was opened in 1925 to finance a rebuilding of the museum, after having been planned on a political level for several decades (Mackeprang 1938 and 1939).

23   These aspects have been brilliantly demonstrated in a recent book by the Norwegian archaeologist, Christian Keller (1978).

24   Based on Jensen and Møller (1939), Reimert (1976), as well as personal communications. Information about professional archaeologists was put at my disposal by the helpful secretariat of the State Committee of the Danish Museums.

BIBLIOGRAPHY

ALMGREN, B. 1965 Das Entwicklungsprinzip in der Archäologie – eine Kritik. *TOR* Vol. XI. Uppsala.

Aarbøger 1912 Nationalmuseet og Provinsmuseerne. *Aarbøger for nordisk Oldkyndighed og Historie.* Copenhagen.

Betænkning No. 152 1956 *Betænkning om en nyordning af de kulturhistoriske lokalmuseers forhold.* Copenhagen.

Betænkning No. 461 1967 *Betænkning om naturfredning I-II.* Copenhagen.

Betænkning No. 517 1969 *En kulturpolitisk redegørelse.* Copenhagen.

Betænkning No. 727 1975 *Betænkning afgivet af udvalget vedrørende revision af museumslovene.* Copenhagen.

BRØNDSTED, J. 1938-40 *Danmarks Oldtid. Vols I-III.* Copenhagen.

—— 1957-60 *Danmarks Oldtid. Vols I-III.* Copenhagen. (Second edition)

—— 1962 *Nordische Vorzeit. Vols I-III.* Neumünster.

CLAUSEN, H.V. 1916 Studier over Danmarks Oldtidsbebyggelse. *Aarbøger for nordisk Oldkyndighed og Historie.* Copenhagen.

DANIEL, G. 1975 *150 Years of Archaeology.* London.

Danmarks statistik & Kulturministeriet. 1979 *Dansk kultur-statistik. 1960-1977.* (Danish cultural statistics) Copenhagen.

DYBDAHL, V. 1965 De nye klasser 1870-1913. *Politikens Danmarkshistorie.* Vol. 12. Copenhagen.

ENGBERG, J. 1973 *Dansk Guldalder. Eller oprøret i tugt-rasp-og forbedringshuset.* Copenhagen.

EGGERS, H.J. 1959 *Einführung in die Vorgeschichte.* Munich.

FORCHHAMMER, J. 1866 Om oldnordiske Samlinger, historiske Museer osv. navnlig i Jylland. *Samlinger til jydsk Historie og Topografie I*. Aarhus.

Hatt,G. 1949 *Oldtidsagre*. (English summary). Det Kgl. Danske Videnskabernes Selskab, Arkæologisk-Kunsthistoriske Skrifter I, 1. Copenhagen.

Hermansen,V. 1931 Oprettelsen af 'Den Kongelige Commission til Oldsagers Opbevaring' 1807. *Aarbøger for nordisk Oldkyndighed og Historie*. Copenhagen.

Hindenburg, G. 1859 Bidrag til den danske Archæologies Historie. Særskilt Aftryk af *Dansk Månedsskrift*. Ny Række Vol. 1 Parts 2 and 3. Copenhagen.

Hvidtfeldt, J. 1949-52 Dansk lokalhistorie gennem 50 år. *Fortid og Nutid*. Vol. XVIII. Copenhagen.

Jensen,C.A. and Møller,J.S. 1939 *Danske kulturhistoriske Museer*. Copenhagen.

Jensen,Steen J. 1975 Det Kongelige Nordiske Oldskrift-Selskabs stiftelse 1825. (The Foundation of the Royal Society of Northern Antiquaries 1825). *Aarbøger for nordisk Oldkyndighed og Historie*. Copenhagen.

Keller,C. 1978 *Arkeologi – wirkelighetsflukt eller samfunnsforming*. Oslo-Bergen-Tromsø.

Kjær, B. 1974 *De første, danske, kulturhistoriske provinsmuseers oprettelse omkring midten af det 19.århundrede*. Ph.D. University of Aarhus (unpublished).

—— 1980 Gamle Thomsens børnebørn. Om oprettelsen af de første danske provinsmuseer. *Fortid og Nutid*, XXVIII, 3.

Klindt-Jensen, O. 1975 *A History of Scandinavian Archaeology*. London.

Kristensen, Møller S. 1942a *Digteren og Samfundet*. Vol. I. Copenhagen.

—— 1942b *Digteren og Samfundet*. Vol. II. Copenhagen.

Kristiansen, K. 1974 En kildekritisk analyse af depotfund fra Danmarks yngre bronzealder (periode IV-V). Et bidrag til den arkæologiske kildekritik. (A Source-critical Analysis of Hoards from Late Danish Bronze Age (periods IV-V). A Contribution to Archaeological Source-criticism.). *Aarbøger for nordisk Oldkyndighed og Historie*. Copenhagen.

—— 1978 A short History of Danish Archaeology. An Analytical Perspective. To appear in *Studies in Scandinavian Prehistory and Early History*, vol. 2. Copenhagen (see note 1).

La cour, V. 1927 *Sjællands ældste Bygder*. Copenhagen.

Larsen, S. 1935 *Et Provinsmuseums Historie*. Odense.

Mackeprang, M. 1938 Nationalmuseets Byg-ningshistorie I. Perioden 1880-1917. *Fra Nationalmuseets Arbejdsmark*. Copenhagen.

—— 1939 Nationalmuseets Bygningshistorie II. Perioden 1917-1933. *Fra Nationalmuseets Arbejdsmark*. Copenhagen.

Mathiassen,T. 1938 Den nye Fredningslov og de første Forsøg på at praktisere den. *Fra Nationalmuseets Arbejdsmark*. Copenhagen.

—— 1948 *Studier over Vestjyllands Oldtidsbebyggelse* (Studies of the Prehistoric Settlement of West Jutland). Nationalmuseets Skrifter Arkæologiskhistorisk Række II. Copenhagen.

—— 1957 Oldtidminderne og fredningsloven. *Fra Nationalmuseets Arbejdsmark*.

—— 1959 *Nordvestsjællands oldtidsbebyggelse*. (The Prehistoric Settlement of Northwestern Zealand). Nationalmuseets Skrifter. Arkæologisk-historisk Række VII. Copenhagen.

Müller,S. 1897 *Vor Oldtid*. Copenhagen.

—— 1898 *Nordische Althertumskunde*. Strassburg.

—— 1904 Vei og Bygd i Sten-og Bronzealderen. *Aarbøger for nordisk Oldkyndighed og Historie*. Copenhagen.

—— 1907 *Nationalmuseet. Hundreda Aar efter Grundlæggelsen*. Copenhagen.

Neergård,C. 1933 Kammerheree N.F.B. Sehested og hans arkælogiske Virksomhed. *Svendborg Amt. Aarsskrift*.

Nielsen,V. 1964 Nyere Museumslovgivning i Danmark. *Fortid og Nutid XXII*. Part 5.

—— 1971 Status for den antikvariske lovgivning. *Fortid og Nutid XXIV*. Part 5.

Oxenvad, N. 1974 F. Sehesteds museum på Broholm. *Fynske Minder*. Odense.

Olrik, H. 1913 Lærernes Bidrag til Oldgranskning og Historieforskning. *Lærerne og Samfundet*.

Petersen, C.S. 1938 *Stenalder-Broncealder-Jernalder*. Bidrag til nordisk Arkæologis Litterærhistorie. Copenhagen.

Quist,J. 1975 Vorbassedrengene. *Fra Ribe amt*. Vol. XIX.

Rasmussen,H. 1966 The Origin and Development of the Danish Folk Museum. In *Dansk Folkemuseum & Frilandsmuseet. History and Activities*. Axel Steensberg in honour of his 60th birthday 1st June 1966. Nationalmuseet.

—— 1979 *Dansk Museumshistorie*. Manuscript. To appear as a monograph in the periodical *Arv & Eje*.

Reimert, E. (ed.) 1976 *Alle Danske Museer*. Copenhagen.

Riismøller, P. 1971 *Sultegrænsen*. Copenhagen.

SKOVMAND, R. 1964 Folkestyrets fødsel. *Politikens Danmarkshistorie*. Vol. II. Copenhagen.

—— 1975 Den folkelige bølge. *Fra Ribe Amt*. Vol. XIX.

STREET-JENSEN, J. 1979 *Korrespondancen mellem C.J. Thomsen og L. Lindenschmit, med en indledning om det arkæologiske miljø ved det 19.århundredets midte*. Manuscript. To appear in German in a book published by Römisch-germanishes Kommission in Mainz.

THOMSEN, C.J. 1836 Kortfattet Udsigt over Mindesmarker og Oldsager fra Nordens Fortid. I '*Ledetraad til nordisk Oldkyndighed*'. Copenhagen.

—— 1837 Kurzgefasste Übersicht über Denkmäler und Althertümer aus der Vorzeit des Nordens. In *Leitfaden zur nordischen Alterthumskunde*. Issued by the Königliche Gesellschaft für Nordische Alterthumskunde.

—— 1848 *A Guide to Northern Archæology*. London.

THORSEN, S. 1979 'Opofrende Venner og farlige Fjender ... 1890 ernes højplyndringer og et bidrag til arkæologiens socialhistorie. Manuscript. *Fortid og Nutid*, XXVIII, 2.

THORLACIUS, B. 1809 *Bemærkninger over de i Danmark endnu tilværende Hedenolds-Höie og Steensætninger*. Copenhagen.

VIBÆK, J. 1964 Reform og fallit, 1784-1830. In *Politikens Danmarkshistorie*. Vol. 10 Copenhagen.

WAD, G.L. 1916 *Fra Fyens Fortid. Samlinger og Studier*. Vol. II. Copenhagen.

WARTHOE-HANSEN, O. 1978 Lokalhistorisk status. *Festskrift til Johan Hvidtfeldt*.

WITT, T. 1977 *Hvad med museerne?* Wormanium.

Aarhus.

WORSAAE, J.J.A. 1843 *Danmarks Oldtid oplyst ved Oldsager og Gravhöie*. Copenhagen.

—— 1844 *Dänemarks Vorzeit durch Alterthumer beleuchtet*. Copenhagen.

—— 1849 *The primeval antiquities of Denmark*. London.

—— 1875 Tale ved det kgl. nordiske Oldskriftsselskabs halvtredsindstyveaarige Stiftelsesfest under H.Maj. Kongens Forsæde paa Amalienborg d.28. Januar. *Aarbøger for nordisk Oldkyndighed og Historie*.

—— 1877 Om Bevaringen af de fædrelandske Oldsager og Mindesmærker i Danmark. *Aarbøger for nordisk Oldkyndighed og Historie*.

—— 1872-77 Le Conservation des Antiquités et des Monuments Nationaux en Danemark. *Mémoires de la Societé Royale des Antiquaires du Nord*. N.S.

—— 1879 On the Preservation of National Antiquities and Monuments in Denmark. Read before the Society of Antiquaries 1879.

—— 1934 *En Oldgranskers Erindringer 1821-47*. Udgivet ved Victor Hermansen. Copenhagen.

ZERLANG, 1977 *Bøndernes Klassekamp i Danmark*. Medusa. Copenhagen.

JVERSEN. P.K. 1968 De Pokalhistoriske foreningers arbejde i tal. 1966-67. *Fortid og Nutid*. Vol XXIII, Parts 5/6.

ØRSNES, M. 1966 Aarbøger for nordisk Oldkyndighed og Historie 1866-1966 (English summary). *Aarbøger for nordisk Oldkyndighed og Historie*.

—— 1969 Forord til genudgivelsen af *Sønderjyske og Fynske Mosefund* af Conrad Engelhardt.

IV
The background to C.J. Thomsen's Three Age System

BO GRÄSLUND

University of Uppsala, Sweden

Like many great discoveries the Three Age System also has its own prehistory. In many European countries, including Scandinavia, there appeared in the sixteenth, seventeenth and eighteenth centuries scholars who were thinking in terms of a Three Age System for the human past, with a Stone Age, a Bronze Age and an Iron Age (Daniel 1943, 1950, 1967, 1976; H. Hildebrand 1886, 1887; B. Hildebrand 1937-38; Petersen 1938; Klindt-Jensen 1975). This was rather to be expected of the antiquaries of that time, even those who were un-acquainted with the ideas of the classical writers. They knew well, from written sources, that the Celtic and Germanic peoples, as well as the Romans, had based their technology on iron. They must have realized, too, that this iron technology lay at the root of their own culture, that they lived in this Iron Age themselves. So it must have been self-evident to them that iron represented the latest stage in this evolution of technology.

At the same time the discovery of the Americas had made people aware that a cultural stage without the knowledge of metals existed, based only on stone and on organic materials. It must, then, have been very easy to conclude that those stone implements and weapons which were found – without any association with metals – almost everywhere in Europe, also belonged to a stage when the use of metals was still unknown. It will have been natural to assume that the use of stone preceded that of metals, for another reason as well. As Sven Nilsson pointed out, there would be no reason for primitive man to continue to use stone implements after having gained access to metals. He also added that this was confirmed by ethnographical observations (Nilsson 1838:1). For those antiquaries who believed in a separate Bronze Age – whether they were influenced by classical writers or not – there was then no other choice than to place this Bronze period between the Stone Age and Iron Age. Considering, also, that at least some observations of find contexts were available to support the Three Age concept, one can hardly characterize this as pure speculation. No doubt the traditional idea of a Three Age System was a fairly logical one, with some sound and reasonable thinking behind it.

How is it, then, that this idea did not find general acceptance in the antiquarian world before C.J. Thomsen formulated it? Perhaps this question is best answered if we look upon it in the light of Thomsen's own work on the Three Age System, and my aim here is to show that no antiquarian before Thomsen had had any opportunity to demonstrate the validity of the Three Age concept and its general widespread significance.

I tried, some years ago (Gräslund 1974: 97-118), to show that Thomsen did not choose his Three Age System just because it was a logical and convenient way of ordering the materials of a museum; that he had not chosen this system as one theoretical model amongst many others, nor in any essential ways been dependent on the old learned tradition, in spite of the fact that he was acquainted with it. Having examined his written works and his correspondence, I arrived at the conclusion that Thomsen's Three Age System was essentially based on his broad experience of the find contexts, probably already as presented at the opening of the Copenhagen museum in 1819, and definitely by 1836, when his views on the subject were at last published in the famous *Ledetraad til Nordisk Oldkyndighed* (Thomsen 1836: 27-90 – Engl. edn 1848: 25-104). This, incidentally, accords with the testimony of J.J.A. Worsaae in his *Danmarks Oldtid* of 1843, which he wrote after having worked for five years as Thomsen's assistant. Worsaae there assures us that it would never have been possible to systematize chronology into a Three Age System, had it not been for the observations of the find contexts (Worsaae 1843: 60; the English edn, *The Primeval Antiquities of Denmark*, is a considerably enlarged and revised version, Worsaae 1849).

From the very start of his antiquarian career Thomsen stressed the importance of observing both which artifacts had been found together and which had never or seldom been found together. He made this clear in many different connections, and I shall cite a few examples. In a letter to J.H. Schröder, a Swedish historian, he wrote in 1821: 'It is evident, that one has not hitherto paid attention to what has been found together'; in the following year he wrote again to Schröder, that 'the antiquaries will never be able to fix a chronology if they don't observe what has been found together' (Gräslund 1974:105). In 1831, in a little pamphlet on the excavation and preservation of prehistoric finds, he stated that 'the greatest caution must be exercised so as to be able to notice the relative position of the different artifacts deposited – the knowledge of which is often more important than the artifacts themselves' (Thomsen 1831: 2; cf the *Ledetraad*, 1836: 87-90; 1848:100-104). The same thought was vividly expressed in a paper of 1832, where Thomsen, complaining that people too often forgot to note in detail the circumstances surrounding the finds, emphasizes that correct observations of the find contexts are more important for research than 'various false glitter' (Thomsen 1832: 420 f.).

Thomsen, in the *Ledetraad*, did not confine himself to establishing the three ages of stone, bronze and iron. The important thing is that he also attributed to each of these stages a large number of different elements, and that he did so, considering the material known at that time, on the whole correctly. All these chronological attributions clearly show how little evolutionary ideas and theoretical models had contributed to Thomsen's Three Age System in general.

A thorough reading of the *Ledetraad* yields a lot of interesting chronological information. Thomsen knew, for instance, that silver was used in the Iron Age, but never in the Bronze Age or Stone Age. But he also knew that gold, like bronze, was already in use in the Bronze Age and even as early as during the transition from the Stone Age to the Bronze Age, and that the use of bronze continued into the Iron Age (Thomsen 1836: 32, 58 ff.; 1848: 30, 64 ff.). He dated glass vessels to the Iron Age but he also noted that glass beads had been used in the Bronze Age and even in the Stone Age (1836: 38, 60 f.; 1848: 64 ff., 68). He had observed that amber was used in the Stone Age (1836: 58; 1848: 65) and that pottery had been produced during each of the three ages (1836: 40, 58, 60; 1848: 41, 65 f.). Thomsen also ascertained that both cremation and inhumation were practised during the Iron Age as well as the Bronze Age but that inhumation was predominant during the Stone Age (1836: 32, 58, 61 f.; 1848: 30, 64 ff.). Furthermore, he was able to date stone-chambered tombs to the Stone Age but small stone cist graves to the Bronze Age (1836: 58, 60; 1848: 64 f.). And he – again quite correctly – could date timber chamber graves (1836: 32, 61; 1848: 30, 68), ship burials (1836: 32; 1848: 30) and horse burials (1836: 61; 1848: 68) to the Iron Age.

These examples of datings in the *Ledetraad* show above all that Thomsen's Three Age System was much more than a simple division of the prehistoric era into three different stages. There is, in fact, a wealth of other information to be found in this book. Most of these datings are in no way the result of any evolutionary speculation. They provide, instead, strong evidence that they have been chiefly based on observations of find contexts, available in sufficient numbers to allow generalized conclusions. It should be noted in this context that Thomsen was well informed about the prehistoric material, not only from Denmark but also from the rest of Scandinavia and from northern Germany, and he justly claimed that his system was valid for the whole Nordic area (1836: 27 ff., 57 f.; 1848: 25 ff., 63 ff.). Thomsen's Three Age System, as set forth in the *Ledetraad*, is the earliest example of comprehensive chronological research based on scholarly methods. It stands out, among other things, as the first reliable and at the same time detailed chronological handbook in the history of archaeology.

Thomsen's Three Age System differs from all of its precursors on another vital point. That is the definition of the two metal ages. The earlier tradition had never been able to master the fact that bronze had already been in use during the transition phase from the Stone Age to the Bronze Age, and had continued to be in use in the Iron Age. This failure, no doubt, was mainly due to the lack of general find observations and it is one important explanation why the earlier tradition never became fully accepted. Thomsen, however, knew from his wide experience that bronze weapons and implements with cutting edges never occurred in the finds together with iron objects, and he made this observation the basis of his definition of the metal ages (1836: 58 ff.; 1848: 65 ff. Cf. letter to B.E. Hildebrand 1937, see B. Hi ebra 1937-38: 730, note 126). This is another example in the *Ledetraad* of a chronological conclusion which could not possibly have been reached by mere speculation. To arrive at such a conclusion needed wide knowledge of the find contexts. This seemingly very simple definition of the two metal ages provides one clue to the success of Thomsen's Three Age System. It is also a good example of his genius and of his ability to make empirical observations and draw general conclusions. We must bear in mind that Thomsen's Three Age System appeared in a situation of almost total chronological ignorance.

Not much is known about the principles of display in the archaeological museums of that time. However, according to the first printed catalogue of the Copenhagen collections, published in 1846, Thomsen at that time had not only a different series of types but also a certain number of closed finds, on display. We know that the same applied in the middle of the century to the Stockholm museum, where the arrangements were influenced by Thomsen (Sorterup 1846: Gräslund 1974:169 f.). In view of Thomsen's emphasis on find contexts, of which we have early documentary evidence, there is reason to believe that he, at least to some extent, applied a similar principle of display in his museum early on. This is also suggested by the fact that Scandinavian colleagues, visiting the Copenhagen collection, were so readily convinced of the validity of the Three Age System that they, like Hildebrand senior and Keyser, began to introduce the system in museums in their home countries, Sweden and Norway, long before details were published (B. Hildebrand 1937-38: 573-84, 611 ff., 677 ff., 711; Andersen 1960: 121 ff.), the find contexts being in fact the only existing evidence. The fact that Thomsen, in 1823 and 1825, invited Professor Büsching in Breslau (Wrocław) to come to the Copenhagen museum to see for himself the evidence for the Three Age System (Seger 1930: 6), seems to indicate that there actually were some closed finds of chronological significance in the exhibition at that time.

Thomsen was fully aware that there were no sharp lines of demarcation between his three Ages. No doubt, his eagerness to point out that transitional stages existed between the Stone Age and Bronze Age, and between the Bronze Age and Iron Age (Thomsen 1836: 38, 60 f.; 1848: 64 f., 67 f.) is to be regarded as further evidence of his empirical way of working.

Why did the archaeological Three Age System have its scientific breakthrough in Denmark, of all countries? Why not in Germany, England, France or Italy, where there had been an older and more vivid tradition of a Three Age System? One part of the answer is that the cultural development in prehistoric Scandinavia had been more uniform than in many other European countries, which – as Worsaae noted – facilitated the understanding of prehistoric Scandinavian prehistory (Worsaae 1846a:117).

Let us, however, bear in mind that the very precondition for a work like Thomsen's is the opportunity to look at a certain amount of representative closed finds and other find contexts. During the first decades of the nineteenth century the National Museum in Copenhagen rapidly grew into the first museum which was anything like representative for the prehistory of a larger area. It is, then, quite logical that the concept of the Three Age System should have originated in Copenhagen, in fact the one and only place where this could have happened 150 years ago. In most other countries it took considerably longer to establish central museums for national antiquities. As Worsaae pointed out in 1846 (Worsaae 1846a: 125 f.; German edn 1846b; cf. Worsaae's autobiography, Worsaae 1934: 128), this development was ndered in countries like Italy and Germany by political disintegration, or just delayed because, in most countries in southern and western Europe which had once been under Roman rule, antiquarian interest in general was focused more on the magnificent Roman antiquities than on the more prosaic native finds. The Copenhagen museum simply was the only museum at that time where you could easily get a survey of sufficient prehistoric material from a large enough area to allow for a chronological synthesis. Christian Jürgensen Thomsen was the first person ever to have had this opportunity and he also had the qualifications to make use of the situation (Gräslund 1974: 91 ff.).

The different rates at which central museums for national antiquities developed in Europe is, no doubt, closely related to the varying rates of acceptance of the Three Age System. Obviously, the early appearance of such collections in Denmark and Sweden played an important part in the prominent position held by prehistoric research in these two countries during most of the nineteenth century. Several antiquaries in Europe hesitated for a long time to adopt the Three Age System. In Germany for instance there were, as late as the 1880s, prominent scholars who were unwilling to accept the idea of a separate Bronze Age and a separate Iron Age. This hesitation could to some extent be explained by the fact that they had few opportunities to examine large and representative materials and find contexts.

Thomsen's Three Age System has often been called a technological model. This is, however, to conceal its real nature, for it is first and foremost a chronological model. There are, neither in the *Ledetraad* nor in the other works of Thomsen, any speculations on or discussions of the technological and economic developments in prehistoric times, such as we find, for example, in Worsaae's or Nilsson's works. Clearly Thomsen chose the raw materials for his classification because they so conveniently served the aim of creating a rough chronological division of prehistoric times. Thomsen's Three Age System basically was a chronological work, being the first ambitious attempt to generalize chronological observations. Its success and its immense influence on archaeology can be attributed to the fact that it was worked out on sound scholarly principles.

BIBLIOGRAPHY

ANDERSEN, P.S. 1960 Rudolf Keyser. *Embets-mann og historiker*. Bergen.

DANIEL, G. 1943 *The Three Ages*. Cambridge.

―― 1967 *The Origins and Growth of Archae-ology*. Harmondsworth.

―― 1975 *A hundred and fifty years of Archae-ology*. London.

―― 1976 Stone, Bronze and Iron. In *To illustrate the Monuments*. Essays on archae-ology presented to Stuart Piggott on the occasion of his sixty-fifth birthday. Lon-don: 36-42.

GRÄSLUND, B. 1974 Relativ datering. *Om krono-logisk metod i nordisk arkeologi*. Tor 16, 1974. Uppsala.

HILDEBRAND, BENGT 1937-38 *C.F. Thomsen och hans lärda förbindelser i Sverige 1816-1837*. Bidrag till den nordiska forn- och hävdaforsknin-gens historia I-II. Stockholm.

HILDEBRAND, HANS 1886 Zur Geschichte der Dreiperiodensystems. *Zeitschrift für Ethno-logie* 18, 1886 Berlin: 357-67.

―― 1887 Treperiodsystemets uppkomst. *Må-nadsblad* 175-77; 1886: 128-39. Stockholm.

KLINDT-JENSEN, O. 1975 *A history of Scandinavian Archaeology*. London.

NILSSON, S. 1838-43 *Skandinaviska Nordens Ur-invånare, ett försök i komparativa ethnografien och ett bidrag till menniskoslägtets utvecklings-historia*. Lund.

PETERSEN, C.J. 1938 *Stenalder, Broncealder, Jer-nalder. Bidrag til nordisk Archæologis Litterærhistorie 1776-1865*. Copenhagen.

SEGER, H. 1930 *Die Anfänge der Dreiperioden-Systems. Schumacher-Festschrift. Zum 70. Ge-burtstage Karl Schumachers*. Mainz: 3-7.

SORTERUP, J.B. 1846 *Kort Udsigt over Museet for nordiske Oldsager*. Copenhagen.

THOMSEN, C.J. 1831 *Om nordiske Oldsager og deres Opbevaring*. Pamphlet (13 pages). Copenhagen.

―― 1832 Untitled paper in *Nordisk Tidsskrift for Oldkyndighed* 1: 420-21.

―― 1836 *Ledetraad til Nordisk Oldkyndighed*. Copenhagen: 27-29.

―― 1848 *Guide to Northern Archaeology*. London.

WORSAAE, J.J.A. 1843 *Danmarks Oldtid oplyst ved Oldsager og Gravhøye*. Copenhagen.

―― 1846a Den nationale Oldkyndighed i Tydskland. Reisebemaerkninger. *Annaler for nordisk Oldkyndighed og Historie*. Copen-hagen. 116-50.

―― 1846b *Die nationale Alterthumskunde in Deutschland*. Copenhagen.

―― 1849 *The Primeval Antiquities of Denmark*. London.

―― 1934 *En Oldgranskeres Erindringer*. Udg. ved V. Hermansen. Copenhagen.

V
The development of the Three Age System: Archaeology's first paradigm[1]
JUDITH RODDEN

The systematic study, classification and chronological ordering of ancient artifacts and monuments are among the fundamental principles of the discipline of archaeology. In the context of the history of the subject, these principles are generally associated with the emergence of the archaeological Three Age System and the birth of scientific archaeology early in the nineteenth century. C.J. Thomsen is generally credited with having been the first to have envisaged and applied, on the basis of the archaeological evidence, a systematic classification of antiquities according to the criteria of material, use and form, which could be correlated with a sequence of temporal periods: the Ages of Stone, Bronze and Iron familiar to every student of archaeology in the last hundred years. Thomsen's schema was first set out in print in the *Ledetraad til Nordisk Oldkyndighed*, published in Copenhagen in 1836.

Should the publication of the *Ledetraad* in fact be considered as a decisive event in the development of the discipline, as archaeology's historical tradition has long accepted? Does Thomsen's scheme for the classification and relative dating of antiquities really represent a major breakthrough in the study of the unwritten past, and, if so, what attitudes did it replace? Did Thomsen's work serve indeed to establish a basic conceptual and methodological framework for his contemporaries, immediate successors, and for later generations of archaeologists? These questions seek to place Thomsen, his work and ideas, in a general context. They may be answered on several levels.

On one level, the answers to these questions are fairly straightforward. Before Thomsen, thinking about antiquities both in Europe and North America can probably be characterized as intellectually fragmented, and often essentially speculative (Daniel, 1968; Willey, 1968; Willey and Sabloff 1974). By contrast, the publication of the *Ledetraad*, and of its translation into German a year later, unified archaeological studies in northern Europe by providing them, in print, with an 'exemplar' or 'paradigm' for contemporary and future archaeologists to follow and develop. Effectively extending its reach and impact to the British Isles and North America were J.J.A. Worsaae's visit to Britain in 1846-47 (Wilkins, 1961), the translation of the *Ledetraad* into

English in 1848 (Ellesmere, 1848), and Adolphe von Morlot's article in 1861 in the influential *Annual Report of the Smithsonian Institution.* In the second half of the nineteenth century, Thomsen's system became *the* system: his basic classification of artifacts arranged by periods was modified and enlarged, amongst others by Worsaae (1843; 1849), Gabriel de Mortillet (Sackett, chapter VII), John Lubbock (1865), John Evans (1872) and Oscar Montelius (Gräslund, 1974, 168-92 and references). But it was not replaced, and came to be challenged only in the 1920s, when anomalous facts produced by the archaeological record required the adoption of ancillary aims: the reconstruction of past 'lifeways', and the delineation of culture processes.

On another level, in order to answer these questions it is important to analyse the nature of the change of thinking crystallized in Thomsen's achievement. If we consider the originality of Thomsen's contribution to archaeology to lie essentially in his successful combination and practical application of ideas in general circulation in his day, then it is necessary to define and to trace the individual histories of the various concepts and beliefs involved, and the chronology of their first appearances and applications to the study of archaeological objects. This paper will attempt this for what are arguably the three most important elements distinguishable in Thomsen's *Ledetraad.* First, and perhaps most important, was 'essentialism' or typological thinking; 'actualism', or, in archaeological terms, the use of ethnographic analogy, constitutes a second basic concept; while 'directionalism', the application of a reasoned or conjectural 'directional' history to the chronological ordering of the past, is the third.

Essentialism and the Emergence of Systematic Archaeology

Thomsen's archaeology shares with the natural history of his time a primary concern with the naming, describing and classifying of objects: in archaeology's case, artifacts. Behind these aims lay a way of looking at things which has been variously termed 'Aristotelian', 'typological', or 'essentialist' (Popper, 1945; Hull, 1965, Mayr, 1972). 'Essentialism' as a philosophic concept is familiar to archaeologists in the context of our traditional definition of an *artifact type* as a mental construct, an 'ideal plan' or 'blueprint', possessing a unique set of features or attributes essential for its definition: 'what makes the thing what it is'. Historians and philosophers of science have long recognized the practical consequences of such thinking, as applied to the definition of 'types' or 'species', and the actual classification of objects (Mayr, 1957; Pratt, 1972; Hull, 1965, 1970). These are as important to understanding 'essentialist' or 'typological' thinking in archaeology, as in palaeontology or biology. They make for familiar problems in practical classification, and may be briefly stated in general terms as follows:

1 As a 'type' is, by definition, hard, fast and unchanging, the application of the type concept in the practical classification of objects of varying forms leads to the recognition of types on the basis of their observable *morphological differences*.
2 'Degree of morphological difference' as a practical criterion of 'type' is inadequate in itself to cope with continuously varying series.
3 The mental construct of a 'type' is subject to continuous revision under the impact of new information.

Essentialism enjoyed a tenaciously successful existence in both 'scientific' and general philosophic thought from St Thomas Aquinas through the nineteenth century. It is only from the mid-sixteenth to the mid-seventeenth centuries, however, that we have the first attempts to name and to classify objects in a manner relevant to Thomsen's scheme several centuries later. The key lay in the general impact of the 'New Science', more specifically of what William Harvey, an early member of the Royal Society, termed 'ocular inspection' of '*Nature* her selfe', upon the Aristotelian 'essentialist' tradition of the Renaissance. The influence perhaps is most clearly seen in the work of the Danish antiquary, Ole Worm. Where he had a clear precedent to follow, as with small objects, their arrangement by class on the shelves of his museum — his 'Cabinet of Naturalia' — is by classic 'Aristotelian' essences: *terrae* (earth), *lapides* (stones), *metal*, etc. (Worm, 1655, bk 1 and frontispiece) [2]. Where he had no guide, as in 'reducing into order that great multitude of stony monuments in his country', Ole Worm

'... first makes a general division of them into two *classes:* namely ... the letter'd monuments, such as consisted of large stones, with inscriptions in Runic or Gothic characters, speaking their occasions and intentions; and unletter'd, which were composed of rude stones, without engravements, but so disposed after a certain manner, as that the beholder might, from the order of their position, collect upon what accidents, and for what ends or uses they had been set up ... Then he subdivides this latter sort into five distinct ranks: namely, into *sepulchra*, tombs, containing the bones of eminent persons defunct; *fora*, places of judicature, where right and justice were administered, according to the laws and customs of the country; *duellorum strata*, cirques or places of duels, or camp-fights; *trophea*, trophies, where battels had been fought, and the enemy defeated; and *comittalia loca*, places wherein kings and supreme commanders were elected by the general suffrages of the people, and inaugurated with great pomp and publick solemnity, such as the rudeness of that nation, and the simplicity of those times, afforded. This scheme being drawn, as the rule of his method, he thenceforward proceeds to examples of each kind: and we are obliged therein to follow him step by step, that so we may the sooner, and without deviation, arrive at a competent degree of satisfaction, whether any, and which of all those different sorts of antique monuments, hath so near a resemblance of *Stone-Heng*, as that we may, from the apparent *similitude* of their forms, infer a probable affinity in their origins and designations.'

(Charleton, 1725, 28-29; citing Worm, 1643, bk 1).

This pattern, of the classification of monuments by observable attributes, and of artifacts by their traditionally accepted properties, continued throughout the seventeenth and early eighteenth centuries. So Ole Worm, in his classification of *lapides* in his museum, included what were in actuality prehistoric stone axes as 'thunderstones' or 'cerauniae', writing

'... so called because they are thought to fall to earth in the lightning flash. They have various shapes, sometimes conical, sometimes hammer- or axe-shaped, and with a hole in the middle. Their origin is disputed; some deny they are meteorites, supposing from their resemblance to iron tools that they are really such tools transformed into stones.'

(Worm, 1655, 74; quoted in Klindt-Jensen, 1975, 23).

In the present context this quotation is particularly relevant in that the description, which is objective, does not make for the classification, which stems from classical thought as represented in Pliny's *Natural History;* and there is the accompanying notion of the transformation of iron tools into stone.

The immediate antecedents to Worm's views are to be found in the early works on mineralogy (Agricola, 1546; Gesner, 1565; de Boodt, 1609; de Laet, 1647); as far as 'cerauniae' are concerned, these reflect a growing scepticism as to the traditional origin of these objects as 'thunderbolts'. These studies also demonstrate the tentative beginnings of attempts at the objective description of artifacts according to such observable criteria as shape and colour. So, for example, Conrad Gesner, in his *De Rerum Fossilium* (1565) still used the classificatory term 'cerauniae', but went to some lengths to describe the objects in question — of which he illustrated four examples — mentioning that they were of varying colours, weights and proportions and that they varied in shape, some resembling hammers or wedges, and others being discoid or claviform.

The disappearance of the 'cerauniae' as a classificatory label may be dated initially as from the publication in 1648 of Ulysses Aldrovandus's *Museum Metallicum*, and is closely related to the discovery of actual primitive peoples who used stone tools (see below). Here the classification of stone artifacts was in terms of the names of familiar tools, as was to be the case with Thomsen: 'knife' and 'axe', for instance. But it was not until the early eighteenth century that the concept of 'cerauniae' was formally abandoned, more or less at the same time that the idea of the transmutation of types was relinquished. The clearest statement to this end was made by the geologist and antiquary, John Woodward (1728). Woodward was vehemently critical of earlier views on stone tools: although these objects 'carry in them so plain tokens of *Art*' and their shapes indicated the purposes for which each was intended, former scholars had been so blinded by preconceptions 'that they have set forth these Bodies as natural Productions of the Earth, under the name of *Cerauniae*'. Woodward continued, drawing upon the contemporary store of ethnographic information, that the stone implements had been made prior to the discovery of iron, and represented all the usual types of tools.

That other relevant preoccupation of late seventeenth-century natural philosophy — a belief in transmutation and the spontaneous generation of materials, types or 'species', has already been mentioned. In natural history a belief in the spontaneous generation of species was prevalent – though not held by John Ray – until well into the eighteenth century. As a theme in sixteenth and seventeenth-century thought, such notions, as cited above with regard to the 'cerauniae', appear in other contexts to which attention has recently been drawn. Abramowicz in a valuable paper (see chapter XIII) has drawn attention to the existence of ideas of spontaneous generation regarding the origin of pottery vessels buried in the earth. As deduced from available references, the time-span for the duration of this view is from the late fifteenth to the mid-eighteenth century, comparable with the period for similar ideas about the 'cerauniae'; and in the broader context, with the theory of the spontaneous generation of animal and plant species (Mayr, 1957; Hoppen, 1976).

The connection between these early classifications and the belief in the transmutation of forms is an important one; as long as it continued, the difficulty of defining types, and of classifying objects, by objective, fixed criteria, remained. Linnaeus broke with tradition, and his conception of the reality, constancy and sharp delimitation of biological species at once established a taxonomic system incompatible with the idea of the transmutation of organisms, and compatible with the popular and generally accepted eighteenth-century doctrine of the 'Great Chain of Being'. Perhaps John Woodward represents a comparable watershed as far as the recognition of the true meaning of fossils in general, and of the 'cerauniae' in particular, are concerned (cf. J.M. Levine, *Dr. Woodward's Shield*, Univ. California Press, 1977). It is only with the early nineteenth century, however, that systematic classifications, based upon objectively defined and constant types, appear in archaeology.

This is not strictly true: an apparent general exception are early attempts at the classification of megalithic monuments, earthworks and barrows, which, from the beginning, were differentiated into types on the basis of objective, observable criteria. Ole Worm's division of 'stony monuments' into 'letter'd' and 'unletter'd' classes, cited above, is a clear and unambiguous case in point. This is an unusually systematic statement; elsewhere in the seventeenth and eighteenth centuries one is essentially dealing with 'working classifications' of field monuments, drawn up for a particular purpose. In the case of John Aubrey, seventeenth-century polymath and pioneer field archaeologist, his 'working classification' of megalithic monuments certainly included 'stone circles' as a class, concerning which he wrote, 'I have arranged these monuments together, for the neer resemblance they have to one another'; and elsewhere, 'to work-out and restore after a kind of Algebraical method, by comparing them that I have seen, one with another; and reducing them to a kind of Aequation' (quoted in Hunter, 1975, 180, notes 4 and 7). Aubrey's search for an ideal 'Aequation' by which his 'less imperfect' (e.g., 'Stone-Heng' and 'Aibury') and 'more imperfect and ruinated' examples might be grouped together, can only be interpreted as a quest for the essential and defining feature of the class. Aside from his unrealized ideal plan – the 'blue-print' defining the type – Aubrey apparently considered associated morphological features, 'ditches and straggling stones' as defining properties (Hunter, 1975, 180).

Later seventeenth-century British antiquaries, writing on megaliths for Gibson's 1695 edition of *Camden's Britannia*, while obviously familiar with, and drawing upon, Aubrey's earlier work, set out informal classifications for typological groupings of megalithic antiquities suitable for their particular regions. Perhaps closest to Aubrey's typology was Sir Robert Sibbald's classification of the megalithic monuments in Scotland and the Orkneys. Sibbald's types included 'circles of stones' ('henge' monuments) and 'obelisks' (single standing-stones) (in Gibson, 1695, 955 and 1085). Edward Lhwyd, writing on Wales, again employs the class 'stone circles'; single chambered tombs, depending upon their size and the inclination of the capstone, are given local names, either *kromlech*, for the larger, generally free-standing monuments, or *kist-vaen*, for the smaller stone cist graves (in Gibson, 1695, 620, 627, and 636-37). The work of Ole Worm was certainly familiar to Lhwyd, as it was to John Aubrey and Walter Charleton before him; and undoubtedly Piggott (1976, 15-16) is correct in suggesting that Worm's work stimulated an interest in, and early comparisons with, the Danish and Swedish counterparts of these monuments. Dom Bernard de Montfaucon (1719-1724) also drew upon northern European comparisons in discussing French megaliths, in this case the Cocherel gallery-grave discovered in 1685 near Dreux. Also in France, Legrand-d'Aussy in the late eighteenth century pioneered a classification of the Breton megaliths, relying, as Lhwyd had done, upon local parlance for type names, in this instance 'menhir' for single standing-stones, and 'dolmen' for chamber-tombs (Daniel, 1960).

John Aubrey was apparently the first to express interest in, and to attempt to classify, another set of field monuments, namely earthworks. Here, Aubrey did explicitly differentiate between types on the basis of differences in form, and in so doing established a tradition which was to last in parts of Britain for more than a century. So he wrote in his *Monumenta Britannica* that Robert Plot, another antiquary and early member of the Royal Society, and Lhwyd's predecessor as Keeper of the Ashmolean Museum at Oxford, 'knew not how to distinguish a Roman camp from a Danish camp till I told him'; 'The Roman Campes are allwayes Square, or at least squarish; and a single worke'; Danish camps (elsewhere Aubrey calls them British) were 'Round, or roundish, and double or treble workes' (quoted in Hunter, 1971, 189; and in Hunter, 1975, 188, note 6). Thomas Tanner systematically applied Aubrey's distinction between Roman and Danish camps to the earthworks of Wiltshire in his *Additions* to Gibson's edition of the *Britannia* (1695, 99-114). In Aubrey's and Tanner's own area — Wiltshire — Colt Hoare, as late as 1812, was characterizing 'earthern-works' as 'of a square or oblong form, bounded by straight lines, and with rounded angles' invariably as Roman camps — an interesting view if one also recalls his professed reluctance to credit the theories of earlier antiquaries in the area. In the interim, Aubrey's original ideas appeared to have held sway in Scotland. There, intellectual tradition attended to both the classical and the scientific in the later seventeenth and eighteenth centuries, and Roman remains were of exceptional interest. Roman camps were recognized by Robert Sibbald on the basis of their square or rectangular form (Sibbald, 1695); as they were to be in the eighteenth century by Sir Walter Scott's fictional antiquary and his immediate predecessors, both fictional and actual (Piggott, 1976, Nos 7 and 8).

There is little in these studies to excite 'measure for measure' comparison with the specific systematic and comprehensive scheme of classification devised by Thomsen. But already it is possible to recognize in these working classifications implications which later profoundly influence the direction of archaeological research. As a philosophical concept, there can be little doubt but that typological thinking based on observation played an operative role in antiquarian studies as from the late seventeenth century. Most noteworthy is the fact that — as an approach — it was applied almost exclusively to the study of field monuments, and not to artifacts [3]. In this situation, one of the first consequences was to stimulate fieldwork, either directly, or indirectly through questionnaires. [4] There was either the need for a 'complete sample' of the occurrences of a type, itself already established as being of 'historical' importance; or, following natural theology and the 'principle of plenitude', the need for a 'complete series', in order to fill any recognizable gaps in God's perfect creation. [5] The fieldwork of Worm, Aubrey, Lhwyd and Sibbald, it can be argued, is cast primarily in terms of the first mould; as regards the second, Colt Hoare's (1812) examination and classification of 'tumuli' or barrows is perhaps most notable.

Colt Hoare's study belongs to Thomsen's own time, and as an essay in classification comes closest in orderliness and thoroughness to Thomsen's own work. Colt Hoare's classification of barrows, in particular, is a model in the exercise of the typological method; [6] and while it owes something to the earlier work of Aubrey and the eighteenth-century antiquary, William Stukeley, it in due course itself became the basis for barrow classification and nomenclature by external form down to the present day (Grinsell, 1953; Ashbee, 1960). Here we have for the first time in archaeology an attempt at a formal classification which depends upon observable, morphological characters for the definition of types, and for the differentiation of one type from another. The concomitant notions of constancy and fixity of type had profound implications for the development of archaeology. In natural history, this led to a concept of species change which inevitably involved abrupt creations and extinctions, whether on a catastrophic (e.g., Buckland), or micro-catastrophic scale (e.g., Lyell), and a 'punctuated' version of the earth's history. The corollary in archaeology was the *invasion model* of cultural change, and once Thomsen 'opened up' objective archaeological classifications to include artifacts in addition to monuments, a chronological ordering of the 'heathen' past by hard and fast 'technological' or 'industrial' periods. [7]

Actualism and Artifactual Interpretation

The use of ethnographic analogy, of the 'comparative approach', of *actualistic comparisons*, lies at the heart of Thomsen's and of more recent archaeological interpretation. Thus Thomsen, in so far as was possible in his *Ledetraad*, classified and named the 'objects of stone' belonging to his 'Heathen Period' by analogy with the form and function of hand-tools in use in his own country in his own day: 1) whetstones, 2) wedges, 3) chisels or gouges, 4) knives and lanceheads, 5) flint flakes and arrowheads, 6) axes, 7) axe-hammers, 8) hammers, 9) slingstones, 10) querns and 11) pendants; Thomsen's other categories of stone tools, as might be expected, follow strictly formal classes: semi-lunar implements, shuttle-shaped stones, nuts or knobs, discs having a hole in the middle, balls and anchors. On another level, Thomsen, in his *Ledetraad* (1836, 58), offers the comparison between the habitual use of stone tools by the Stone Age inhabitants of northern Europe and modern 'savages'. Eleven years earlier, in a letter to Johann Gustav Büsching, an antiquarian colleague of Breslau (now Wrocław, Poland), Thomsen — less inhibited, perhaps, than when he wrote for publication — stated more freely and fully:

'It seems clear to me that in an early period, all of northern Europe — Scandinavia, most of Germany, France and England — was inhabited by actually very similar and very primitive races. That these correspond to the wild North Americans in many respects, is certain. They were war-like, lived in the forest, were not acquainted with metals (or only sparingly so), divided themselves into large groups, and were partly slain, partly subjugated and partly pushed back into hinterlands and remote areas.'

(quoted in Seger, 1930, 4).

In building up a coherent picture of the use of ethnographic comparison in archaeological interpretation prior to Thomsen, it is obvious that the nature of the original sources upon which the comparisons were based should be considered, if only in a preliminary manner. Potentially, there were three quite different kinds of reference material available to seventeenth- and eighteenth-century Europeans upon which analogies with contemporary 'primitive' peoples could be drawn: 1) descriptive or narrative reports by explorers, travellers or early colonists; 2) contemporary illustrations, most generally commissioned to accompany such accounts, voyages or atlases; and 3) ethnographic collections, made by collectors, colonists or others (e.g., traders) who visited the newly-discovered lands. Piggott (1976, Nos 2, 4 and 6) has commented on the early use (as from the later sixteenth century in Britain) of drawings of American Indians to suggest the appearance of ancient Britons; while tools and weapons are depicted in these illustrations along with other artifacts, they are not shown either as frequently or with a degree of precision which, ideally, one would like to suggest as being likely to lead to tangible application; and in the absence of any definite reference, it is difficult to evaluate the importance of these representations in the interpretation of British prehistoric artifacts. Almost certainly the published reports which these illustrations accompanied were the primary sources used by seventeenth-century antiquaries. Such usages ultimately led to the establishment of a 'tradition': initially, this reflects comparatively specific reference to the sources; later, these were accepted as given.

The first century of the exploration of America saw the beginnings of the interrelationship. Comments upon the Carib Indians, dating from Columbus's second voyage to the New World, include, 'they do not work the wood with iron or with steel, which they lack, but with sharply-pointed stones fitted with a wooden handle' (Morison, 1963, 235). In the same area, but half a century later, Oviedo y Valdés (1959, 26 and 29) pointed out: 'there are other weapons of reed grass, or straight light canes, on the point of which they fix a flint tip'; and, 'after they have killed the animals, since they do not have knives with which to skin them, they quarter them and cut them to pieces with stones and flints.' Such accounts of the New World proved tremendously popular, including, in Britain: Richard Hakluyt's *Divers Voyages touching the Discoverie of America* published in 1582, Peter Martyr's *Decades of the New World*, and Thomas Hariot's *A briefe and true report of the new found Land of Virginia* (1588), the volume for which John White made the well-known series of water-colour paintings of North American Indians and with which the hypothetical early Britons were compared almost at once, as mentioned above. Often going into many editions, they frequently repeated the pro-colonizing 'formula' of the native Americans 'having no edge weapons of iron or steel to offend us withal.'

These early sources provided the primary basis for the comparison of 'primitive' tools with prehistoric ones; and the first objective realization that a time could have existed in human history 'that knew not yet the use either of Iron or of any Metal' (Montfaucon, 1719-1724). Historically, comparisons between prehistoric artifacts and the tools of contemporary primitive peoples first became widespread in the second half of the seventeenth century. The use of more sweeping analogies, involving interpretation of 'levels' of economic, social or political development, such as employed by Thomsen (quoted above) and later nineteenth-century archaeologists, dates in the main from the eighteenth century and the philosophic historians of the French and Scottish Enlightenments (see below). In natural history, the concept behind the use of these types of comparison has been termed 'actualism' by Hooykaas (1959) and, following him, Rudwick (1971).

The principle behind the approach may be briefly stated: the observation of *actual phenomena* — those existing at the present day or during recorded human history — can provide a reliable guide to the interpretation of the past. [8] Actualism is, therefore, only a method or approach to evidence, and its results and conclusions are comparably circumscribed. Applied to the point of absurdity, it implies that no phenomena could have existed in the past except for those which can be witnessed in the present, and indeed these must have been present in the past to a similar degree. The need for qualification and explanation, therefore, is inherent in the application of the actualistic method. This is a particular requirement of comparisons on the 'general' level — where systems, and not objects, are being reconstructed. In this section I shall restrict myself to the interpretation of objects based upon the comparison of prehistoric and contemporary artifacts.

British antiquaries began making comparisons between the stone arrowheads and axes in their collections and those in 'contemporary' use by American Indians as early as 1656. William Dugdale (1656, 778) in all likelihood was drawing upon Amerindian parallels in reconstructing the hafting of his Oldbury flint axe when he conjectured:

'they being at first so made by the native Britans, and put into a hole, boared through the side of a staff, were made use of for weapons, inasmuch as they had not then attained to the knowledge of working iron or brass to such uses.'

Thirty years later, Plot was using actual ethnographic specimens as a basis for his interpretations: writing on stone celts he comments, 'how they might be fastened to a helve, may be seen in the Musaeum Ashmoleanum, where there are several Indian ones of the like kind,

fitted up in the same order as when formerly used' (Plot, 1686, 397).
Regarding that other category of familiar stone tools, flint arrowheads, Lhwyd wrote from Scotland in 1699, where apparently he
had just seen Sibbald's 'elf-arrows':

'I doubt not but you have often seen of those arrowheads they ascribe to elfs or
fairies: they are just the same chip'd flints ye natives of New England etc. head
their arrows with, at this day: and there are also several stone hatchets found
in this kingdome, not unlike those of the Americans.'

(quoted in Gunther, 1945, 420; and Piggott, 1976, 19).

Such specific comparisons, based either upon written sources or
upon actual objects in European collections, are not limited to Great
Britain or to the seventeenth century. Kilian Stobaeus, Professor of
Natural Science at Lund, writing in 1738, also made use of actual
American Indian tools — in this case from Louisiana — in his interpretation of Swedish flint artifacts (Klindt-Jensen, 1975, 38); but
Stobaeus's comparisons were for the more general purpose of elucidating a very ancient phase in Scandinavia's past. Heizer (1962a) cites
similar examples from France and Germany in the eighteenth century.
This is not unexpected: from around the middle of the eighteenth
century it is probably fair to say that specific comparisons, as cited
above, between American Indian and ancient European stone artifacts virtually cease. The implications had come to be taken for
granted, and attention was now directed towards more general comparisons between the behaviour and institutions of 'primitive' peoples
and the conjectural stages of Europe's remote past.

A Directionalist Ordering of the Past: the Three Age System

When coming to speak in general terms in his *Ledetraad* about the ages
to which his antiquities might be referred, Thomsen (1836, 57; Ellesmere, 1848, 63-64) begins: 'Our collections are however still too recent
and our facts too few for the drawing of conclusions ... The remarks
which we now proceed to offer must therefore be viewed merely in the
light of conjectures, destined to be confirmed or rectified in proportion
as a more general attention is devoted to the subject.' Thomsen was
proceeding cautiously; the writing of a conjectural history of the past,
based upon a record dug from the earth, was a risky business, and was
also recognized as such by the geologists of the period. Colt Hoare
resolutely refused to undertake the task. [9] Thomsen had the advantage
of writing in 1836, and not in 1812: in a historiographically 'wide-
open' Denmark where both Enlightenment 'universal' history and
and nationalist romanticism could play a role, and not in Whig
England, where there was a little need either for 'universal' histories
with their implications of progress and improvement, or, by this date,
Druidical romanticism; and possibly with the benefit of a larger, or

more comprehensive, record of systematic observations of find contexts and associations upon which to draw conclusions (Gräslund,
1974, and chapter 4 *supra;* Klindt-Jensen, 1975, 57). Certainly the
completeness of the record as it was being recovered from the earth
was being continuously extended all over Europe, as was the nature of
the actualistic comparisons involved in its interpretation. When combined with the growing implications of an 'evolutionary', 'progressive', or '*directional*' pattern of the past, the conclusions made were
initially hesitant, but obvious.

The quest for a comprehensible past — preferably one following a
trend or overall pattern — in the eighteenth and early nineteenth
centuries has been well surveyed by historians for history (Bury, 1932;
Teggart, 1949; Collingwood, 1946; Bock, 1956), anthropologists for
anthropology (cf., most recently, Harris, 1968), archaeologists for
archaeology (Daniel, 1943, 1950; Piggott, 1960; Heizer, 1962a), and
historians of science for geology, biology and palaeontology (Gillispie,
1951; Haber, 1959; Toulmin and Goodfield, 1965; Rudwick, 1972).
When applied to objects dug from the earth, whether fossils or artifacts, the terms 'evolution' and 'progress' as we understand them, are
inappropriate for the period under consideration. As regards 'evolution', the mechanism for the steady unfolding of clearly differentiated
biological species remained to be discovered; and as Daniel (1943;
1950) has rightly noted, comes regularly to be applied to cultural
change only a quarter of a century after the publication of Thomsen's
guidebook. 'Progress' is very much an Enlightenment term, but its
confounding sense of satisfaction or dissatisfaction for any particular
direction of change in terms of moral, aesthetic or other value judgements renders the use of the term inappropriate in any analysis of ideas
outside the Age of the Enlightenment *per se*, without substantial
qualification. Rudwick (1971) employs the term *directionalism* in the
context of the history of science, as one being more neutral yet
descriptive of overall trends or patterns through time. This term is
more suitable to our purposes, for it is generally applicable to archae-
ologistical constructions such as Thomsen's, as well as to the early
conjectural 'universal' and 'national' histories that were being written
in the eighteenth and early nineteenth centuries.

Directionalist thinking about the human past in the late seventeenth, eighteenth and early nineteenth centuries — especially when it
incorporated a scheme characterized by successive stages of increasing
technological, economic or social complexity — had a basis both in a
logical and reasoned estimation of what man's primitive condition
must have been (i.e., inductive reasoning), and in deduction, founded
upon observation and comparison of available evidence. So, for example, the Scottish Enlightenment historian, William Robertson, relied
upon the American Indian to provide the prototype examples for his
successive stages of 'Progress'; and, exceptionally, upon European

artifacts for the justification that such a history had a 'universal' reality (Robertson, 1777; Hoebel, 1960). In all likelihood, Robertson was following the earlier French Enlightenment historian Antoine-Yves Goguet in part in his reference to artifacts, and to a 'universal' history with a pre-metal using age succeeded by one characterized by gold, silver and copper. Goguet's book, *De l'Origine des Lois, des Arts et des Sciences, et de leurs progrès chez les anciens peuples* (1758), ran into three French editions, and was translated into English and published, significantly, in Edinburgh in 1761.[10] The connection between contemporary primitive humanity and the earliest periods of history — involving reason, ethnography and archaeology, is even more explicit in Cornelius de Pauw's *Recherches Philosophiques sur les Ameriquains, ou Mémoires Intéressantes pour servir a l'Histoire de l'Espèce Humaine*, which was published first in Berlin in 1768-69, and appeared in at least six more editions, in addition to an English translation of 1806. In this work, de Pauw, a friend of Diderot and d'Alembert, wrote of 'les haches de pierre qu'on déterre en Suède, et en Allemagne, a des très-grandes profondeurs, et qui doivent etre extrêmement anciennes, ayant eté employées avant l'invention du fer et du cuivre', and that savages of the New World also made use of such artifacts at the present day.

In arguing deductively from the contemporary ethnographic record, as well as inductively, for the existence of a pre-metal using industrial stage, Robertson, Goguet and de Pauw were making use of observations reaching back to the first discovery of America. Reference has already been made to the frequent mention, by explorers and settlers in the late fifteenth and sixteenth centuries, of the absence of steel or iron weapons among the Indians of the New World. By the second half of the seventeenth century, the logical extension of these reports to the concept of a time in the history of mankind when tools had been made out of stone, was being suggested; by the eighteenth, it was being regularly employed — not only by Enlightenment historians — but by antiquaries and the writers of 'national' histories. The names of the antiquaries are familiar ones: Dugdale (1656), Woodward (1728) and Lyttleton (1773) in Great Britain; Montfaucon (1719-1724), Jussieu (1730) and Mahudel (1740) in France; Eckhart (1750) in Germany; and Stobaeus (1738) in Scandinavia. The notion of a Stone age, and subsequently of successive Bronze and Iron ages, then, was already well established prior to the nineteenth century, and it should come as no surprise that Thomsen, and others engaged in the writing of conjectural 'national' histories in northern Europe, should incorporate it into their own work.

It is to be expected as well that the use of actualistic comparisons of a more general kind should become more commonplace, and be cast with reference to the 'universal' stages of the Enlightenment historians: viz. hunting, pastoralism and farming (Turgot); or savagery, barbarism and civilization (Montesquieu, Ferguson and Robertson). The importance of this aspect of Enlightenment thought in the writing of 'histories' of northern Europe remains to be systematically explored. There can be no doubt, however, that Sven Nilsson's directionalist scheme for early societies (Nilsson, 1838-43; Petersen, 1938; Klindt-Jensen, 1975) — savages, nomads and farmers — represents an attempt to apply Enlightenment 'universal' history to the 'national' history of Scandinavia: Nilsson's 'savages' are, in fact, his Stone Age hunters and fishers, whose lifeways he also reconstructed employing actualistic comparisons in accepted Enlightenment manner. Thomsen's own indebtedness to the Enlightenment in this respect is less well seen. But it may be noted that Thomsen also equates the Stone Age with 'savagery'; and that his reconstruction of their way of life, previously quoted, is already familiar by the middle of the eighteenth century.

The Nature of Thomsen's Contribution

In assessing the nature of Thomsen's contribution to archaeology, this paper thus far has focussed upon the historical background to his work, and attempted to trace the development of those ideas and concepts which together constitute the foundation of his achievement. Three basic conceptions are involved:

1) *Essentialism*, or typological thinking. First objectively applied to the study of archaeological monuments. The systematic classification of artifacts employing the type concept began only with Thomsen, and depended upon the recognition of artifacts for what they were, objective description, and abandonment of the conceptions of 'Aristotelian' essences and transmutation.

2) *Actualism*. Tacit acceptance of the validity of ethnographic comparison lay behind the identification of artifacts as tools, deductive arguments for the existence of stone, bronze and iron technological stages, and conjectures on the customs and institutions of early peoples.

3) *Directionalism*. Belief in an underlying directional pattern to change in the human past was necessary for the chronological ordering of the 'prehistoric' past by successive technological stages.

As an interdependent complex, these historically separate concepts were accepted as a *paradigm* by archaeologists in the later nineteenth and earlier twentieth centuries; this paradigm both governed research and defined the general direction of scientific thought. The originality of Thomsen's achievement was that the *Ledetraad* was the first instance of these ideas – which had historically lengthy individual existences – being presented together as a complex and in print. It was as a complex that these ideas were recognized and accepted as being relevant to archaeology.

The question may now be asked: does Thomsen's contribution to archaeology then constitute a 'revolution' in the discipline (Kuhn, 1962; Greene, 1971; Mayr, 1972)? It may be described as such if it is accepted that Thomsen's 'bundle' of ideas did indeed constitute a paradigm which was followed by the archaeological community in the later nineteenth century; and if it is acknowledged that, as a scientific revolution, it took several centuries to achieve. The success of Thomsen's 'package' lay in its acceptability — it was the right thing at the right time; basically, that package named, described and classified, but did not seek to explain.

NOTES ON THE TEXT

1   For an interest in the history of the Three Age System, I owe a very great deal to Professor Glyn Daniel, and also to Professor Stuart Piggott; I am also deeply indebted to Professors John Howland Rowe and the late Robert F. Heizer, of the University of California at Berkeley, for suggestions as to references and for many stimulating discussions; and, most particularly, to my husband for a very considerable amount of practical help and valuable criticism during the writing of this paper.

2   A fair comment upon type classifications, strictly applied, is the inevitable and familiar category for the otherwise unclassifiable objects: Ole Worm's *varia*.

3   At least in Great Britain and Scandinavia.

4   Both Lhwyd and Sibbald relied heavily upon these in compiling their contributions to the *Britannia*.

5   The early and influential rationalist philosopher, Spinoza, argued that 'every fact of existence must be held to have its roots in the eternal order' (Lovejoy, 1936); he included man's products in his scheme (Harris, 1968).

6   In his classification of barrows, Colt Hoare first differentiates between *long* barrows and *circular* (= round) barrows. Circular barrows were further subdivided into the following main types: *bowl* barrows, *bell* barrows, '*druid*' barrows (= disc); and *pond* barrows (Hoare, 1812, 20-23).
   A second class of objects, where differences in shape and size were used as differentiating criteria, was the associated pottery. Colt Hoare (1812, 25-27) recognized as separate types: 1) *sepulchral or funereal urns* (= collared urns); 2) *drinking cups* (= bell beakers); and 3) *incense cups* (also grape cups).

7   'Heathen': pre-Christian; and because northern Europe was not incorporated into the Roman Empire, 'prehistoric'.

8   The term originated with Hooykaas and was subsequently picked up by Rudwick. Their concern was to analyse the various conceptions of *uniformitarianism* employed in the great Lyellian debate on geological processes and agencies of the 1830s and 1840s. Rudwick has defined four *logically distinct* types of 'uniformity' and their opposites, while recognizing that there may be more:

   a)   *theological*
        (in relation to the creative activity of God) — Naturalistic *vs.* Supernaturalistic;
   b)   *methodological*
        (correspondence/analogy with actual phenomena) — Actualistic *vs.* Non-actualistic;
   c)   *rate* of action — Gradualistic *vs.* Saltatory;
   d)   overall *pattern* — Directional *vs.* Steady-state (the original meaning of 'uniformitarianism').

9   'I have wandered as little as possible into the regions of fancy and conjecture, and I have endeavored throughout my whole progress to adhere most scrupulously to my motto, and to SPEAK FROM FACTS, NOT THEORY', concluded Colt Hoare in the now classic report of his barrow excavations with William Cunnington (Hoare, 1812, 254). It is significant that a conjectural dating of their barrows according to contents was suggested to Cunnington and Colt Hoare, but ultimately discarded. The suggestion came from the Rev. T. Leman of Bath, and in its references recalls

the ideas of the 'universal' historians discussed below:

'I think we distinguish three great eras by the arms of offence found in our barrows. 1st those of bone and stone, certainly belonging to the primeval inhabitants in their savage state, and which may be safely attributed to the Celts. 2nd those of brass, probably imported into this island from the more polished nations of Africa in exchange for our tin, and which may be given to the Belgae. 3rd those of iron, introduced but a little while before the invasion of the Romans.'

(quoted in Cunnington, 1975, 76).

10 Goguet (1761, vol. 1, 140-61, quoted in Heizer, 1962b, 14-21) clearly argues a three age technological model in which agriculture and 'all the mechanical arts...owe almost all their improvements to the discovery and use of metals':

'All nations were originally in the same state of ignorance. We have incontestable, proofs of this, independent of the testimony of historians. A kind of stones commonly called *thunderstones*, are still preserved in a great many cabinets ... It is evident from inspection alone, that these stones have been wrought by the hands of men ... This is something more than a mere conjecture ... It is well known, that tools of stone have been in use in America from time immemorial ... They are frequently found ... There must then have been a time, when the people of these countries were ignorant of the use of iron, as the people of America were before the arrival of the Europeans ... Metallurgy, however, was an early discovery amongst the nations who applied to agriculture ... These countries were the first where mankind settled, and formed themselves into powerful monarchies. I am however of opinion, that, in these ages, they understood only the working of a few metals, as gold, silver and copper. Iron, that metal so necessary, and at present so common, was long either unknown, or but little used.'

Goguet's sources included Scripture, the classical authors, accounts of travellers such as Dampier, artifacts, and the fund of general knowledge which existed at his time concerning the natives of the New World.

BIBLIOGRAPHY

AGRICOLA, GEORGIUS (Bauer, George) 1546. De natura fossilium. In *De ortu et causis subterraneorum; de natura eorum quae effluunt ex terra; de natura fossilium; veteribus et noviis metallis; Bermannus, sine De re metallica Dialogus*, pp. 171-380. Basle.

ALDROVANDVS, ULYSSES 1648. *Musaeum Metallicum*. Compiled by Bartholomew Ambrosinus. Bologna.

ASHBEE, PAUL 1960. *The Bronze Age Round Barrow in Britain*. London.

BOCK, KENNETH E. 1956. *The Acceptance of Histories. Toward a Perspective for Social Science*. University of California Publications in Sociology and Social Institutions, vol. 3, no. 1. Berkeley and Los Angeles.

BOODT, ANSELMUS BOETIUS DE 1609. *Gemmarum et Lapidum Historia*, ... Hanover.

BURY, J.B. 1932. *The Idea of Progress: An Inquiry into its Origin and Growth*. New York.

CHARLETON, WALTER 1725. *Chorea Gigantum: or, the most famous Antiquity of Great Britain, vulgarly called Stone-Heng, standing on Salisbury-Plain, restored to the Danes*. 2d edn. London.

COLLINGWOOD, R.G. 1946. *The Idea of History*. Oxford.

CUNNINGTON, ROBERT H. 1975. *From Antiquary to Archaeologist: A biography of William Cunnington, 1754-1810*. Edited by James Dyer. Princes Risborough, Aylesbury, Buckinghamshire.

DANIEL, GLYN E. 1943. *The Three Ages: An Essay on Archaeological Method*. Cambridge.

—— 1950. *A Hundred Years of Archaeology*. London.

—— 1960. *The Prehistoric Chamber Tombs of France: A Geographical, Morphological and Chronological Survey*. London.

—— 1968. One Hundred Years of Old World Prehistory. In *One Hundred Years of Anthropology*, edited by J.O. Brew, pp. 57-93. Cambridge, Mass.

DUGDALE, WILLIAM 1656. *The Antiquities of Warwickshire, illustrated; from records, leiger-books, manuscripts, charters, evidences, tombes and armes: beautified with maps, prospects, and portraictures*. London.

ECKHART, JOHANN GEORG VON (Eccardus) 1750. *De origine Germanorum eorumque vetustissimis coloniis, migrationibus ac rebus gestis libri duo. Ex Schedis manuscriptis viri illustris edidit, figuras aeri incisas adiecit. et praefatus es Christianus Ludovicus Scheidus*. Göttingen.

ELLESMERE, EARL OF, ed. and trans. 1848. *Guide to Northern Archaeology*, the Royal Society of Northern Antiquaries of Copenhagen. London.

EVANS, JOHN 1872. *The Ancient Stone Implements, Weapons and Ornaments of Great Britain*. London.

GESNER, CONRAD 1565. *De Rerum Fossilium, Lapidium et Gemmarum maximè, figuris et simili-*

tudinibus Liber: non solùm Medicis, sed omnibus rerum Naturae ac Philologiae studiosis, utilis et iucundus futurus. Zurich.

GIBSON, EDMUND (ed. and trans.) 1695. *Camden's Britannia.* London.

GILLISPIE, CHARLES COULSTON 1951. *Genesis and Geology: A Study in the Relations of Scientific Thought, Natural Theology, and Social Opinion in Great Britain, 1790-1850.* Harvard Historical Studies, vol. 58. Cambridge, Mass.

GOGUET, ANTOINE YVES 1758. *The Origin of Laws, Arts, and Sciences, and their Progress among the Most Ancient Nations.* 3 vols, translated by R. Henry (vol. 1), Dr Dunn (vol. 2) and A. Spearman (vol. 3). Edinburgh, 1761. First published as *De l'Origine des Lois, des Arts et des Sciences, et de leurs progrès chez les anciens peuples* in Paris.

GRÄSLUND, BO 1974. *Relativ datering: om kronologisk metod i nordisk arkeologi.* Tor, vol. 16. Uppsala.

GREENE, JOHN C. 1971. The Kuhnian Paradigm and the Darwinian Revolution in Natural History. In *Perspectives in the History of Science and Technology,* edited by Duane H.D. Roller, pp. 3-25. Norman.

GRINSELL, L.V. 1953. *The Ancient Burial-Mounds of England.* 2d edn, rev. London.

GUNTHER, R.T. 1945. *Life and Letters of Edward Lhwyd: Second Keeper of the Musaeum Ashmoleanum.* Early Science in Oxford, vol. 14. Oxford.

HABER, FRANCIS C. 1959. *The Age of the World: Moses to Darwin.* Baltimore.

HARIOT, THOMAS 1588. *A briefe and true report of the new found land of Virginia: of the commodoties there found and to be raysed, as well marchantable ... Directed to the Adventurers, Favourers, and Welwillers of the action, for the inhabiting and planting there.* London.

HARRIS, MARVIN 1968. *The Rise of Anthropological Theory: A History of Theories of Culture.* New York.

HEIZER, ROBERT F. 1962a. The Background of Thomsen's Three-Age System. *Technology and Culture* 3 (1962): 259-66.

—— (ed.) 1962b. *Man's Discovery of his Past: Literary Landmarks in Archaeology.* Englewood Cliffs, N.J.

HOARE, SIR RICHARD COLT. 1812. *The Ancient History of South Wiltshire.* London.

HOEBEL, E.A. William Robertson: An 18th Century Anthropologist-Historian. *American Anthropologist* 62 648-55.

HOOYKAAS, R. 1959. *Natural Law and Divine Miracle. A Historical-Critical Study of the Principle of Uniformity in Geology, Biology and Theology.* Leiden.

HOPPEN, K. THEODORE 1976. The Nature of the Early Royal Society: Parts I and II. *British Jnl for the Hist. of Science* 9: 1-24 and 243-73.

HULL, DAVID L. 1965. The Effect of Essentialism on Taxonomy — Two Thousand Years of Stasis (I). *British Journal for the Philosophy of Science* 15: 314-26.

—— 1970. Contemporary Systematic Philosophies. *Annual Review of Ecology and Systematics* 1 19-54.

HUNTER, MICHAEL 1971. The Royal Society and the origins of British archaeology: Parts I and II. *Antiquity* 45 113-21 and 187-92.

—— 1975. *John Aubrey and the Realm of Learning.* London.

JUSSIEU, ANTOINE DE. 1725. De l'Origine et des Usages de la Pierre de Foudre. *Histoire de l'Académie Royale des Sciences* for 1723 (Mémoires de Mathématique et de Physique section: 6-9). Paris.

KLINDT-JENSEN, OLE 1975. *A History of Scandinavian Archaeology.* London.

KUHN, THOMAS, S. 1962. *The Structure of Scientific Revolutions.* International Encyclopedia of Unified Science, vol. 2, no. 2. Chicago and London.

LAET, JOHANNES DE 1647. *De Gemmis et Lapidus, Libri Duo: Quibus praemittitur Theophrasti Liber de Lapidieus Graece et Latine cum Brevibus Annotationibus.* Leiden.

LOVEJOY, ARTHUR O. 1936. *The Great Chain of Being: A Study of the History of an Idea.* Cambridge, Mass.

LUBBOCK, JOHN 1865. *Pre-historic Times: as illustrated by Ancient Remains, and the Manners and Customs of Modern Savages.* London and Edinburgh.

LYTTLETON, CHARLES Bishop of Carlisle. 1773. Observations on Stone Hatchets. *Archaeologia* II: 118-23.

MAHUDEL, NICOLAS 1740. Les Monumens les Plus Anciens de l'Industrie des Hommes, et des Arts reconnus dans les Pierres de Foudre. *Histoire et Mémoires de l'Académie Royale des Inscriptions et Belles-Lettres, Institut de France* 12: 163-69.

MAYR, ERNST 1957. Species Concepts and Definitions. In *The Species Problem.* Publication No. 50 of the American Association for the Advancement of Science, edited by Ernst Mayr: 1-22. Washington.

—— 1972. The Nature of the Darwinian Revolution. *Science* 176: 981-89.

MONTFAUCON, DOM BERNARD DE 1719-24. *Antiquity Explained, and Represented in Sculptures.* Translated into English by David Humphreys. 5 vols. London, 1721-22. First published as *L'Antiquité Expliquée, et Représentée en Figures,* in 5 vols, in Paris.

MORISON, SAMUEL ELIOT. ed. and trans. 1963. *Journals and other Documents on the life and voyages of Christopher Columbus.* New York.

MORLOT, CHARLES ADOLPHE VON 1861. General Views on Archaeology. *Annual Report of the*

Board of Regents of the Smithsonian Institution ... for the year 1860: 284-343.

NILSSON, SVEN 1838-43. *Skandinaviska Nordens Ur-invånare, ett försök i komparativa Ethnografien och ett bidrag till menniskoslägtets utvecklings-historia.* Lund.

OVIEDO Y VALDÉS, GONZALO FERNÁNDEZ DE 1526. *Natural History of the West Indies.* Translated and edited by Sterling A. Stoudemire. University of North Carolina Studies in the Romance Languages and Literatures, no. 32. Chapel Hill, 1959. First published as *De la natural hystoria de las Indias* in Toledo.

PAUW, CORNELIUS DE 1768-69. *Recherches philosophiques sur les Amériquains, ou Mémoires intéressantes pour servir à l'histoire de l'espèce humaine.* Berlin.

PETERSEN, CARL S. 1938. *Stenalder, Broncealder, Jernalder: Bidrag til nordisk Arkaeologis Litteraerhistorie 1776-1865.* Copenhagen.

PIGGOTT, STUART 1960. Prehistory and Evolutionary Theory. In *Evolution After Darwin*, edited by Sol Tax, vol. 2, *The Evolution of Man: Man, Culture and Society*, pp. 85-97. Chicago.

—— 1976. *Ruins in a Landscape: Essays in Antiquarianism.* Edinburgh.

PLOT, ROBERT 1686. *The Natural History of Stafford-shire.* Oxford.

POPPER, KARL R. 1945. *The Open Society and Its Enemies*, vol. 1, *The Spell of Plato.* London.

PRATT, VERNON 1972. Biological Classification. *British Journal for the Philosophy of Science* 23: 305-27.

ROBERTSON, WILLIAM 1777. *The History of America.* 2 vols. London.

RUDWICK, MARTIN R.S. 1971. Uniformity and Progression: Reflections on the Structure of Geological Theory in the Age of Lyell. In Duane H.D. Roller (ed.), *Perspectives in the History of Science and Technology*, 209-27. Norman.

Rudwick

—— 1972. *The Meaning of Fossils: Episodes in the History of Palaeontology.* London.

SEGER, HANS 1930. Die Anfänge des Dreiperioden-Systems. In *Schumacher-Festschrift: Zum 70. Geburtstag Karl Schumachers:* 3-7. Mainz.

SIBBALD, SIR ROBERT 1695. The Thule of the Ancients. In *Camden's Britannia*, edited and translated by Edmund Gibson: 1089-1102. London.

STOBAEUS, KILIAN 1752. Ceraunii Betulique Lapides dissertatione historica illustrati. 1738. Pt 4 of his *Opuscula in quibus Petrefactorum, Numismatum et Antiquitatum Historia illustratur, in unum volumen collecta.* Danzig.

TEGGART, FREDERICK J., (ed.) 1949. *The Idea of Progress. A Collection of Readings.* Rev. edn, with an intro. by George H. Hildebrand. Berkeley and Los Angeles.

THOMSEN, C.J. 1836. Kortfattet Udsigt over Mindesmaerker og Oldsager fra Nordens Fortid. In *Ledetraad til Nordisk Oldkyndighed:* 27-87. Copenhagen.

TOULMIN, STEPHEN, and GOODFIELD, JUNE 1965. *The Discovery of Time.* London.

WILKINS, JUDITH (Rodden) 1961: Worsaae and British Antiquities. *Antiquity* 35: 214-20.

WILLEY, GORDON R. 1968. One Hundred Years of American Archaeology. In *One Hundred Years of Anthropology*, edited by J.O. Brew: 29-53. Cambridge, Mass.

WILLEY, GORDON R., and SABLOFF, JEREMY A. 1974. *A History of American Archaeology.* London.

WOODWARD, JOHN 1728. *Fossils of all Kinds, Digested into a Method Suitable to their mutual Relation and Affinity . . .* London.

WORM, OLE (Wormius, Olaus) 1643. *Danicorum Monumentorum Libri Sex: E spissis antiquitatum tenebris et in Dania ac Norvegia extantibus ruderibus eruti ab Olao Worm.* Copenhagen.

—— 1655. *Museum Wormianum. Seu Historia rerum rariorum, tam Naturalium, quam Artificialium, tam Domesticarum, quam Exoticarum, quae Hafniae Danorum in aedibus Authoris servantur.* Leiden.

WORSAAE, J.J.A. 1843. *Danmarks Oldtid oplyst ved Oldsager og Gravhøie.* Copenhagen.

—— 1849. *The Primeval Antiquities of Denmark.* Translated, and applied to the illustration of similar remains in England by William J. Thoms. London and Oxford.

VI
Giants and pygmies: the professionalization of Canadian Archaeology [1]

BRUCE G. TRIGGER
McGill University, Montreal, Canada

In 1853, a 37-year-old Scotsman named Daniel Wilson arrived in Toronto, Canada, with his wife and children, so that he might occupy the chair of History and English Literature at University College at the even then meagre salary of £350 a year. Although he had been unable to find suitable employment in his native land, this talented and versatile scholar was already recognized as one of Europe's most accomplished archaeologists of the new school based on the work of Christian Thomsen (Hale, 1893; Wrong and Langton, 1901; Simpson, 1963; McIlwraith, 1964; Trigger, 1966a). In 1848, he had published *Memorials of Edinburgh in the Olden Time*, a two-volume collection of his pencil sketches of old and recently demolished buildings in the Scottish capital accompanied by an account of interesting events in the history of the city. In 1851, he published *The Archaeology and Prehistoric Annals of Scotland*, following which he was awarded the honorary degree of Doctor of Laws by the University of St Andrews. That book was the first major effort to apply the Scandinavian Three Age system to the study of British archaeology. In it, Wilson broke with the prevailing tradition of British antiquarianism and correctly saw the work of Thomsen as constituting 'the foundation of archaeology as a science'. He had made use of his position as an honorary secretary of the Society of Antiquaries of Scotland to collect information about standing monuments and artifacts found throughout Scotland, which he studied when feasible typologically. Wilson divided his book into four sections, which he devoted to the Stone (Primeval), Bronze (Archaic), and Iron Ages and to the Christian period. Within each section, individual chapters were assigned to various classes of data – tombs, fortifications, dwellings, weapons, vessels, ornaments, art, religion, and domestic life. He also advocated that the display of artifacts at the British Museum should be organized on the basis of Thomsen's system and advocated the repeal of the Treasure Trove law in Scotland, which he demonstrated had encouraged the destruction of many artifacts made of precious metals. Wilson's decision to leave Scotland was obviously taken most reluctantly and after his hopes of obtaining a suitable academic or administrative position there had been exhausted.

Archaeology in Canada before 1850

Substantial European settlement in what is now southern Ontario had begun only after the American Revolution. By 1850, however, the agricultural settlement of this region was complete and a period of more complex social and economic development was under way. Nevertheless, the cultural and intellectual attainments of all parts of Canada lagged far behind those of Great Britain and the east coast of the United States, where European settlement had progressed more rapidly than in Canada. Because of the work of eastern institutions, archaeological investigation throughout the United States was considerably ahead of what it was in Canada. Southern Ontario remained a new society that was preoccupied with practical matters and in which men of talent and ability were quickly absorbed into business or public life. Art, literature, and other pursuits that did not have immediate practical application were viewed as suitable avocations rather than vocations for any man worthy of respect. Also the historian R.S. Harris (1976: 87) has observed that prominent Canadians of that period were so involved in the political and religious controversies of the day that they were rarely able to appreciate the timeless world of scholarship.

Yet prior to Wilson's arrival in Canada, there had been a growing, if minor, interest in archaeology in the various colonies that in 1867 were to become the founding provinces of Canada. As early as 1696, the French merchant Charles Aubert de La Chesnaye recorded the discovery of Indian tools in the course of European agricultural operations in Quebec (Martijn, 1978:12). The oldest surviving archaeological collection in Canada appears to be a group of stone artifacts, including some magnificent projectile points, dating from the Archaic period (2000 to 3000 BC), unearthed in 1700 by workmen at Bécancour, midway between Montreal and Quebec City. They are still preserved in the small museum of the Ursuline sisters at Trois-Rivières (Ribes 1966). Yet the quality of the intellectual life of the thinly-populated colony of New France is best indicated by the fact that it did not contain a single printing press prior to the British conquest in 1760.

Later, French Canadians tended to be most interested in archaeological problems that were related to their own colonial history. In 1844, the Jesuit Pierre Chazelle had securely identified the stone ruins of two mission headquarters that his order had abandoned in Ontario prior to 1651. In the 1850s, Father Félix Martin and Father Joseph-Charles Taché, the latter of Laval University, explored the country around these missions and studied Indian sites associated with them. Taché excavated sixteen Huron ossuaries, or bone pits, but no account of his work has survived. The records of Martin's *Voyages et Recherches* are preserved in manuscript (A.E. Jones, 1906: 7; Kidd, 1952: 4; Martijn, 1978: 13).

In Ontario and the Maritime Provinces, farmers and other interested individuals assembled private collections of Indian artifacts
during the first half of the nineteenth century. Such materials were
included in the short-lived museum that Abraham Gesner, the in-
ventor of kerosene, opened in St John, New Brunswick, in 1842
(Noble, 1972: 5; Connolly, 1977: 7). Beginning in the 1830s, Iroquoian ossuaries in Ontario were dug into by curiosity-seekers, some of
whom had genuine scientific interests. Yet no local journals were being
published that could record the results of such activities, even if there
were a desire to do so. What is known comes from brief newspaper
accounts, publications in foreign journals, or later compilations of
recollections (e.g., Bawtree, 1848; Dade, 1852; Van Courtland, 1853).

In 1849, a group of provincial land surveyors, civil engineers, and
architects living in and near Toronto took the first steps to found the
Canadian Institute (later the Royal Canadian Institute). It was incorporated in 1851 and became the most influential of a series of
natural history societies that were established by professional men with
scientific interests in different parts of Canada (*Canadian Journal*
1852a). The Natural History Society of Montreal, which was formed
in 1827, also began to function more actively in the 1850s, and both
the Natural History Society of New Brunswick, in St John, and the
Nova Scotian Institute of Natural Science, in Halifax, were founded
in 1862. The Antiquarian and Numismatic Society of Montreal,
which was at first exclusively interested in numismatics, was also
founded that year. Each of these societies had some members who
were interested in archaeology and they published journals in which
archaeological papers began to appear. In 1852, the Canadian Institute distributed a circular (also reproduced in its periodical *The
Canadian Journal* 1852b) urging the recording of Indian sites, which
it was anticipated would be discovered in considerable numbers in the
course of railway construction. It also urged the donation of artifacts
to the society's museum, then in process of formation. The circular's
strong emphasis on mounds and earthworks reflected the influence of
E.G. Squier's *Aboriginal Monuments of the State of New York*, which the
Smithsonian Institution had published in 1849. Although the circular
was unsigned, it was drafted by Sandford Fleming, a civil engineer
who was later to devise the present world-wide system of standard
time. [2]

Daniel Wilson

As soon as Daniel Wilson arrived in Canada he began to take an
interest in the country's archaeology. Following a visit to Canada, his
friend Robert Chambers, the anonymous author of *The Vestiges of
Creation*, wrote to Wilson, 'I had been mourning over you as banished,
cut off from all congenial pursuits . . . but here I find you fit into your

own favourite tastes as aptly as though Graeme's slough had marked out the line of your Toronto railway!' (Trigger, 1966a: 22). Wilson sought to acquaint Canadians with what was happening in Europe and to promote work of similar quality in Canada (Wilson, 1854). He urged the careful excavation and recording of archaeological discoveries (Wilson, 1855: 346-47; 1856: 517-18). He also began to take measurements of Indian skulls (as he had already done with prehistoric Scottish ones) and published an article in *The Canadian Journal* urging the establishment of a Canadian collection of prehistoric crania (Wilson, 1855; 1857). This work was to result in Wilson's far-reaching critique of the conclusions of Samuel Morton's *Crania Americana*, which had appeared in 1839.

In the summer of 1855, Wilson made the first of several difficult trips as far west as Fond du Lac, on the shores of Lake Superior, where he examined prehistoric Indian copper mines. About the same time, he investigated Indian remains discovered along the north shore of Lake Erie.[3] In 1860, Egerton Ryerson, Chief Superintendent of Education for Canada West (i.e., roughly southern Ontario), carpingly noted that 'in his leisure moments [Wilson] has devoted himself to disembowelling the Cemeteries of the Indian tribes in seeking up Tomahawks, Pipes and Tobacco which may be found there and writing essays upon them' (Harris, 1976: 87). In fact, Wilson did not set out to excavate archaeological sites in Canada any more than he had done so in Scotland. His method, like that of Thomsen, was to study the archaeological record as it was available to him from chance finds, publications, and museum collections.

Wilson began to observe many parallels between the archaeological remains found in the Old and the New Worlds, beginning with similarities in pottery. Having been trained in the tradition of the Scottish Enlightenment, he generally interpreted these as evidence of independent parallel evolution resulting from psychic unity, rather than ascribing them to diffusion from one hemisphere to another. He also believed that the Canadian Indians' way of life exemplified what European societies had been like in early prehistoric times, and that white pioneer society recapitulated certain aspects of life in the European Dark Ages. Hence, while Wilson continued to study the archaeology and physical anthropology of the native peoples of eastern Canada, his interests rapidly expanded to embrace the ethnography and languages of the entire New World. He also expressed enlightened views about racial mixture and the acculturation of Indians to white ways that were of considerable social and humanitarian importance.

These new interests helped Wilson to edit an improved second edition of *The Prehistoric Annals of Scotland*, published in 1863, but they found their fullest expression in *Prehistoric Man: Researches into the Origin of Civilisation in the Old and New Worlds*. This book appeared in 1862, was revised in 1865, and largely rewritten in 1876. Although it was one of the first major attempts to synthesize the culture-history of the New World, it also signalled the shift of Wilson's interest from archaeology *per se* to the broader perspective of anthropology in the modern American sense. *Prehistoric Man* was well received in the United States and also influenced, so Horatio Hale (1893: 260) informs us, German anthropologists. In 1882, an American reviewer described it and *The Prehistoric Annals of Scotland* as 'training-books for the present generation of scholars' (Starr, 1882: 307), while the New York State archaeologist A.C. Parker (1907: 460) compared Wilson's works in importance with those of Lewis H. Morgan and the American archaeologists E.G. Squier and E.H. Davis, stating that 'with those works, a new epoch dawned'. Justin Winsor (1889: 376-77) viewed *Prehistoric Man* as being an American counterpart of Sir John Lubbock's *The Origin of Civilization*. He complained, however, that although it was the evident result of long study, the book was 'not well fortified with references'. This lack no doubt resulted from the limited library resources that were available to Wilson in Toronto.

One reason why Wilson's interests became pan-anthropological and hemispheric in scope was that he had found too few data assembled for Ontario or any other delimited portion of the New World, for him to apply there the relatively detailed artifact-based approach that he had employed in Scotland. Nor were the lithic artifacts of North America as susceptible to chronological interpretation as the stone, bronze, and iron ones of Europe had been. Rather than undertake the slow and relatively unrewarding task of assembling necessary data, by carrying out excavations and recording surface finds, Wilson sought to deal with broader or different problems for which sufficient data were at hand. In a study of the Huron Indians who had lived not far north of Toronto until the seventeenth century, that Wilson (1884) wrote late in his life, archaeological data were scarce and used only to illustrate arguments based on historical and ethnographic sources. This was typical of antiquarian scholarship in North America at this period (Trigger, 1970).

In the course of his academic career, Wilson was drawn into defending the interests of his college and the cause of secular education in Ontario. He was also active in championing various university reforms, including latterly the admission of women to university lectures. His skill in practical matters came to be greatly admired. In 1880, he was appointed second president of University College, an office that by 1887 had evolved into the first presidency of the reorganized University of Toronto. Wilson's growing administrative burden cut into the time that was available for his 'favourite study' of anthropology. Although he was able to visit Europe several times and the United States quite frequently, he came to feel cut off from the mainstream of scientific development. It is significant that he felt it necessary to ask the British ethnologist, E.B. Tylor, to prepare an appendix dealing with archaeology for a popular book on *Anthropology* that he, Wilson, published in the Humboldt Library series in 1885 – this for a scholar who had once been one of Europe's foremost pre-historians! Wilson's sense of isolation was exacerbated by the fact that his intellectual sympathies remained British and European. He was more often critical than approving of the reasoning of American anthropologists. Yet Wilson (1885; 1892) continued to produce major anthropological studies until his death in 1892.

It is perhaps typical of the adverse environment in which Wilson conducted his anthropological research that a semi-official biography written a few years after he died slandered his scholarly work, with Philistine pride, as being 'more diffuse than accurate' and stated that had he remained primarily a scholar 'the real man would have been submerged' (Wrong and Langton, 1901: 204). It is also indicative of this environment that Wilson never established (or, to my knowledge, tried to establish) a permanent teaching position in archaeology or anthropology at the University of Toronto.

John William Dawson

Another prominent Canadian academic who interested himself in prehistoric archaeology was John William Dawson, principal of McGill University from 1855 to 1893 (Trigger, 1966b). Dawson was born in Nova Scotia and studied geology at the University of Edinburgh. Although he had worked with the eminent British geologist, Charles Lyell, in the Maritime Provinces in 1841, and therefore must have been familiar with Lyell's uniformitarian approach, Dawson's religious convictions inclined him to a catastrophist view of geology. After 1859, he also became an outspoken opponent of biological evolution. In addition, Dawson was interested in general problems of prehistory as they affected the literal interpretation of the Bible. He produced two books dealing piously with the Hebrew scriptures and the Holy Land in the light of archaeology and natural history (Dawson, 1860a, rewritten 1877; 1888).

In 1859, Dawson published a description and discussion of a complete Iroquoian pottery vessel from Pontiac County, Quebec, that had been deposited in the museum of the Natural History Society of Montreal. The following year, he recorded most of the information that is now available concerning an important Iroquoian site (subsequently known as the Dawson site) which came to light adjacent to the McGill University campus in what is now the centre of Montreal. This occurred when excavations for building purposes were being made there (Dawson, 1860b; 1861; Pendergast and Trigger, 1972). He also ensured that much of the material collected at that site made its way into museums. Great interest was aroused by this find, since it yielded a small amount of apparently early European goods and seemed to be located in the right place to be the remains of the Indian village of Hochelaga, that had been visited and described by the French explorer Jacques Cartier in 1535. This find sparked off Dawson's interest in American Indian archaeology and ethnology; however, he tended to interpret all data in terms of what he knew about the Dawson site.

Dawson's biblical and Indian interests were brought together in his *Fossil Men and their Modern Representatives: An Attempt to Illustrate the Character and Condition of Prehistoric Man in Europe by those of the American Races*. This book was first published in serial form in 1874 and was reissued in revised book form in three editions between 1880 and 1888. Dawson proposed, as Wilson had done earlier, to use the customs of living primitive peoples to illustrate the nature of life in prehistoric times. What distinguished *Fossil Men...* from most contemporary works of this sort was Dawson's unhappiness with the idea of cultural evolution. Although he observed that when Europeans first arrived in North America its 'Stone Age' tribes were living at many different cultural levels, he concluded that there was no evidence that cultures of different degrees of complexity had not co-existed throughout history. He argued that few archaeological sites known so far were well stratified; hence many primitive ones might have been used as the workshops or hunting camps of more advanced peoples. Dawson believed, as Joseph-François Lafitau had done long before, that earliest mankind had been free from 'degradations' such as polytheism, atheism, polygamy, and cannibalism. He believed degeneration to be as characteristic of human history as progress and identified the leading forces promoting progress as being the 'God-given genius' of gifted individuals and the example set by more civilized peoples.

Although Dawson's writings may have appealed to religious fundamentalists, they exerted little lasting influence on the development of archaeology inside or outside of Canada. Dawson's interest in prehistoric archaeology was only a small part of the broad spectrum of his interests, most of which were related to the natural sciences. Also, Canadian prehistory was of concern to him only as part of the defence of his fundamentalist religious views. Hence he was not particularly inclined to encourage teaching and research in prehistoric archaeology for their own sake at McGill. However, his son, George Mercer Dawson, who became director of the Geological Survey of Canada, was later to encourage that organization to conduct the earliest archaeological as well as ethnographic reconnaissance work in western Canada (Noble, 1972: 22, 25, 27, 30-31). He also published the first significant account of archaeological sites west of the Rocky Mountains (G.M. Dawson, 1891).

Hereafter, archaeological research in Quebec was long confined to the contributions of amateur archaeologists, such as William D. Lighthall, Aristide Beaugrand-Champagne, and R.W. McLachlan, who mainly published speculative studies or accounts of individual finds in local journals. In 1887, various French-Canadian clergymen submitted brief notices of finds of artifacts in different parts of Quebec province to the *Naturaliste Canadien*, but this practice did not persist. In 1894, the writer Alphonse Gagnon published a volume of essays intended to popularize North American archaeology among French readers, but his book dealt scarcely at all with Canada.

Archaeology in the Maritime Provinces

Beginning in 1863, John M. Jones (1863) and William Gossip (1864) published accounts of the well-organized excavations that members of the Nova Scotian Institute of Science had carried out in the shell-mounds of St Margaret's Bay and at Cole Harbour, Nova Scotia. This work followed the publication by the Smithsonian Institution, in 1861, of an English translation of an article by A. von Morlot on the shell-middens of Denmark and the Swiss lake dwellings. This publication stimulated extensive research by Jeffries Wyman on shell-mounds along the east coast of the United States (Willey and Sabloff, 1974: 50). The excavation of shell-heaps remained popular for some time in Nova Scotia and New Brunswick and widespread interest in this phenomenon in the United States and Europe encouraged a reciprocal exchange of information with archaeologists in these areas (Connolly, 1977: 9-11). Although most work by amateur archaeologists in the Maritime Provinces was devoted to describing burials and individual artifacts, George Matthew's (1884) stratigraphic digs in a prehistoric village site at Bocabec, New Brunswick, must rank as the most careful excavation recorded in Canada in the nineteenth century. Two distinct strata of occupation were identified and activity patterns were distinguished by observing the relationship between artifacts and the floor plans of houses. In 1900, Matthew also published a pioneering study of the geographical origin and distribution of lithic materials that the Indians of New Brunswick had used to make artifacts. In 1909, William McIntosh, the first full-time curator of the New Brunswick Museum, published an analysis of 2,500 fragments of aboriginal pottery from that province.[4] Matthew and others were in contact with Daniel Wilson and John William Dawson as well as with foreign scholars, and notices of their activities appeared in American and European journals. Yet, in spite of the development of significant archaeological collections, no posts were established exclusively for archaeological research in either the museums or the universities of the region. Moreover, the likelihood of this happening diminished as economic conditions deteriorated in the Maritimes beginning in the latter part of the nineteenth century. Instead, interest in archaeological studies gradually waned and was virtually extinct by 1914.

David Boyle

In 1884, David Boyle was appointed archaeological curator at the Canadian Institute Museum. In 1887 he received a salary from the Ontario Government and thus became the first professional archaeologist in Canada (Orr, 1911). Boyle was born in Scotland and had come to Canada at the age of fourteen. He taught in a school in the small town of Elora, Ontario, before opening a bookstore in Toronto in 1883. While in Elora, he read about the archaeological discoveries that were being made in the Near East, which inspired him to begin to assemble an extensive and valuable collection of Indian artifacts. In Toronto this growing collection was installed in the Canadian Institute building, until it was finally removed to the new Provincial Museum. After 1886, Boyle visited many parts of Ontario, trenching mounds and persuading farmers and amateur collectors to donate their finds to the museum. He also profited intellectually from his association with Daniel Wilson and with the distinguished ethnologist Horatio Hale, who had come from the United States and worked as a lawyer in the village of Clinton, Ontario. Boyle can be regarded as Wilson's leading student in archaeology and the man who carried on Wilson's interest in the subject in Ontario.

By the time of his death, in 1911, Boyle had assembled a collection of more than 32,000 artifacts from across Ontario, most of them surface finds. Like most archaeologists in the United States at that time, he classified these artifacts in terms of provenance, material, and function. Like them, he also exhibited little awareness of time depth or cultural sequences. Similar classificatory procedures were proposed by Professor Loring W. Bailey (1887), an amateur archaeologist at the University of New Brunswick. He classified artifacts according to the material used and whether they came from coastal or inland sites. In 1887, Boyle began to edit the *Annual Archaeological Report for Ontario*, in which artifacts that had been received by the museum were recorded. Reports describing archaeological work in the province were also published. The *Annual Archaeological Report* thus became the first Canadian journal devoted primarily to archaeology. It continued to be published until 1926 and in later years was handsomely illustrated.

Although primarily a museum man, Boyle gathered about him and gave direction to a group of serious amateur archaeologists who carried out site surveys and excavations (some of them with professional thoroughness) in various parts of Ontario. Boyle published their reports in his journal. The most important of his contributors was Andrew F. Hunter, who, around the end of the nineteenth century, systematically recorded 637 Iroquoian sites in northern Simcoe County, the historic homeland of the Huron Indians. Hunter noted the location of each site, classified it according to function, noted its size, and sought to estimate whether it yielded many, few, or no

European goods as a clue to its relative age. This was probably the most comprehensive archaeological survey of an historic tribal area that had so far been carried out in North America. Hunter's survey was noted by the American archaeologist William Beauchamp and set a high standard for the latter's general survey of archaeological sites in New York State (Noble, 1972: 16; Hunter, 1900; Beauchamp, 1900: 16). Other members of Boyle's group were William G. Long, who excavated mounds in the Trent Valley, Colonel George E. Laidlaw, who recorded mainly Iroquoian sites in Victoria County (adjacent to the area where Hunter worked), and William J. Wintemberg, the craftsman son of a German blacksmith from New Dundee, who in his spare time returned from Toronto to survey sites around his birthplace in southwestern Ontario (Kidd, 1952: 71-72; Trigger, 1978b).

Western Canada

In 1881, a group of amateur archaeologists in Manitoba began to pursue an interest in small burial mounds in the southern part of the province, which they interpreted in terms of the soon to be discredited hypothesis which maintained that all such remains in North America were the work of a vanished race of Mound-Builders. One of the Manitoba archaeologists, the geologist Henry Montgomery, had previously conducted archaeological investigations in Ontario and another, the Reverend George Bryce, was to become president of the Royal Society of Canada, which had been founded in 1882 (Noble, 1972: 22-23; Bryce, 1885). In British Columbia, local amateur archaeologists began to study Indian burials, kitchen middens, and rock art in the 1890s. Journals in eastern Canada as well as in the United States and Britain published the reports of these workers (Hill-Tout, 1895; Carlson, 1970; Noble, 1972: 30-31). During the early part of the twentieth century,however, amateur work in both of these provinces, as in Quebec and the Maritimes, tended to slow down, while no professional archaeology emerged.

Smith and Wintemberg

In 1910, pressure from Canadians interested in archaeology and ethnology resulted in the federal government establishing a separate anthropological department within the Geological Survey of Canada, which as noted above, had already been collecting data on these topics. From this department, the present National Museum of Man was to develop; the department was strongly supported by the Royal Society of Canada and from a committee of the British Association for the Advancement of Science that had been formed to promote ethnological research in Canada. The first committee, which had commissioned Franz Boas to study the tribes of British Columbia, had been created when the British Association met in Montreal in 1884. It had been chaired by the British ethnologist E.B. Tylor, but the management of its affairs was left in the hands of Daniel Wilson, John William Dawson, and Horatio Hale. When the British Association met in Canada for the third time, in 1909, this committee was placed under the chairmanship of the Reverend George Bryce (Cole, 1973: 40-43).

Edward Sapir, a 26-year old linguist and student of Boas's, who had completed his doctorate at Columbia University the previous year, was made director of the new anthropology department. He, in turn, appointed Harlan I. Smith as the department's archaeologist. Born in Michigan in 1872, Smith had studied at the University of Michigan and had excavated in the American Midwest, before beginning work in British Columbia in 1897 as archaeologist with the Jesup North Pacific Expedition of the American Museum of Natural History (Wintemberg, 1940; Leechman, 1949). He is particularly remembered for his efforts to interpret material from sites by projecting ethnographic information back into prehistory. In 1895, this led him to analyse artifacts from the Fox Farm site, in Kentucky, in terms of a series of functional categories (Smith, 1910).

Although Sapir has been accused of ignoring the work of Canadian pioneer and local anthropologists (M. Barbeau cited in Cole, 1973: 43), he appointed the enthusiastic but poorly schooled Wintemberg as a full-time preparator under Harlan Smith in 1912. Wintemberg already shared Smith's interest in the functional interpretation of archaeological evidence and the two men became close friends and colleagues. At the Roebuck site, Smith taught Wintemberg how to excavate and record sites in a more professional manner. This excavation, which lasted from 1912 to 1915, was the largest and most systematic one to have been conducted up till then in Canada east of the Rocky Mountains. In spite of his frail health, for many years Wintemberg carried out arduous archaeological surveys and excavated sites in the Atlantic Provinces, central Canada, and on the Prairies. The latter work has been credited with stimulating the development of amateur archaeology in the province of Saskatchewan (Noble, 1972: 25).

William Wintemberg's most systematic work was his study of Iroquoian archaeology. He published in detail his findings at six major sites, in the same format that Smith had used for the Fox Farm site. Wintemberg acquired a sufficiently detailed knowledge of the archaeology of southwestern Ontario for him to recognize regional variations and infer a developmental sequence that research subsequently has confirmed is correct for the middle and late Iroquoian periods (1300 to 1650). Unlike contemporary archaeologists in the United States, he perceived the *in situ* development of Iroquoian cultures, although his diffidence (perhaps reflecting his awareness of his lack of formal education) was such that he adhered to the opinion of A.C. Parker, who maintained that the earliest Iroquoian cultures derived by hypothesized migrations from the southern United States. Wintemberg remained primarily interested in the functional interpretation of archaeological data, although his interpretations, like those of Harlan Smith, tended to remain on a relatively superficial level (Rouse, 1972: 147). Not until shortly before his death in 1941 was he beginning to take account of the interest in defining archaeological cultures and working out cultural chronologies that were associated with the American Midwestern Taxonomic Method (Willey and Sabloff, 1974: 112-113). This tardiness is surely in large part an indication of the relative isolation in which he was working.

Prior to World War II, there were only a few full-time research positions in archaeology in Canada and these were associated with museums. Government support for archaeological work remained very limited throughout Canada, in spite of lavish appropriations for this purpose, especially in connection with job-creating programmes, in the neighbouring United States. In 1938, the Anthropology Department, which had developed at the University of Toronto under the direction of the ethnologist T.F. McIlwraith, began to conduct excavations at the Pound site, near Aylmer, Ontario. After the war, J. Norman Emerson, a Canadian trained at the University of Chicago, was appointed as a full-time archaeologist within the department. He initiated a vigorous programme of fieldwork aimed at establishing a sound cultural chronology for Ontario Iroquoian archaeology. He also began to train students at the graduate and undergraduate levels. Since the war, there has been a considerable increase of interest in archaeology and, after 1960, archaeologists began to find employment in increasing numbers in university departments, museums, and government services across Canada. There are now over 100 professional prehistoric archaeologists at work in the country (Trigger, 1976).

Discussion

Archaeology in Canada and the United States began as the study of the prehistory of the American Indian. It was generally assumed that Indian cultures had been static prior to the arrival of Europeans and that they had a shallow time-depth; hence archaeological finds were interpreted in terms of what was known about the ethnography of tribes that had lived in the same area in historic times. Archaeological finds in the Maritime Provinces were ascribed to prehistoric Micmacs; those in southern Ontario to prehistoric Iroquoians and Algonkians. Such beliefs led most North American archaeologists to concentrate first on studying geographical and functional variations in their data, while paying scant attention to chronological problems (Trigger, 1978a: 75-95). The development of archaeology in the Old World nevertheless had demonstrated that the accurate construction of chronologies for prehistoric periods was an essential prerequisite for scientific archaeology.

Prior to 1850, archaeological finds generally went unrecorded in Canada for lack of any opportunity to publish them. After that time, natural history societies began assembling archaeological collections and a fund of information about Canadian archaeological discoveries began to be recorded in local journals. Most articles were simply descriptions of artifacts and are of relatively little importance, but some recorded excavations of varying degrees of competence. Yet, in spite of a widespread casual interest in 'Indian relics', there were no spectacular prehistoric remains in Canada that, like the great mounds in the central United States, could arouse heated public controversies and so help overcome the reluctance of officials to authorize the expenditure of funds on archaeological research. Nor did archaeology in Canada find wealthy private patrons. Although influential and respected scholars, such as Daniel Wilson and John William Dawson, published books on archaeology – and Wilson's anthropological work was recognized as important far beyond the borders of Canada – neither of them managed to establish a single university post in prehistoric archaeology. Still later, when small amounts of public money were made available for anthropological research, it was generally believed that it was more important to record the vanishing customs of living Indian peoples than to excavate their prehistoric remains, which it was mistakenly argued would endure in the ground for centuries (Jenness, 1932: 71). Hence ethnography was encouraged at the expense of archaeology.

Yet, in the 1880s, a few archaeologists began to be appointed to museum posts. They were mostly self-trained, but quickly set new standards for archaeological research. David Boyle systematically collected artifacts that were being ploughed out of the ground across southern Ontario and classified them according to provenance, material, and assumed use, as was done between 1840 and 1914 by archaeologists in the United States, during what Willey and Sabloff (1974: 42) have called the Classificatory-Descriptive period of American archaeology. Boyle and his American contemporaries accomplished much the same work of preliminary data collection, description, and elementary functional analysis as had been performed in Europe by the so-called antiquarians. The work of the latter had provided the basis on which Christian Thomsen, by working out rudimentary sequences of cultural change, could initiate the development of scientific archaeology. This was necessary work that Wilson, though trained in the principles of Thomsen and Worsaae, had neither the time nor the patience to accomplish. An increasing emphasis on excavation and a more self-conscious concern with the functional interpretation of artifacts dominated the small circle of professional archaeologists in Canada until prehistoric archaeologists began to obtain university teaching positions after World War II. Then, as had happened a few decades earlier in the United States, Canadian archaeologists began to appreciate the importance of establishing detailed cultural chronologies. Within a few years, archaeological research, at least in southern Ontario, had drawn abreast of, and (by drawing on its own unique heritage) in some aspects surpassed, what was being done in adjacent parts of the United States.

Summary

One prerequisite for the development of scientific archaeology was the establishment of an antiquarian-style data base. Attitudes peculiar to Americanist archaeology long delayed the development of an interest in chronology (the hallmark of scientific archaeology) in both Canada and the United States. Nevertheless, the accomplishments of the antiquarian or descriptive period, in terms of growing knowledge of regional variation and a functional understanding of artifacts, laid the basis for the rapid development of prehistoric archaeology that occurred after 1914 in the United States and, largely because of insufficient financial support and different research priorities, only after 1945 in Canada.

NOTES

1 *Published Sources*. The first comprehensive survey of the history of Canadian archaeology known to me is Jenness, 1932. A longer and more recent survey is Noble, 1972, reprinted in more accessible but somewhat altered form, without the section on British Columbia, and without many useful references, as Noble, 1973. The institutional background of the development of Canadian archaeology is given in Cole, 1973. Connolly, 1977 provides a detailed survey of archaeology in Nova Scotia and New Brunswick as reflected in publications between 1863 and 1914. Martijn, 1978 traces the history of archaeology for Quebec, while Kidd, 1952 has done the same for Ontario and Carlson, 1970 for British Columbia. Chamberlain, 1889 provides a valuable annotated bibliography of early archaeological publications in Canada. Work for foreign expeditions and foreign archaeologists in Canada that has not contributed to the institutional development of Canadian archaeology is not surveyed in this paper. Nor do I consider work done by Canadian archaeologists abroad. Professor Gerald Killan, of King's College, London, Ontario, has written a comprehensive biography of David Boyle (*David Boyle: From Artisan to Archaeologist*) which should be published in the near future.

2 Noble (1972: 15) suggests that this statement was drafted by Daniel Wilson; however, Wilson did not arrive in Canada until 1853. It was noted in an obituary of David Boyle (Orr 1911) that before 1875 Fleming had tried to assemble a collection of Indian artifacts for the Canadian Institute but had met 'with no measure of success'.

3 Wilson, 1856; cf. letter of D. Wilson to David Laing, 8 September 1855, cited in Piggott and Robertson, 1976, item 71.

4 Much earlier, Daniel Wilson had expressed interest in the archaeological evidence for long-distance trade in marine shells in North America.

BIBLIOGRAPHY

BAILEY, L.W. 1887 On the Relics of the Stone Age in New Brunswick. *Bulletin of the Natural History Society of New Brunswick* 5: 1-16.

BAWTREE, E.W. 1848 A Brief Description of Some Sepulchral Pits, of Indian Origin, Lately Discovered Near Penetanqueshene. *The Edinburgh New Philosophical Journal* 45: 86-101.

BEAUCHAMP, W.M. 1900 *Aboriginal Occupation of New York*. Albany: Bulletin of the New York State Museum 7, no. 32.

BRYCE, GEORGE 1885 The Mound Builders: A Lost Race Described. *Manitoba Historical and Scientific Society, Transactions* 18: 1-20.

Canadian Journal 1852a Account of Foundation of the Canadian Institute. *Canadian Journal* 1: 3-5.

—— 1852b Plan to Collect Information concerning Indian Remains. *Canadian Journal* 1: 25.

CARLSON, R.L. 1970 Archaeology in British Columbia. *B.C. Studies* nos. 6-7: 7-17.

CHAMBERLAIN, A.F. 1889 Contributions Towards a Bibliography of the Archaeology of the Dominion of Canada and Newfoundland. *Annual Archaeological Report for Ontario 1889*: 54-59.

COLE, DOUGLAS 1973 The Origins of Canadian Anthropology, 1850-1910. *Journal of Canadian Studies* 8: 33-45.

CONNOLLY, JOHN 1977 Archeology in Nova Scotia and New Brunswick between 1863 and 1914 and its Relationship to the Development of North American Archeology. *Man in the Northeast* 13: 3-34.

DADE, C. 1852 Indian Remains — Being a Description of an Indian Burial Ground in Beverly Township, Ten Miles from Dundas. *Canadian Journal* 1: 6.

DAWSON, G.M. 1891 Notes on the Shuswap People of British Columbia. *Proceedings and Transactions of the Royal Society of Canada* 9, Series I, Section ii: 3-44.

DAWSON, J.W. 1859 On a Specimen of Aboriginal Pottery in the Museum of the Natural History Society of Montreal. *Canadian Naturalist and Geologist* 4: 186-90.

—— 1860a *Archaia: or, Studies of the Cosmogony and Natural History of the Hebrew Scriptures*. Montreal.

—— 1860b Notes on the Aboriginal Antiquities Recently Discovered on the Island of Montreal. *Canadian Naturalist and Geologist* 5: 430-49.

—— 1861 Additional Notes on Aboriginal Antiquities Found at Montreal. *Canadian Naturalist and Geologist* 6: 362-73.

—— 1877 *The Origin of the World*. Montreal.

—— 1880 *Fossil Men and their Modern Representatives*. Montreal (third edition, 1888).

—— 1888 *Modern Science in Bible Lands*. Montreal.

GAGNON, ALPHONSE 1894 *Etudes archéologiques et variétés*. Levis.

GOSSIP, WILLIAM 1864 On the Occurrence of Kjoekkenmoedding on the Shores of Nova Scotia. *Proceedings and Transactions of the Nova Scotian Institute of Science* 1: 94-99.

HALE, HORATIO 1893 Sketch of Sir Daniel Wilson. *Popular Science Monthly* 44: 256-65.

HARRIS, R.S. 1976 *A History of Higher Education in Canada, 1663-1960*. Toronto.

HUNTER, A.F. 1900 Sites of Huron Villages in the Township of Tay. *Annual Archaeological Report for Ontario, 1889*: 51-82.

HILL-TOUT, CHARLES 1895 Later Prehistoric Man in British Columbia. *Proceedings and Transactions of the Royal Society of Canada* 1, Series II, Section ii: 103-22.

JENNESS, DIAMOND 1932 Fifty Years of Archaeology in Canada. *Royal Society of Canada, Anniversary Volume, 1882-1932*: 71-76. Toronto.

JONES, A.E. 1907 '*8endake Ehen*' or Old Huronia. Toronto: Fifth Report of the Bureau of Archives for the Province of Ontario.

JONES, J.M. 1863 Kitchen-middens of St. Margaret's Bay, Nova Scotia. *Annual Report of the Smithsonian Institution*: 370-71.

KIDD, K.E. 1952 Sixty Years of Ontario Archeology. In *Archeology of Eastern United States*, J.B. Griffin (ed.): 71-82. Chicago.

LEECHMAN, DOUGLAS 1949 Bibliography of Harlan I. Smith, 1889-1936. *Annual Reports of the National Museum, 1939-1947*: 8-14. Ottawa: Department of Mines and Resources.

MCILWRAITH, T.F. 1964 Sir Daniel Wilson: A Canadian Anthropologist of One Hundred Years Ago. *Transactions of the Royal Society of Canada* 2, Series IV, Section ii: 129-36.

MCINTOSH, WILLIAM 1909 Aboriginal Pottery of New Brunswick. *Bulletin of the Natural History Society of New Brunswick* 27: 110-20.

MARTIJN, C.A. 1978 Historique de la Recherche archéologique au Québec. In *Images de la Préhistoire du Québec*, C. Chapdelaine (ed.): 11-18. Montreal: Recherches Amérindiennes au Québec.

MATTHEW, G.F. 1884 Discovery of a Village of the Stone Age at Bocabec. *Bulletin of the Natural History Society of New Brunswick* 3: 6-29.

—— 1900 A Quarry and a Workshop of the Stone Age in New Brunswick. *Proceedings and Transactions of the Royal Society of Canada* 6, Series II, Section ii: 61-69.

NOBLE, W.C. 1972 One Hundred and Twenty-five Years of Archaeology in the Canadian Provinces. *Bulletin of the Canadian Archaeological Association* 4: 1-78.

—— 1973 Canada. In *The Development of North American Archaeology*, J.E. Fitting (ed.): 49-83. New York.

ORR, R.B. 1911 Dr. David Boyle. *Annual Archaeological Report for Ontario, 1911:* 7-8.

PARKER, A.C. 1907 *Excavations in an Erie Indian Village and Burial Site at Ripley, Chautauqua County, New York.* Albany: New York State Museum Bulletin 117.

PENDERGAST, J.F. and B.G. TRIGGER 1972 *Cartier's Hochelaga and the Dawson Site.* Montreal.

PIGGOTT, STUART and M. ROBERTSON 1977 *Three Centuries of Scottish Archaeology.* Edinburgh.

RIBES, RENÉ 1966 Pièces de la période archaïque trouvées vers 1700 dans la regione de Bécancour. *Cahiers d'archéologie québecoise* 2, no. 1: 22-34.

ROUSE, IRVING 1972 *Introduction to Prehistory.* New York.

SIMPSON, W.D. 1963 Sir Daniel Wilson and the *Prehistoric Annals of Scotland:* A Centenary Study. *Proceedings of the Society of Antiquaries of Scotland* 96: 1-8.

SQUIER, E.G. 1849 *Aboriginal Monuments of the State of New York.* Washington: Smithsonian Contributions to Knowledge 2, ix.

STARR, F. 1882 Anthropological Work in America. *Popular Science Monthly* 41: 289-307.

TRIGGER, B.G. 1966a Sir Daniel Wilson: Canada's First Anthropologist. *Anthropologica* 8: 2-28.

—— 1966b Sir John William Dawson: A Faithful Anthropologist. *Anthropologica* 8: 351-59.

—— 1970 The Strategy of Iroquoian Prehistory. *Ontario Archaeology* 14: 3-48.

—— 1976 The Archaeological Base in Canada: Training, Facilities, Opportunities. In *New Perspectives in Canadian Archaeology*, A.G. McKay (ed.): 185-201. Ottawa: Royal Society of Canada.

—— 1978 a *Time and Traditions: Essays in Archaeological Interpretation.* Edinburgh.

—— 1978 b William Wintemberg: Iroquoian Archaeologist. In *Northeastern Anthropology in Memory of Marian White*, William Engelbrecht and D.K. Grayson (eds), pp. 5-21. Rindge: Occasional Papers in Northeastern Anthropology, No. 5.

VAN COURTLAND, E. 1853 Notice of an Indian Burying Ground, Bytown. *Canadian Journal* 1: 160-61.

WILLEY, G.R. and J.A. SABLOFF 1974 *A History of American Archaeology.* London and San Francisco.

WILSON, DANIEL 1848 *Memorials of Edinburgh in the Olden Time.* Edinburgh.

—— 1851 *The Archaeology and Prehistoric Annals of Scotland.* London.

—— 1854 Remarks on some Coincidences between the Primitive Antiquities of the Old and New World. *Canadian Journal* 2: 213-15.

—— 1855 Hints for the Formation of a Canadian Collection of Ancient Crania. *Canadian Journal* 3: 345-47.

—— 1856 Discovery of Indian Remains, County Norfolk, Canada West. *Canadian Journal*, N.S. 1: 511-19.

—— 1857 Supposed Prevalence of One Cranial Type Throughout the American Aborigines. *Canadian Journal* N.S. 2: 406-35.

—— 1862 *Prehistoric Man.* London.

—— 1863 *The Prehistoric Annals of Scotland.* London.

—— 1884 The Huron-Iroquois of Canada: A Typical Race of American Aborigines. *Proceedings and Transactions of the Royal Society of Canada* 2, Series I, Section ii: 55-106.

—— 1885 *The Right Hand: Left Handedness.* London.

—— 1892 *The Lost Atlantis and other Ethnographic Studies.* New York.

WINSOR, JUSTIN 1889 *Narrative and Critical History of America*, Vol. I. Boston.

WINTEMBERG, W.J. 1940 Harlan Ingersoll Smith. *American Antiquity* 6: 63-64.

WRONG, G.M. and H.H. LANGTON (eds) 1901 *Review of Historical Publications Relating to Canada.* Toronto.

VII
From de Mortillet to Bordes: a century of French Palaeolithic research

JAMES R. SACKETT

University of California, Los Angeles, USA

French archaeology may never again offer the drama or intellectual excitement provided by the heroic age which culminated in the official endorsement in 1859 of Boucher de Perthes' evidences for the antiquity of man. But it was one thing to demonstrate the existence of the Palaeolithic world, and quite another to establish a discipline for attacking its archaeological record in an organized fashion. The history of this discipline in France may be divided into three periods, or eras, which respectively began shortly before 1870, shortly after 1900, and about 1950. Such divisions are of course arbitrary. Nonetheless, each of them conveniently serves to characterize a marked advance in the degree of refinement with which prehistorians excavated and processed their data and an equally marked change in the manner they went about classifying and interpreting them. By extension, each represents a distinct stage in what might be termed the logic of inquiry of French Palaeolithic research.

As Laming-Emperaire (1964) so richly documents, it was in the 1860s that there emerged in France a self-conscious science of prehistory with its own proper congresses, journals, and researches. This formative period is inevitably associated with the name of Gabriel de Mortillet (1821-1899), owning both to the ubiquitous role he played as prehistory's chief editor and publicist and the rousing claims he so boldly pronounced for the new science's responsibilities and potential. The era was never in fact so uniform in thought and thrust as de Mortillet's own writings suggested or as prehistorians during the era which followed sometimes characterized it when highlighting the novelty of their own achievements. Yet his successive publications, culminating in *La Préhistorique* (1883) and *Le Musée Préhistorique* (1881) (in whose writing Adrien de Mortillet was a major collaborator), clearly served as a frame of reference for the work of his contemporaries. And his dominant themes were largely theirs. One was a lively interest in the significant palaeoethnological questions posed by Stone Age culture history, sustained by considerable optimism regarding the relative ease with which these could be illuminated by comparative ethnography. A second, closely related to the first, was the attempt to order the archaeological record in terms of a scheme of phases, or 'epochs', which embodied the developmental doctrines of late nineteenth century evolutionism. Whether these doctrines derived from evolutionary thought in geology more than in cultural anthropology can be debated. Judging from his fondness for the great capitalized abstractions of the day, in particular Progress (which invariably hinders clear thinking about the alternate forms developmental change may take), it is unlikely that de Mortillet himself worried overmuch about the distinction between the two.

Mortilletian systematics represented the first enlightened attempt to grasp something of the full range proffered by the Stone Age archaeological record and, as such, deserves recognition as a major achievement (an excellent review of its development may be found in Daniel 1975: 99-109, 122). Nonetheless, close examination of its design and substance can be a highly disconcerting experience for the modern student. Its epochs, even though they bear such familiar names as Mousterian and Magdalenian, do not in fact constitute discrete industrial complexes like those we recognize today, but instead represent intergrading temporal phases within the unilinear evolution of what seems to have been regarded as a single unbroken Palaeolithic cultural tradition. The definition of these phases, although well illustrated by depictions of individual artifacts, betrays no rigorous knowledge of either artifact typology or industrial variation. And even their temporal ordering is based more upon consideration of how Stone Age technology should logically have evolved than upon concrete stratigraphical evidence. This thinness of fact and method is richly documented in Smith's (1966: 5-21) splendid survey of the history of Solutrean research, which remains the only detailed case-study of the era written by someone with intimate knowledge of the data involved. Even more telling would be a similarly detailed examination of the logic and empirical naiveté responsible for the ultimate failure of Mortilletian systematics to give explicit recognition in the form of one or more epochs to the distinctive Aurignacian-Perigordian block of cultures (an issue briefly sketched in Sackett 1965: 1-30). This we now know occupies more than half of the entire Upper Palaeolithic, exhibiting considerably more stratigraphical and artifactual heterogeneity than that displayed by the Solutrean and Magdalenian cultures which succeed it.

It was, in fact, a debate over this last issue, the extraordinary *bataille de l'Aurignacien*, that most clearly signals the beginning of a new era. Its chief protagonist was Henri Breuil (1877-1961), whose opening shot, 'Essai de stratigraphie des dépôts de l'age du Renne' (1905), and culminating masterpiece, 'Les subdivisions du Paléolithique supérieur et leur signification' (1913), serve to bracket the rather turbulent passage from the age of de Mortillet to the ensuing period. The historian of archaeology would discover a rich vein to mine in this controversy, including Breuil's sarcasm, Peyrony's stratigraphical committees (the findings of whose site visits were sometimes noted down on the spot by a lawyer), and, on the opposing side, the attempts of Adrien de Mortillet and Paul Girod to defend the Mortilletian tradition by alternating strategic silences with righteous indignation and, ultimately, downright fraud (see Breuil, 1913: 167). But we should not allow these dramatic events to divert our attention from the quieter but more fundamental revolution in research strategy of which Breuil's brilliant syntheses are but a single expression and which, as one quickly perceives in working through the pages of the *Bulletin* of the then newly founded Société Préhistorique Française, would in any case have crushed the old ways under the sheer bulk of its empirical results. What was emerging was the school of thought that was to dominate French prehistory right through World War II and which continues to influence the conduct of research even today. It is difficult to find a label other than 'traditional' for this school's approach and the period it dominates, both because it was essentially synonomous with French prehistory as such, and because it cannot be identified with the name of any individual. (This last follows from the strong regional emphasis of the period, which guaranteed that no single scholar could play a commanding role in France as a whole comparable to that once enjoyed by de Mortillet.)

The traditional school was France's version of what one sometimes hears referred to as *straight archaeology*. In this approach researchers tend to dismiss palaeoethnological interpretation as mere speculation, and — invoking the principle of unripe time — defer the writing of culture history to some unspecified point in the future 'when the data are in'. They cultivate instead a narrow devotion to the empirical content of the archaeological record, engaging in intensive programs of excavation and preoccupying themselves with the typology of artifacts and the structure of the sites from which they derive. The object of their work is to construct schemes of time-space systematics. Here the basic task is to define the artifactual similarities and differences among assemblages and, taking advantage of whatever light can be shed by stratigraphy, to seriate them into regional sequences which at least potentially can be brought into alignment with one another by cross-correlation. The craft-like involvement with stone tools and strata reflected in Victor Commont's sophisticated pre-World War I investigations into the Lower Palaeolithic of the Somme Valley typifies the straight archaeologist at his best (see Bordes and Fitte, 1953). However, perhaps the most remarkable product of this genre of research by the French school was the regional succession of cultural traditions worked out by Denis Peyrony (1869-1954) in the famous Perigord rockshelters of southwestern France. Among his other achievements, this prodigious excavator was the first to recognize synchronous, interstratifying industries within the Middle Palaeolithic; additionally, he succeeded in establishing the industrial successions which lay within the Solutrean and Magdalenian traditions on a much firmer empirical base than Breuil had furnished them with in 'Les Subdivisions'. But most important was Peyrony's seriation of the deposits at La Ferrassie and Laugerie-Haute, which revealed that the Aurignacian complex was vastly more complicated than Breuil had imagined. Instead of representing three intergrading temporal phases, it constituted two distinct traditions — the Aurignacian *sensu stricto* (Breuil's middle phase) and the Perigordian (Breuil's lower and upper phases) — which evolved as parallel phyla through a succession of more or less synchronous industrial stages. (A useful crash course on the formidable topic of Aurignacian-Perigordian systematics is furnished by Movius 1974: 87-91.)

Now, although the work of Peyrony and his counterparts elsewhere constitutes the most productive era of French Palaeolithic research, it is in many respects the least well understood of any of our periods. For one thing, there are no sophisticated treatments of its development comparable to those which Laming-Emperaire (1964) and Daniel (1975) have provided for the formative era and the heroic age which preceded it. Space-time systematists, stolidly beating the path of the archaeological record, obviously do not make as good press as de Mortillet's grand vision of the past or as Boucher de Perthes' rewriting of the Book of Genesis. But even more important is the fact that the seemingly obvious business of conducting straight archaeology is not in reality so obvious after all. Straight archaeologists are almost invariably preoccupied with the details of regional sequences; this lends a strongly arcane and parochial element to their writings which puts them beyond the grasp of the reader unfamiliar with the specific data involved. Moreover, since they are directed toward colleagues who presumably share the same body of assumptions regarding the nature of the archaeological record and of archaeological inquiry itself, these writings seldom if ever treat issues of method and theory in an explicit fashion. Assumed to be understood because they are familiar, these, too, usually go unstated.

But it is clearly necessary that we attempt to understand the assumptions held by traditional French prehistory and the methodology to which they gave rise. Without such understanding the bridge of thought and achievement which connects de Mortillet's era with our own cannot be reconstructed save in terms of a mere chronicling of its major excavations and publications. Equally important, such understanding has quite pragmatic ramifications in current research. For it is the traditional school's artifacts which fill our museums and its systematics which continue to provide the idiom of much of our own thought and effort. And yet we can find this legacy somewhat impoverished and confining. For one thing, the classifications it produced do not always hold. The impression of substance and order given by the stately march of traditions and industries over its regional sequences turns out to be oversimplified and even misleading. Equally important, neither the data nor the theoretical direction left to us by the designers of these schemes seem to conform with the needs of an era which is once again turning to the palaeoethnological questions which were set aside when the formative era came to a close. Presumably an understanding of why this is so is prerequisite to gaining a clearer perception of what we ourselves are, and should be, doing. Thus the question of what constituted the logic of inquiry of French Palaeolithic research during the first half of this century may fairly be regarded as having the highest priority both to those who wish to write its history and to those who need to understand it in order to go further. There should be profit then in devoting to this question the bulk of the pages which remain, even though their restricted scope dictates that many of the issues involved be oversimplified and that what are in many instances impressionistic guesses be presented as assertions.

In essence, the aims and procedures of traditional French Palaeolithic research were no different from those of any other field of straight archaeology. But in this case a distinctive turn was lent to the enterprise by the assumption that the attack upon the archaeological record should in some manner emulate the approach that earlier had been used with such great success by palaeontologists in unravelling the fossil record. The most singular and explicit expression of this belief was the grounding of systematics upon *fossiles directeurs*, that is, diagnostic artifact types whose restricted distributions in the archaeological record were believed to delineate the major cultural traditions and industries which make up their successive temporal subdivisions. The analogue between artifactual *fossiles* and the 'index' or 'zone' type-fossils employed by palaeontologists is obvious, and use of the term in fact dates back to the explicitly geological formats in which Mortilletian systematics were framed. However, as is the case with so many of the terms archaeologists borrow today from the physical and natural sciences, the label in itself largely served an idiomatic function. It was applied simply to whatever one considered to be diagnostic for purposes of space-time classification and its usage consequently varied from one researcher to the next depending upon the tasks that happened to engross him. A dedicated fieldworker like Peyrony preferred to regard the *fossile directeur* as a discrete and highly specific artifact type which possessed equally discrete and specific stratigraphic significance. On the other hand, in the writings of sophisticated laboratory typologists like those of the Brive school (e.g., Bourlon, M. and J. Bouyssonie, 1912), it assumed the more idealized role of a representative form that summarized in normative fashion the major morphological themes which characterized a much broader block of distinctive typological intergradation.

However, while the *fossile* itself may suggest a metaphor, it floated on the surface of a deeper and more implicit current of thought in systematics which did in fact accept palaeontology as a model. The key notion at work here was that fundamental patterning in the artifactual and fossil records is essentially the same and that, as a consequence, culture history can be regarded and accounted for in essential *organic* terms. This notion more specifically entailed two unspoken assumptions. The first was that a direct parallelism exists between the cultural and organic worlds of such a kind that we can expect to find a one-to-one correlation between archaeological and natural stratigraphy. The second was that any given cultural complex, like any given palaeontological complex, should be more or less invariant in the manner in which it expresses itself. This last means that the cultural entities recognized in archaeological systematics are to be regarded as *natural* categories, which — in the manner, say, of organic species – are inherently discontinuous and do not modify their form from one context to the next. It follows from this that a specific tradition should give rise to but one characteristic type of industry in any specific block of time and space in the archaeological record. As we shall see, no matter how much such assumptions seem alien to most modern prehistorians, the grounds for making them were understandable and even perhaps sound. Yet their practical consequences were manifold, serious, and restrictive.

Their most immediate impact is manifested in the interrelated domains of data collection and classification. For, despite the fact that excavation techniques in the period under consideration constitute a stratigraphic revolution in comparison to those of its predecessor, prehistorians nonetheless still grossly underestimated the complexity of their archaeological record. This in part arose from their assumption of a one-to-one correlation between cultural and natual stratigraphy. It was deemed sufficient, as a result, to excavate a site only in terms of its more obvious stratigraphic units, that is, the usually thick zones of relatively homogeneous sedimentological composition which represent the major episodes of its history of deposition and, by extension, of regional environmental evolution. Palaeoecological data recovered were mainly confined to representative specimens of large mammals, these being considered the more sensitive indicators of the climatic succession which accompanied that evolution. And the artifact assemblages themselves were collected with little or no regard to the vertical, let alone the horizontal, tool distributions within these major stratigraphic zones. This last point is of particular significance because we know from modern excavation in similar (and indeed, sometimes the same) deposits that such zones more often than not incorporate several distinct archaeological horizons which can vary significantly in their tool types and type frequencies.

Equally important, given the invariant manner in which any time-space segment of a cultural tradition was assumed to express itself, it followed that the classificatory procedures which accompanied such zone-oriented excavation could safely be pursued in an essentially qualitative manner. In other words, the differences which distinguished one archaeological industry from another were assumed to be sufficiently clear-cut for observation of the simple presence or absence – or at most, impressionistic guesswork regarding the relative frequencies – of the key *fossiles* tool forms to be considered sufficient for most taxonomic purposes. Moreover, the distinction between describing assemblages and classifying them into industries and traditions was operationally blurred, since the established *fossiles* were employed in such a manner as to define simultaneously both their formal content and their genetic affiliations. Thus no clear line was drawn between what we regard today as the distinct realms of artifact typology (and general typological description) and ordering assemblages. It is not surprising therefore that the analytic circularism inherent in such thinking fed back into the sampling procedures that accompanied excavation itself. In brief, since the data requirements of *fossile* classification were limited, there was a strong tendency to overlook the supposedly 'banal' areas of typological variation in favour of the established *fossiles* — a tendency so strong in fact that a large proportion of the artifacts initially recovered never found their way back to the laboratory at all. (One of the sadder if more informative exercises in the history of archaeology would be to excavate the spoil heaps of our predecessors in order to discover the amount and kind of artifactual material so many of them discarded.)

The net effect of such procedures was to greatly restrain, and even to a considerable extent, predetermine, what a prehistorian would see. Having segregated his assemblages only in global terms with reference to the broad stratigraphical zones, he masked and averaged out the subtle interoccupational differences within them that would have been revealed by stratigraphical sampling conducted at a higher level of resolution. At the same time, having discarded so much of the banal element, his attention in viewing these global assemblages necessarily concentrated upon the *fossiles* which were the sole items that had consistently been saved. Inevitably, therefore, the artifact assemblages available to him for any given time period within a region tended to exhibit a homogeneous and quite stereotyped aspect. And when in turn those from different time periods were compared they as inevitably appeared to exhibit fairly distinct qualitative breaks in the manner in which the *fossiles* delineated temporal phasing in the regional cultural succession. In brief, prehistorians literally created in the empirical sense an archaeological record that did in fact parallel the fossil record in consisting of a straightforward succession of invariant stages which could be simultaneously identified and defined by a series of index *fossile* forms. It would be an exaggeration to claim that they therefore were capable of observing as excavators only what they had already assumed to be true as taxonomists. But it is fair to state

that their sampling and classificatory procedures dramatically reduced their ability to perceive novelty or to appreciate the more subtle
kinds of variability and alternate patterns that might find expression in
archaeological deposits.

Let us turn briefly from the realm of data gathering and classification to that of interpretation. I have argued elsewhere that the
assumptions and procedures outlined above largely precluded the
attempt to deal systematically with the archaeological record in what
a modern prehistorian would regard as culturally meaningful terms
(Sackett, 1968: 65-67). In part my argument calls for modification. In
particular, that traditional prehistorians avoided palaeoethnological
questions such as Stone Age economics and demographic patterns in
favour of a 'humanistic' emphasis upon matters of ideology and
aesthetics I would no longer attribute to the organic model. The
absence of the former is typical of straight archaeology as a genre of
research, which, as we have seen, dismisses such questions on the
grounds of unripe time. And the importance of the latter was no doubt
dictated by the truly spectacular discoveries of burials, ritual equip-
ment, and art made during the era, whose impact upon the intellectual
life of the time was great indeed. Nonetheless, while straight archaeology does not require that we breathe ethnographic life into the past,
the genetic time-space schemes it generates do in fact represent a kind
of culture historical model-making. In other words, the definition of
traditions and industries necessarily entails making certain assumptions about the manner in which cultural process and pattern express
themselves in the archaeological record. And here it can be fairly
argued that the organic model promoted restrictive, and indeed unrealistic expectations regarding the form these should assume.

Its most obvious reflection was an important error of misplaced
concreteness frequently built into traditional systematics, which seem
to imply that it is the artifacts and assemblages themselves that are the
agents of culture history — evolving and hybridizing as if, like living
organisms, they were capable of sexual reproduction. Movius (1953:
188), among others, has commented how so often one encounters in
the traditional schemes the curious spectacle of tools interacting
among themselves and of industries fusing into some sort of matri-
monial alliances. Here perhaps we may again be dealing as much with
metaphor as model. However, model surely lies behind two much
graver assumptions which did indeed thwart the design of schemes
which were meaningful in culture historical terms.

One was that, since prehistoric cultural complexes necessarily
behave as natural units which can assume but a single form at any
specific time and place, it follows that any systematic artificial variation that may be seen within a given tradition in a given region must
be assigned temporal significance and construed so as to reflect a linear
succession of industries. A necessary correlate of this is that dissimilar

industries which occupy the same block of space and time, in other words, which 'interstratify' within a given regional sequence, must necessarily belong to distinct traditions. In brief, all significant variability observable in the archaeological record must be significant in *phylogenetic* terms. Thus functional variability, that is, industrial differences which reflect alternate complexes of activities which might simultaneously have been pursued by one and the same culture and which therefore might entail non-linear variability within a tradition, was by definition excluded from systematics. The second equally grave assumption that followed from an organic model is that the culture dynamics which lay behind the genetic groupings of the traditional schemes could be 'explained' simply by referring it to variables arising from the the world of nature. Most often this was done implicitly, and simply involved the attempt to establish as narrow a correlation as possible between cultural and natural stratigraphy. However, when the opportunity arose, particularly in those cases where two or more distinct industries were found to interstratify (a situation wherein a more culturally sensitive model would at least have suggested the possibility of functional variability), the phylogenetic integrity of their respective traditions was preserved by attributing them to distinct lines of biological evolution among prehistoric men themselves.

In that block of the archaeological record with which I am most familiar, the Upper Palaeolithic of Perigord, Denis Peyrony's work would seem to be fairly consistent with the idealized picture of the traditional logic of inquiry just described. He by no means conforms to it in every respect. In particular he was far ahead of his time in the degree of stratigraphical control he exercised in many of his excavations and the relative completeness of the artifact assemblages he recovered. It was, in fact, the exercise of comparatively refined field methods which allowed him to perceive the distinctiveness of the Aurignacian and Perigordian complexes, which rarely appeared clearly segregated in the more loosely controlled excavations of his contemporaries. And yet his highly formulaic publications on Aurignacian-Perigordian systematics provide some of the most telling illustrations of the organic model at work (e.g., Peyrony, 1933; 1936). One cannot help but be struck by the stereotyped quality artifact assemblages assumed under his perfunctory, *fossile*-oriented descriptions, the schematic precision with which they are slotted into the stages of the two parallel industrial successions, and the manner in which these stages are correlated in turn with specific climatological horizons distinguished by supposedly unique depositional and faunal characteristics; there even appears a biological argument which attributes the parallel phyla to distinct races of Upper Palaeolithic men. One senses almost a robot-like quality in the manner in which *fossiles*, developmental stages, geological horizons, and races are made fully complementary parts of a closed mechanical system in which there seems no room at all for the untidiness that attends more realistic culture historical classification. An organic cast of thought is equally revealed by Peyrony's subsequent interpretation of certain 'Perigordian of the IInd group' assemblages as by-products of hybridization between the Aurignacian and the Perigordian (1964). For these were characterized, not by artifacts in which the distinctive typological themes of the two phyla actually merged, but instead simply by the joint appearance of some of their respective *fossile* diagnostics. In other words, he apparently assumed that the mixture of two cultures need not be expressed any differently than would be the mixture of two faunal complexes, and that *fossile* tool types were no more likely to lose their integrity as natural categories in the case of the former than would animal species in the case of the latter.

While readers more familiar with other regions must judge whether the organic model was in fact truly ubiquitous in French prehistoric research during the traditional era, it was in any event not confined exclusively to Perigord. For example, Movius's (1953: 163-64) depiction of Breuil's Lower Palaeolithic scheme which emerged during the 1930s suggests a particularly striking example of the model at work. Here the notion of supposedly distinct parallel phyla of flake tool and core-biface traditions was reinforced both by a biological argument (entailing their supposed association with distinct-palaeoanthropic and neanthropic lines of hominid evolution) and by the manner in which preconceptions born of *fossile* systematics prevented fieldworkers from recognizing the fact that co-occurrences of the two tool components was a reasonable expectation, rather than an anomaly that needed to be accounted for in terms of periodic hybridization between distinct cultural traditions. Such thinking, furthermore, was by no means exclusively a French phenomenon, but seems in fact to have been common in all fields of Palaeolithic research (see, for example, Isaac, 1972: 168-71). It is tempting to speculate in this connection whether the traditional legacy is still to be seen in the inclination of researchers at the Olduvai Gorge to assume that their Acheulian and Developed Oldowan need be attributed to distinct phyletic lines, respectively *Homo erectus* and *Homo habilis* (e.g., Leakey, 1971).

Now, before attempting to account for the reasons why traditional French prehistory took the path it did, we must examine briefly the nature of the era which succeeded it. By 1950 the traditional approach had begun to retreat before several fundamental advances in research strategy. In part these have involved efforts to greatly enchance the overall quantity and quality of data that were realized from the archaeological record. Excavation techniques have come to assume the character of stratigraphical dissection whereby assemblages are segregated with reference to the specific occupational horizons and minimal sedimentological components that can be observed in site deposits. All lithic material, including unused tool blanks and industrial debris, is saved in these assemblages, and they are accompanied both by fully documented provenance information and by representative samples of faunal, palynological, and sedimentological data. This last information has been employed to develop a new *chronostratigraphical* approach to space-time systematics, wherein the design of regional sequences entails a holistic level-by-level correlation of the site stratigraphies involved, founded as much upon their palaeoenvironmental (especially sedimentological) contents as upon the seriational information provided by their occupational horizons alone (e.g. Bonifay, 1956; Laville, 1975). While it could be argued that such advances in the technology of prehistoric research are simply refinements of earlier sampling and analytic procedures, their combined effect has nevertheless been to cause a leap in the degree of resolution with which prehistorians are able to observe and control the archaeological record.

No less important, this effort has been complemented by the development of a new approach to systematics that has had an equally profound effect. In brief, the traditional concept of the qualitative *fossile directeur* has been set aside in favour of the notion that it is the relative frequencies of several tool types viewed in the ensemble, rather than the simple presence or absence of a few of them viewed individually, that is essential to refined systematics. The basic idea is not new. But it was François Bordes (1950) who first saw clearly that translating the notion of 'diagnostic' into quantitative terms was not simply a matter of counting, but instead that it required the introduction of two new elements into the methodology of systematics. One is that artifact typology and assemblage ordering must constitute distinct procedures, in other words, that the definition of an assemblage's formal content must be operationally distinguished from the definition of its genetic affiliations to other assemblages in space-time systematics. As we have seen, this distinction was never clearly made in the traditional approach, since it was the inherently circular role of *fossile directeurs* to define simultaneously an assemblage's content and assign it within some larger ordering scheme. The second is that artifact classification must be extended to the entire range of formal variation occupied by recognizable tools rather than simply to those specific areas which potentially possess the greatest diagnostic value in assemblage ordering. This 'banalization' of artifact classification in the form of a standardized *comprehensive typology* makes it possible for every artifact lying within the stated range to be assigned to a specific category and subsequently counted. Obviously, without this criterion of comprehension, which was by no means consistently recognized in traditional systematics, quantitative statements about relative tool frequencies lost most of their meaning.

Armed with its comprehensive type-lists and some relatively simple techniques of statistical description, Bordesian systematics has greatly enhanced our knowledge of the archaeological record. Two examples of outstanding importance have been Bordes' (1961) own re-definition of the Mousterian as a complex of four distinct phyla or traditions which interstratify at random, and Denise de Sonneville-Bordes' (1960) monumental reappraisal of traditional Aquitanian material and systematics dating from Peyrony's era. Of even greater interest from the perspective of this essay are the results currently being achieved now that a reasonably abundant number of artifact assemblages obtained by the new recovery procedures are available for Bordesian analysis whose space-time systematics rests, not upon archaeological seriation alone, but upon the more holistic and delicate chronostratigraphical approach described above (see Laville, Rigaud, and Sackett, 1980). For this work has not simply brought refinement to the traditional schemes. Instead, it is revealing that the archaeological record is a vastly more complicated affair than the traditional model led one to expect, and that it can, in fact, involve fundamentally different kinds of patterning. To point to but one key example of the new results, it has become clear that in the Upper Perigordian the traditionally recognized *fossiles* seem not to be time-bound in any narrow sense at all, but instead to come and go in successive cultural strata in no predictable fashion whatever. Equally important, the relative proportions of the formerly 'banal' tools with which these associate from one assemblage to the next exhibit no consistent patterns, nor — regardless of whether it is defined in terms of the individual *fossiles* or the overall quantitative make-up of the assemblages in which they occur — does there appear to be any meaningful correlation between industrial variation and the alternating climatic types which make up regional environmental successions. In this case then a functional, not a phyletic explanation is obviously needed if such variability is to be explained (Rigaud, 1978). In short, we no longer expect to see an archaeological record comprising simple linear successions of stereotyped industries which, whether in individual or parallel phyla, succeed one another over time exactly in step with natural environmental change.

No specific new model has yet been generated to conform with these new expectations. In this connection it is relevant to note that the Bordesian revolution which began the present era entailed a change in method, not theoretical perspective, and that much of the traditional legacy may still in fact remain. Thus, except where the evidence is unequivocal, as in the case of the Upper Perigordian example noted above, phyletic rather than functional explanations continue to be preferred in accounting for situations where unlike industries are seen to interstratify. And again, some of the claims made for the inherent integrity of the so-called 'morphological' tool classes which make up Bordesian type-lists are not unlike those made for natural categories.

Nonetheless, that the Bordesian revolution had led us to a renewed interest in palaeoethnology is obvious to anyone familiar with the current scene. The emphasis placed upon cultural-ecological reconstruction in the Abri Pataud research program (Movius, 1974), the horizontal exposure of activity areas at the extraordinary open site of Pincevent (Leroi-Gourhan and Brézillon, 1966), debate over the expression of style and function in artifact assemblages (e.g., Sackett, 1979), and the use of ethnographic analogy in analysing prehistoric butchering patterns (Rigaud, 1978) are but a few of the signs of a basic shift now under way toward new directions of research. It is to be hoped that enthusiasm over such new developments does not make us forgetful of the legacy of our predecessors. In order to fully understand that legacy we must close this essay by looking once again at the traditional school, this time not with respect to the logic of inquiry itself but rather with regard to the conditions which promoted its development.

There is no single or simple answer to the question of why French prehistory during the traditional period adopted what we have referred to as an organic model. It is not enough to point out that Gabriel de Mortillet's original occupation was malacology and that Mortilletian systematics in general had strong palaeonotological overtones. For the literature of the formative era reveals as strong as interest in anthropology as in geology. This interest only slackened near the turn of the century, when the passing of cultural evolutionary theory left in its wake no useful palaeoethnological models for archaeologists whose data referred to an epoch of culture history so far removed from any obvious ethnographic parallels. And, as one can find documented in Mercier's (1966) fine small volume, early twentieth-century anthropology in France would seem to have lacked the data base, theoretical interests, and even institutional arrangements required to maintain an active alliance with prehistory. In any case, the adoption of an essentially palaeontological frame of reference would have offered several attractions at a time when prehistorians were turning from palaeoethnology to the narrower concerns of straight archaeology. To the extent that the strongly empirical bent of straight archaeology fostered a spirit of scientism – that is, the desire to assume the trappings of an already established and prestigious science – prehistorians at the turn of the century might easily have looked to palaeontology in much the same manner as self-consciously scientific archaeologists today look toward ecology and systems theory. Then too, a palaeontological approach would have introduced a welcome element of reductionism. By suppressing consideration of the complex culture historical reality which lay behind the archaeological record, the organic model reduced the number of variables with which prehistorians had to contend and simultaneously served to break up their task into the more manageable units that suffice when the aims of analysis extend no further than the ordering of artifacts themselves.

But, in any event, there were sound empirical reasons why an identification with geology and, by extension, with palaeontology must have seemed obvious and profitable. To the same degree that the ethnographic background of Stone Age life might seem remote and abstract, so the geological reality of its archaeological record was immediate and concrete. The Palaeolithic comes to us enveloped in a previous geological epoch, and Pleistocene deposits – whether they appear in a rockshelter, stream terrace, or open-air station – present sedimentological and stratigraphic problems that far surpass those normally encountered by archaeologists working in later time periods. Thus to conduct Palaeolithic fieldwork almost inevitably means to become occupied with a geological frame of reference. And, in turn, just as a humanistic perspective led seventeenth-century virtuosi to regard figured stones as the 'coins of nature', so might a geological perspective prompt a twentieth-century archaeologist to conceive of artifacts in a fairly literal sense as the fossils of history. It is by no means irrelevant to this last point that, even in the minds of modern pre-historians (e.g., Leroi-Gourhan, 1945: 472), stone tools do often seem to possess a life of their own in the sense that the evolution of lithic technology displays a kind of internal logic whose patterns are intrinsic to it and can to a great extent be studied without direct reference to the cultural background in which they functioned.

Finally, it bears stressing that the traditional approach did indeed work. To be sure, one can quickly grow impatient when working through the literature of that era in discovering the number of pre-historians in whom the love of system released the passion for uni-formity, and how often, as a result, systematics functioned to keep the data at a distance in the very act of ordering them. But at the same time the traditional approach did emphasize empirical research and it did provide a coherent and internally consistent framework within which the contents of the archaeological record could be described and compared in an orderly manner. In doing so it laid the foundation for our own efforts, and it is of secondary importance that its expec-tations regarding the nature of patterning inherent in that record were, at least in our eyes, wrong. The traditional approach should be applauded for its efficacy rather than censured for its limitations.

BIBLIOGRAPHY

BONIFAY, EUGÈNE 1956 Les sédiments détritiques grossiers dans le remplissage des grottes—Méthode d'étude morphologique et statistique. *L'Anthropologie* 60: 447-61.

BORDES, FRANÇOIS 1950 Principles d'une méthode d'étude des téchniques de débitage et de la typologie du Paléolithique ancien et moyen. *L'Anthropologie* 54: 19-34.

——— 1961 Mousterian cultures in France. *Science* 134: 803-10.

BORDES, FRANÇOIS and PAUL FITTE 1953 L'atelier Commont. Album de 188 dessins de Victor Commont avec une étude de l'atelier. *L'Anthropologie* 57: 1-45.

BOURLON, M. and J. and A. BOUYSSONIE 1912 Grattoirs carénés, rabots et grattoirs nucléiformes. Essai de classification des grattoirs. *Revue Anthropologique* 22: 473-86.

BREUIL, HENRI 1905 Essai de stratigraphie des dépôts de l'Age de Renne. *C.R. Congrès Préhistorique Française*, Perigueux. 74-80.

——— 1913 Les subdivisions du Paléolithique supérieur et leur signification. C.R. *14ème Congrès International d'Anthropologie et d'Archéologie Préhistorique*, 1912 Geneva, 165-238.

DANIEL, GLYN 1975 *A Hundred and Fifty Years of Archaeology*. London.

ISAAC, GLYNN LL. 1972 Early phases of human behaviour: models in Lower Palaeolithic archaeology. In D.L. Clarke (ed.), *Models in Archaeology*: 167-99. London.

LAMING-EMPERAIRE, A. 1964 *Origines de l'Archéologie Préhistorique en France*. Paris.

LAVILLE, HENRI 1975 *Climatologie et Chronologie du Paléolithique en Périgord: Etude sédimentologique de dépôts en grottes et sous abris*. Memoir No. 4, Etudes Quaternaires. Editions du Laboratoire de Paléontologie Humaine et de Préhistoire. Université de Provence.

LAVILLE, HENRI, JEAN-PHILIPPE RIGAUD, and JAMES SACKETT 1980 *Rockshelters of the Perigord: Geological Stratigraphy and Archaeological Succession*.

LEAKEY, MARY 1971 *Olduvai Gorge. Volume III: Excavations in Beds I and II, 1960-1963*. Cambridge.

LEROI-GOURHAN, ANDRÉ 1945 *Evolution et Techniques. II: Milieu et Techniques*. Paris.

LEROI-GOURHAN, ANDRÉ, and MICHEL BRÉZILLON

——— 1966 L'Habitation Magdalénienne No. 1 de Pincevent, près Montereau (Seine et Marne). *Gallia Préhistoire* 9: 263-385.

MERCIER, PAUL 1966 *Histoire de l'Anthropologie*. Le Sociologue no. 5. Paris.

MORTILLET, GABRIEL DE 1883 *Le Préhistorique: Antiquité de l'Homme*. Paris. (2nd edn. 1885, third–in collaboration with A. de Mortillet—1909).

MORTILLET, GABRIEL DE and ADRIEN DE MORTILLET 1881 *Le Musée Préhistorique*. Paris. (2nd edn. 1903).

MOVIUS, HALLAM L. Jr 1953 Old World prehistory: Paleolithic. In A.L. Kroeber (ed.), *Anthropology Today*. Chicago: 163-92.

——— 1974 The Abri Pataud program of the French Upper Paleolithic in retrospect. In G.R. Willey (ed.), *Archaeological Researches in Retrospect*. Cambridge: 87-116.

PEYRONY, DENIS 1933 Les industries aurignaciennes dans le bassin de la Vézère. Aurignacien et Périgordien. *Bulletin de la Société Préhistorique Française* 30: 543-59.

——— 1936 Le Périgordien et l'Aurignacien. (Nouvelles Observations). *Bulletin de la Société Préhistorique Française* 33: 616-19.

——— 1946 Une mise au point au sujet de l'Aurignacien et du Périgordien. *Bulletin de la Société Préhistorique Francaise* 43: 232-37.

RIGAUD, JEAN-PHILIPPE 1978 The significance of variability among lithic artifacts: a specific case from southwestern France. *Journal of Anthropological Research* 34: 299-310.

SACKETT, JAMES 1965 *Aurignacian culture in the Dordogne: a study in archaeological systematics*. Unpublished Ph.D. dissertation, Harvard University.

——— 1968 Method and theory of Upper Paleolithic archeology in southwestern France. In L. and S. Binford (eds), *New Perspectives in Archaeology*. New York: 61-83.

——— 1979 A prologue to style in lithic archeology. In R. Tringham (ed.), *Lithic Analysis in Archaeology*, New York.

SMITH, PHILIP 1966 *Le Solutréen en France*. Mémoire no. 5, Publications de l'Institut de Préhistoire de l'Université de Bordeaux. Bordeaux.

DE SONNEVILLE-BORDES, DENISE 1960 *Le Paléolithique Supérieur en Périgord*. Bordeaux.

VIII
The concept of culture in European archaeological literature

C. F. MEINANDER

University of Helsinki, Finland

The word 'culture' deserves to be examined from a purely linguistic point of view, as an example of how quite an ordinary word in one language, here the Latin verb *colere* (to cultivate), has been taken up by other languages. From this word, during centuries of use in those languages and their common structure of thought, has emanated a focal word and a whole skein of words and concepts. The word culture is used nowadays in so many senses that it is remarkable that it still meets the demands we make on a word, namely that it has to be understood by everyone using it.

Here is what E. B. Tylor wrote in 1871: 'Culture or Civilization, taken in its wide ethnographic sense, is that complex whole which includes knowledge, belief, art, morals, laws, customs and other capabilities and habits acquired by man as a member of society.' Tylor's work, a German edition of which appeared in 1873, was extremely important to the development of Anglo-Saxon anthropological research. His presentation is, as was customary in his day, mainly evolutionistic and leaves little space for descriptions of specific peoples and their culture. Indeed, he mentions that tribes and peoples each have their own culture, but he only sees them as examples of stages of universal evolution. In subsequent editions of the book this basic approach was not changed.

In history, research and historiography the word culture was soon given another meaning: as early as the eighteenth century it was regarded as the opposite of barbarism with the supplementary connotation of education, enlightenment, morals. Cultural history, the history of civilization, was conceived as the opposite and an end product of political history. Johann Gottfried Herder (1744-1803) wrote that the individual has his *Bildung*, his education, whereas the people has culture. At the same time it was stated or claimed that German culture was not the same as French culture, not to mention Chinese or Eskimo culture. This is really a purely German matter as in France they did not write or talk about culture but about civilization. This caused confusion as the German-speaking area began to include customs, religion and art under the heading culture, but laws, constitution and science under the heading civilization, whereas the French speakers did not make this distinction.

In the middle of the nineteenth century German historians meant by culture everything which it still represents in ordinary speech (I imagine that this goes for all European languages), but in addition the word came to have a special significance. In his work *Geschichte des Altertums* of which the first part appeared in 1884, Eduard Meyer divides his history into chapters headed 'die ägyptische Kultur', 'die asiatischen Kulturen', 'die griechische Kultur'; he further distinguishes the Trojan, the Syrian, the Mycenaean and the Middle-East cultures. I quote: 'Wenn zwei ursprünglich unabhängige Kulturen in Berührung treten...so enstehen...auf einander fortschreitende Kulturkreise. Zwei solche Kreise...es sind der ostasiatische und der der Mittelmeervölker.' We see here the already developed notion that historical evolution is divided into cultures which, in their turn, can be combined into *Kulturkreise* (culture provinces). Whether or not Eduard Meyer was the first to divide the course of events of world history into clutures I have not discovered, but at all events he had followers, among whom Oswald Spengler with his work *Untergang des Abendlandes* and Arnold Toynbee were the most popular. The latter, in *A Study of History*, interprets civilizations as ontological entireties, as operative units of history, 'the intelligible units in history'.

We find that the specific concepts of culture had ripened and acquired their meaning in history as well as in the anthropological sciences as early as the 1880s, probably already a few decades earlier.

A scientific study that we must not forget in this context is philology. Philology has in many respects had a decisive effect on the formation of archaeological theories, particularly as many of the earlier archaeologists had a philological education, unless they were natural scientists. One of the central themes of comparative philology was the reconstruction of the presumed Indo-European or Finno-Ugrian primitive language and at the same time an identification and description of the peoples speaking this language. With the support of linguistic criteria the primitive people (*Urvolk*) and culture (*Urkultur*) were reconstructed long before archaeology was of any help. It is possible to establish quite clearly that in the earliest archaeological publications, where the author deliberately operates with archaeological cultures, the main interest lies in these same questions concerning the *Urvolk*, the Indo-Germanic or Indo-European or Aryan and the Finno-Ugrian.

In archaeology, when we use the term 'culture', it has a special significance. V. Gordon Childe (1929) was the first to define an 'archaeological culture', but the concept was in use in the whole of Europe two or three decades before he came on the scene. I myself prefer to use David Clarke's definition of 1968: 'An archaeological culture is a polythetic set of specific and comprehensive artifact types which consistently recur together in assemblages within a limited geographic area.' In this paper I shall deal with the question of how that concept originated and spread in the terminology of archaeology. My argument is based exclusively on the archaeological literature of the last century, and I shall begin with the remotest part of Europe, namely my own country, Finland.

Finland

Of particular significance are the following three authors: Aarne Mikael Tallgren (1885-1945), Aarne Äyräpää (1887-1971) and Carl Axel Nordman (1892-1972).

Äyräpää (Europaeus) put forward the idea of archaeological cultures in an article 'Fornfynd från Kyrkslätt och Esbo Socknar' (1922); in an earlier article (1917), he had referred to the Kitchen Midden Culture, the Harpoon Culture (= Maglemose), the Megalith Culture and the Battle-Axe Culture. This article being a review of newer Scandinavian literature, the terms he used were exact translations of the Scandinavian terms. It does not mean, therefore, that the concept of cultures had as yet been introduced into Finnish research; the terms Battle-Axe Culture and Comb-Pottery Culture were used for the first time by Äyräpää in an article in 1919.

Carl Axel Nordman kept pace with Äyräpää. His doctoral thesis 'Studier i gånggriftskulturen' appeared in 1918. In it the word culture occurs rarely and wholly in accordance with the example set by Sophus Müller. In 1921 and 1922, however, Nordman wrote two articles – 'Pohjoismaisia kivikauden kysymksiä' and 'Some Baltic Problems' – in which we find all the Finnish Stone Age cultures whose names are still in use: the Suomusjärvi Culture, the Comb-Pottery Culture, the Battle-Axe Culture, and the Kiukais Culture.

Comparison of the terminology in the works of Tallgren with that of Nordman and Äyräpää presents some difficulty since many of Tallgren's works have been translated into French. Thus, Tallgren calls Ananino both an *époque* and a civilization. The latter term is apparently a translation of the Finnish *kulttuuri*, culture, judging from the fact that Tallgren refers to a 'couche de civilisation' meaning a culture layer. Besides, Tallgren writes in 1919 about the Minoussinsk, the Pianobor and the Ananino civilizations. Yet, in his article 'La Pontide préscytique', which appeared in 1926, he uses the word culture, although sparsely, and civilization not at all. In 'Zur Archäologie Eestis' published in 1922, in German, Tallgren uses the terms Kunda Kultur, Pernausche Knochenkultur, Burtnieksche Knochenkultur, Bootaxtkultur and Somusjärvi Kultur.

In his doctoral thesis 'Die Kupfer-und Bronzezeit' (1911) Tallgren applied the term culture only to the Fatjanovo Culture; otherwise using it rather in a chronological sense: the stone culture, the copper culture, the bronze culture; he does, however, refer to the Einzelgrab-kultur, the Südrussische Kultur and the Tripolje Culture, as well as to the Fatjanovo Culture.

Tallgren may have borrowed the name 'Fatjanobo-Kultur' from Spičyn, who used it as early as 1903. Gorodcov used the terms 'Fatja-novskaja kultura', 'Donetskaja kultura' and 'Semjanskaja kultura' in his work about the Bronze Age of Russia in 1913.

The earliest occurrences I have found of the term 'Tripolje Culture' is in a lecture V. V. Hvojko delivered in 1899 and published in 1901. There he distinguishes between two cultural stages on the southern Dnieper and calls them *Kultura A* and *Kultura B*. At the Pan-Russian congress in Jekaterinoslav in 1905 (the transactions were published in 1907) Hvojko speaks of 'Tripolskaja Kultura'. At the same congress E.P. von Stern also used the term 'Tripolskaja kultura', but in inverted commas.

In the words of Julius Ailio we find the word culture used in quite an original sense. What we now term cultures Ailio calls groups in his doctoral thesis 'Die steinzeitlichen Wohnplatzfunde' (1909). Thus, he refers to 'die ostfinnische Gruppe', 'die aländische Gruppe', 'die Gruppe von Alastaro', 'die Gruppe von Kiukainen', 'die in engeren Sinne arktische Kulturgruppe'. He uses the word culture in a purely technological sense: Schieferkultur, Feuersteinkultur, Basic Kultur; the terms have, in a sense, a chorological but not a chronological meaning. Ailio's natural science background becomes apparent here.

To sum up, we can say that the concept 'archaeological culture' came into common use in Finland in 1922 with the works of Tallgren, Nordman and Äyräpää; in 1929 Gordon Childe defined it in much the same way. Prior to 1922 the term was seldom used and had differing connotations. Nordman certainly acquired his apparatus of ideas from Denmark where he worked under Sophus Müller from 1911 to 1918. Äyräpää was strongly influenced partly by Müller, partly by German research. Two archaeologists of great importance to Finnish research were the Norwegian, A. W. Brögger, and the Swede, Nils Aberg, both of whom accepted the idea of 'archaeological cul-ture', the former in 1909 and the latter in 1918.

Sweden

Where Sweden is concerned we find that, with one important excep-tion, Montelius did not write about cultures. His view of culture was evolutionistic and chronological, in much the same way as was E. B. Tylor's view of ethnology. At the beginning of this century, however, a new generation came on the scene. In particular, I want to mention Knut Stjerna, whose very important 'Before the Stone Cist Age' came out in 1912, and Oscar Almgren whose 'Some Swedish-Finnish Stone Age Problems' appeared the same year. In both these articles the term culture is used, alternating with civilization: Dwelling-Place Culture, Battle-Axe Culture, Megalith Culture, Kitchen Midden Culture, Gorodischte Culture. Stjerna, it would appear, applied the word civilization to the *hunting cultures* but used 'culture' where agriculture was concerned. Almgren uses the term culture consistently and gives it an explicit ethnic meaning.

In his article in *Fornvännen* (1906) Almgren does not use the word culture at all in this sense, nor does T. J. Arne in an article (1909) on Sweden's first boat-axe grave. In his doctoral thesis, published in 1918, 'Das nordische Kulturgebiet', Nils Åberg discusses some 20 cultures, all of them Central European, but it must be remembered that Åberg worked in Germany during the First World War. We might say that the cultures with which Åberg filled the Neolithic of Central Europe remind one of a war game with marching army corps and brigades inspired by the dramatic reality of that war.

Norway

Both Stjerna and Almgren could have received, and probably did receive, their inspiration from 'Die Herkunft der Germanen' by Koss-inna (1911) or from the Kossinna circle in general. A. W. Brögger seems, nevertheless, to have had an alibi: his thesis 'The Arctic Stone Age' appeared as early as 1909. In it are found such terms as the Magdalenian Reindeer Culture, the South-Norwegian Nöstvet Cul-ture, the Baltic Dwelling-Place Culture, the Arctic-Baltic Slate Cul-ture. The only instance of a place-name being coupled with the word culture is the Nöstvet Culture, about which more later. Brögger sharp-ly rejects the theory of a culture being associated with a certain race. All the same, he equates – seemingly almost unaware of it himself – the Arctic population and the Arctic Slate Culture, so, at least in this case, giving culture an ethnic compass. The idea of the Arctic Slate Culture as representing a specific people appears in one of Brögger's earlier works, 'Studier over Norges Stenalder' (1906), in which he refers to what Olof Rygh stated in 1874.

The term Nöstvet Culture was used for the first time by Andreas M. Hansen in *Landnam i Norge* (1904) where he writes: 'The dwelling-place finds from Kristianastrøket present a particularly developed culture – an original and independently developed stone age culture.' In his doctoral thesis of 1906 Brögger in a way disclaims the term Nöstvet Culture. 'I do not refrain from observing that the word Nöstvet Culture should not be used, as it could easily be misunder-stood. The term 'older stone age' is better and more reliable.' It is evident that Brögger did not in these works given the concept of culture an ethnic sense, but he nevertheless uses the word culture as an operative concept.

Denmark

When Sophus Müller wrote his 'De Jydske Enkeltgrave fra Stenal-deren' in 1898 he did not make these burial places constitute a culture; on the whole, he does not write about cultures there. But when he comes back to the same subject in 1913, in 'Sönderjyllands stenalder', he frequently uses the terms Single Grave Culture and Collective Tomb Culture. He does it mainly in polemical arguments against Gustaf Kossinna, and it is thus apparent that the terms have been taken from Kossinna's 'Die Herkunft der Germanen' (1911). Müller does not polemicize against Kossina's thesis on the ethnic contents of the archaeological cultures: he seems, on the contrary, to have accepted this principle. He argues only against the Megalith Culture being equated with the Indo-Germanic Urkultur.

In other aspects, Müller has used this concept of culture with restraint. His work during the first decade of this century relating to the prehistory of Europe, which appeared in many languages, contains a compilation in tabular form entitled *Übersicht der prähistorischen Kulturgruppen;* individual groups are not labelled cultures, but are given a proper name: Hallstatt, Villanova, Dipylon. As chapter headings we find the more traditional titles: The Egyptian Culture, The Assyrian and Babylonian Culture, The Culture of the West-Semitic peoples, The Culture of Asia Minor, The Ancient Aryan Culture, The Ancient Indian Culture, The Persian Culture; but what we call archaeological cultures are missing.

When Sarauw published the Maglemose find in 1904 he did not use the term 'Maglemose Culture' but referred instead to 'this new Stone Age Culture which Worsaae characterized as the older Stone Age of Denmark or the Kitchen Midden Age', and further, to 'the Culture before us in the Maglemose find'. For Sarauw the term Maglemose had here a mainly chronogical connotation. Knud Friis-Johansen, who in 1919 published the find of Svaerdborg Mose, did not write about a Maglemose Culture either, but in 1924 H.C. Broholm used the names Lyngby Culture (after Gustav Schwantes), Maglemose Culture and Kitchen Midden Culture.

The archaeological concept of cultures developed vigorously only with Therkel Mathiassen and Johannes Brøndsted in the 1930s. It is possible that they were at that time already influenced by British research, particularly by V. Gordon Childe. The fact that C. A Nordman, coming from Denmark in 1918, introduced the concept in Finland indicates that it was more commonly accepted there than the literature would suggest.

To follow the concept 'an archaeological culture' in Western Europe presents some difficulties since the word culture has such a powerful rival in the word civilization. In *La préhistoire française*, a work published as recently as 1976, the terms *groupes*, *cultures* and *civilisations* are used indiscriminately to signify the same thing, no ethnic conclusions being arrived at as a rule.

Where Great Britain is concerned, I would refer to Bruce Trigger's recently published *Time and Tradition* (1978), in which he devotes a whole chapter to an analysis of the concept 'an archaeological culture', and in particular to its history from an Anglo-Saxon point of view. According to Trigger (p. 83), O.G.S. Crawford (*Man and his Past*, 1921) would have been the first to use such an expression in its Central European sense, in a manner which assumed wide-spread familiarity with the concept. M.C. Burkitt used the term in 1923 and 1926 in *Our Early Ancestors*, apparently as a loan translation from Central European literature. Burkitt's attitude towards the work of V. Gordon Childe is not clear to me; he quotes Childe but not his *The dawn of European civilization*. Nor do I find it quite clear what real role Childe played in European archaeological research before the Second World War. I have an impression that his importance has been overestimated in Great Britian.

It is obvious that the use of the word culture by Nordic archaeologists during the second decade of our century was inspired by German terminology and especially by Kossinna's works. In reality, there was a much older tradition to fall back on. At the international congress for anthropology and archaeology in 1874 in Stockholm, Oscar Montelius gave a lecture entitled 'Sur les souvenirs de l'âge de pierre des lapons en Suède'. Writing about Olof Rygh, Montelius refers to 'la civilisation arctique de la pierre' and 'la groupe arctique de l'âge de la pierre'. It should be noted that Montelius never used these expressions later, although he continued to accept the idea that the 'arctic' slate tools could be associated with the Lapps.

The passage by Rygh quoted by Montelius is included in the annual report of the museum in Christiania (Oslo) for 1866. I quote (p.100): 'Spears and arrowheads of this peculiar kind are not uncommon in Norway; also knives of the same stone and of an extraordinary shape have been found. It is assumed that they did not belong to the same culture and people as did the usual well-known Stone Age objects, which are in keeping with those from Denmark and southern Sweden as far as the shape and material are concerned. They are found mostly in Tromsö and Finmarken Amter, where the usual stone objects are very rare. They cangthus plausibly be attributed to the Lapps.' This is, as far as I know, the earliest use of the word culture in this sense and with an ethnic connotation. In 1871 Rygh goes on to say: '. . . may we assume two stone age cultures and two stone age peoples. One of these cultures might be called the arctic one. There are good reasons to attribute the arctic culture to the Lapps.'

Hans Hildebrand, too, was early in the field. In 'Bidrag till spännets historia' (1870) he coins many names of cultures, among them the La

Tène Culture, 17 years before Furtwängler. He does not, however, give the name any ethnic significance, properly speaking. The expressions Hallstatt, Villanovan and La Tène Culture are then taken over by Undset (1881) and Lissauer (1887) with an explicit reference to Hildebrand. For them these cultures have, however, a purely chronological meaning. This usage was continued also by Hoernes (1889), Jelinek (1894) and Penka (1897).

That the concept of cultures entered into Neolithic research comparatively late was probably mainly because it was not until the 1890s that attempts were made to divide Neolithic material into separate groups. For a long time only the Nordic megalith tombs and the Swiss lake-dwelling sites were known. It was possible to start a proper classification only when on the one hand the Bandkeramik, on the other hand the Corded Ware had been identified. Klopfleisch from south Germany has been called the 'father' of Bandkeramik. Corded ware was for the first time treated in considerable detail by A. Götze (1891); in his works mention is made of 'die Kultur der Bandkeramik', 'noch andere neolithische Kulturen', 'die Kultur der thüringer Schnurkeramik', 'die thüringer Gruppe der Bandkeramik'. Götze's doctoral thesis of 1891 is wholly devoted to describing and classifying the corded ware, and he does not try to associate it with any specific people; this gives his presentation a strictly objective character.

What, in this context, was in fact Kossinna's role? We can disregard the fact that he was certainly not objective in his nationalistic frenzy and that his style was distasteful. His first work was a lecture in Kassel in 1895 (published in 1896): 'Die vorgeschichtliche Ausbreitung der Germanen in Deutschland'. It is mainly a collection of statements with a philological basis – in the first instance a kind of manifesto. The archaeological material is very meagre, the Stone Age being omitted altogether. But his principle of interpreting archaeological cultures is already in evidence, and he will not allow his concepts of people and language groups to be questioned. His famous thesis that distinctly delimited archaeological cultures always coincide with specific peoples ('scharf umgrentzte archäologische Kulturprovinzen decken sich zu allen Zeiten mit ganz bestimmten Völkern und Völkerschaften') was not presented until 1911, but the principle itself and the method of work were clearly formulated some 16 years earlier. And it was Kossinna's 1911 article which made the term 'archaeological culture' catch on in various parts in Europe, although not always with acceptance of Kossinna's conclusions.

Kossinna's definition does not differ much from Childe's. Both considered that by a cultural region was meant the region pertaining to a people. Neither of them invented his definition, it was applied already in the 1860s for example by Olof Rygh. The thesis seems to have been in a sense implicit in the whole of archaeological research, implying that prehistoric finds enabled you to ascertain the nationality of those responsible for them. This idea goes as far back as the seventeenth century. What is new, however, is that one no longer sought to make assertions founded on separate objects; cultures were used as operative units.

One of the starting points of this study was to try to determine whether the archaeological concept of culture emanated from anthropology or from the study of history. If I have not reached any final conclusion, it is partly because I have an insufficient knowledge of anthropological literature. Indeed, I have not in any of the earlier examples cited references to anthropological literature. On the contrary, it seems that anthropology during the entire nineteenth century was based on an evolutionistic concept of culture, whereas in archaeology this concept plays a markedly idiographic role. I thus find it most likely that the archaeological concept of culture derived from the corresponding concept in historiography.

On the other hand, we have to remember that throughout the second half of the nineteenth century archaeology and anthropology – and to a slightly lesser extent, history – shared the same debating ground. The international archaeologists' congress which played an important part in the forming of theories as well as of terminology were common to archaeologists and anthropologists. Thus neither has been ignorant of the other's concepts and definitions. It would seem essential to find out the importance to German archaeology and particularly to Kossinna of Leo Frobenius and the 'culture doctrine' he worked out during the last years of the nineteenth century, a subject K.H. Jacob-Friesen (1928) touches upon to some extent.

The criticism directed at Kossinna and of the thesis that culture and people are synonymous runs like a *leitmotif* through archaeological literature from one decade to the next. During the last ten years this criticism has in the main turned most energetically on the application of the word culture in archaeology. Among the critics we find such authoritative archaeologists as Glyn Daniel (1971), Evžen Neustupný (1976) and Anders Hagen (1970). Before the advent of radiocarbon dating, some 30 years ago, a culture was a necessary chronological instrument. By assigning a certain object to a certain culture we also arrived at its age. The age of the culture was mainly determined by its relation to other cultures. The radiocarbon datings enabled us to date a find without asking to which culture it might belong.

All the same, I still believe in the usefulness of the concept of 'culture'. It was originally adopted because within the same region were found antiquities whose interrelationship it was not possible to determine and which apparently belonged to different social traditions. It was a concept that helped to distinguish between the megaliths and the Einzelgrabkultur, between a dwelling-place and a battle-axe culture, between Hügelgräberkultur and Urnenfelderkultur. It thus had a clearly antithetic use.

That cultures often have been given a meaning which does not correspond to what a prehistoric people professed is a different matter. We have believed in peoples and great migrations which have not existed. A philological world of concepts, families of languages and language stages have been projected on to archaeology without any real correspondence. When reaction sets in we are ready to deny the whole paradigm.

I believe in the usefulness of cultures simply because all science implies generalizations. Science assumes that we should, in accordance with what we know, draw our conclusions about the unknown. Backed up by an archaeological site already examined we should be able to comment on sites not yet excavated. That is conditional upon our being able to give validity to our statements by setting limits in time and space, and we need a terminology adapted for this purpose.

Archaeologically, 'culture' is just such a term; it gives the limits in time and space for our statements about prehistory. Culture is a necessary operative concept, but we should not be led into believing that the cultures we postulate will always correspond to a certain social structure such as a people or a tribe or a language group.

BIBLIOGRAPHY

ABERG, N. 1918. Das nordische Kulturgebiet in Mitteleuropa während der jüngeren Steinzeit. *Arbeten utg. med understöd af Vilhelm Ekmans universitetsfond, Uppsala*, 22: 1.

AILIO, J. 1909. *Die steinzeitlichen Wohnplatzfunde in Finland*. Helsingfors (Helsinki).

ALMGREN, O. 1906. Upplands stenåldersboplatser. *Fornvännen*.

―― 1912 Några svensk-finska stenåldersproblem. Ett orienteringsförsök. *Antikvarisk tidskrift för Sverige*, 20: 1.

ARNE, T.J. 1909. Stenåldersundersökningar. *Fornvännen*.

BAILLOUD, G. and P. MIEG DE BOOFZHEIM. 1955. *Les civilisations néolithiques de la France*. Paris.

BANG, K. 1974. Om Kulturbegrebet. *Kontactstencil* (Organ for Nordiska Arkeologis-tudenter), Nr. 8. Copenhagen.

BERGMANN, J. 1972. Ethnos und Kulturkreis. Zur Methodik der Urgeschichtswissenschaft. *Prähistorische Zeitschrift*, 47-2.

―― 1974. Zum Begriff des Kulturkreises in der Urgeschichtswissenschaft. *Prähistorische Zeitschrift*, 49: 1.

BRJUSSOW, A.J. 1957 *Geschichte der neolitischen Stämme im europäischen Teil der USSR*. Berlin.

BRÖGGER, A.W. 1906. Studier over Norges stenalder. *Videnskabs-selskabets Skrifter. Mat. nat. Klasse 1906:* 1. Christiania (Oslo)

―― 1909. Den arktiske stenalder i Norge. *Videnskabs-selskabets Skrifter. Hist. filos. Klasse 1909:* 1. Christiania (Oslo).

BROHOLM, H.C. 1924. Nye Fund fra den ældre Stenalder. *Aarböger*.

BRONDSTED, J. 1938. *Danmarks Oldtid 1: Stenalderen*. Copenhagen.

BRUNN, W.A. von 1953. Frühe soziale Schichtungen im nordischen Kreis und bei den Germanen. *Festschrift des Römisch-Germanischen Zentralmuseums in Mainz*, Band III.

BURKITT, M.C. 1923. *Our Forerunners*. London.

―― 1926. *Our Early Ancestors*. Cambridge.

BURSCH, F.C. 1953. Vorgeschichte als Kulturgeschichte. *Actes C.I.S.P.P. Zurich, 1950*. Zurich.

CHILDE, V.G. 1925. *The Dawn of European Civilization*. London.

―― 1929. *The Danube in Prehistory*. Oxford.

―― 1942. *What happened in History*. Harmondsworth.

C.I.S.P.P. 1976. *La préhistoire française, II: Les civilisations néolithiques et protohistoriques de la France*. CNRS (Paris).

CLARK, G. 1961. The Dawn of Culture, in S. Piggott (ed.), *The Dawn of Civilisation*. London.

CLARKE, D.L. 1968. *Analytical Archaeology*. London.

DANIEL, G.E. 1950. *A hundred years of archaeology.* London.
—— 1975. *A hundred and fifty years of archaeology.* London.
EGGERS, H.J. 1950. Das Problem ethnischer Deutungen in der Frühgeschichte. *Festschrift Wahle:* 49-59. Heidelberg.
EUROPAEUS, A. 1917. Indoeurooppalaiskysymys ja kivikauden tutkimus. *Valvoja.* Helsinki.
—— 1919. Suomen vanhimmat kiviaseet. *Historiallinen aikakauskirja.* Helsinki.
—— 1922. Fornfynd från Kyrkslätt och Esbo socknar. *SMYA-FFT* XXXII: 1. Helsingfors (Helsinki).
FRIIS-JOHANSEN, K. 1917. Jordgrave fra Dyssetid. *Aarbøger.*
—— 1919. En boplads i Sværdborg Mose. *Aarbøger.*
GORODCOV, V.A. 1913. Kultury bronzovoj epohi v Srednej Rossij. *Otcet' imperatorskago rossijskogo istoriceskago museja 1912.* Moscow.
GÖTZE, A. 1891. *Die Gefässformen und Ornamente der neolithischen schnurverzierten Keramik im Flussgebiete der Saale.* Jena.
—— 1900. Neolithische Studien. *Zeitschrift für Ethnologie,* XXXII.
—— 1909 *Die vor- und frühgeschichtlichen Alterthümer Thüringens.* Würzburg.
HAGEN, A. 1970a. Om arkeologiens Kulturbegrep. *Kuml.*
—— 1970b. Refeksjoner om noen arkeologiske problemstillinger og tolkningsmuligheter. *Viking.*
HANSEN, A.M. 1904. *Landnåm i Norge.* Christiania (Oslo).
HARRIS, J.C. 1971. Explanation in prehistory. *Proc. Prehist. Soc.,* 37: 1.
HEIERLI, J. 1901. *Urgeschichte der Schweiz.* Zurich.
HILDEBRAND, H. 1870. Bidrag till spännets historia. *Antikvarisk tidskrift för Sverige,* IV.
—— 1880. *De förhistoriska folken i Europa. En handbok i jämförande fornkunskap.* Stockholm.
HOERNES, M. 1889a. Grabhügelfunde von Glasinac in Bosnien. *Mitt. d. Anthrop. Ges. in Wien,* XII.
—— 1889b. La Tène-Funde in Nieder-Österreich. *Mitt. d. Anthrop. Ges. in Wien,* XIX.
—— 1892. *Die Urgeschichte des Menschen.* Leipzig.
—— 1909. *Natur- und Urgeschichte des Menschen,* Vol. II. Leipzig.
HVOJKO, V.V. 1901. Kamennyj vek' srednago Pridneprov'ja, *Trudy XI arheologiceskago sezda. Moskva 1899.* Moscow.
—— 1907. Nacalo zemledelija i bronzovyj vek' v' Srednem' Pridneprov'e, *Trudy XIII arheologiceskago sezda b Ekaterinoslave 1905.* Moscow.

JACOB-FRIESEN, K.H. 1928. Grundfragen der Urgeschichtsforschung. *Veröffentlichungen der Urgeschichtlichen Sammlungen des Landesmuseums zu Hannover,* I.
JAHN, M. 1953. Die Abgrenzung von Kulturgruppen und Völkern in der Vorgeschichte. *Ber. Abh. Sächs. Ak. Wiss. zu Leipzig: Phil. Hist. Klasse.* 99: 3.
JELINEK, B. 1894. Materialen zur Vorgeschichte und Volkskunde Böhmens. *Mitt. d. Anthrop. Ges. Wien,* XXIV.
KENDRICK, T.D. and C.F.C. HAWKES. 1932. *Archaeology in England and Wales 1914-1931.* London.
KILIAN, L. 1960. Zum Aussagewert von Fund- und Kulturprovinzen. *Światowit,* XXIII.
KLEJN, L.S. 1971. Was ist eine archäologische Kultur? *Ethn. Arch. Z.,* 12.
—— 1976. Das Neolithicum Europas als ein Ganzes. *Jahresschrift Halle,* 60.
—— 1977. A panorama of theoretical archaeology. *Current Archaeology,* 18: 1.
KLOPFLEISCH, F. *See* Neumann, G. 1932.
KOENEN, K. 1895. *Gefässkunde der vorrömischen, römischen und fränkischen Zeit in den Rheinland.* Bonn.
KOSSINNA, G. 1895. (Kossinna's Kassel lecture). Die Vorgeschichtliche Ausbreitung der Germanen in Deutschland. *Zeit. des Vereins für Volkskunde 6 Jg. 1896.*
—— 1902. Die indogermanische Frage archäologisch beantwortet. *Zeit. für Ethnologie,* XXXIV.
—— 1911. Die Herkunft der Germanen. Zur Methode der Siedlungsarchäologie. *Mannus,* 6.
KROEBER, K.L. and C. KLUCKHOHN. 1952. Culture, a critical review of concepts and definitions. *Papers of the Peabody Museum, Harvard,* XLVII: i.
LINDEMAN, F. 1891. Rede gehalten am Sarge Otto Tischlers. *Schriften der Phys. Ökon. Ges. zu Königsberg in Pr.*
LISSAUER, A. 1887. *Die prähistorischen Denkmäler der Provinz West-Preussen und der angrenzenden Gebiete.* Leipzig.
MALMER, M.P. 1963. *Jungneolithische Studien.* Lund.
MANDERA, H.E. 1965. Zur Deutung neolithischer Kulturen. Nassauische Annalen, 76.
MATHIASSEN, T. 1934. Primitive Flintredskaber fra Sämsö. *Aarbøger.*
—— 1936. En Vestjydsk Megalitbygd. *Aarbøger.*
—— 1937. Gudenaa-Kulturen. *Aarbøger.*
MENGHIN, O. 1952. Urgeschichtliche Grundfragen, *Historia Mundi,* I.
MEYER, E. 1884-1902. *Geschichte des Altertums,* I-IV. Stuttgart.
MONTELIUS, O. 1874. Minnen från lapparnes stenålder i Sverige. *Kungl. Vitterhets historie*

och antikvitetsakademiens Månadsblad, 31.

—— 1876. Sur les souvenirs de l'age de la pierre des lapons en Suède. *Congrès international d'anthropologie et d'archéologie préhistorique. Compte rendu de la 7e session, Stockholm 1874.*

Much. M. 1893. *Die Kupferzeit in Europa und ihr Verhältnis zur Kultur der Indogermanen.* Jena.

Müller. S. 1898. De Jydske Enkeltgrave fra Stenalderen. *Aarbøger.*

—— 1905. *Urgeschichte Europas.* Strasbourg.

—— 1907. *L'Europe préhistorique.* Paris.

—— 1908. *Världskulturen* red. af Aage Friis, Vol. II.

—— 1913. Sönderjyllands Stenalder. *Aarbøger.*

Neumann. G. 1932. Dr Friedrich Klopfleisch Professor der Kunstgeschichte an der Universität Jena, Begründer der thüringischen Urgeschichtsforschung. *Mannus*, XXIV.

Neustupny. J. 1960. Some suggestions concerning archaeological records and archaeological cultures. *Światowit*, XXIII: 31ff.

Nordman. C.A. 1915. Till frågan om den förhistoriska arkeologins metod. *Nya Argus.*

—— 1918. Studier öfver gånggriftkulturen i Danmark. *Aarbøger*, 1917.

—— 1921. Pohjoismaisia kivikauden kysymyksiä. *Aika.*

—— 1922. Some Baltic problems. *JRAI*, LII.

Otto. K.H. 1953. Archäologische Kulturen und die Erforschung der konkreter Geschichte von Stämmen und Völkerschaften. *Ethnographisch-Archäologische Forschungen*, Band I. Berlin.

Peake. H. 1922. *The Bronze Age and the Celtic World.* London.

Penka. K. 1893. Die Heimat der Germanen. *Mitt. d. Anthr. Ges. in Wien* XXIII.

—— 1897. Zur Paläoethnologie Mittel- und Südeuropas. *Mitt. d. Anthr. Ges. in Wien* XXVII.

—— 1910 (?). Die Entstehung des neolithischen Kultur Europas. *Beiträge zur Rassenkunde.* Leipzig.

Reinecke. P. 1902. Neolithische Streitfragen. Ein Beitrag zur Methodik der Prähistorie. *Zeit. Ethnol.*, XXXIV.

Renfrew. A.C. 1974. British prehistory: changing configurations, in A.C. Renfrew (ed.), *British Prehistory*, London.

Rygh. O. 1867. Foreningen til Norske Fortidsmindesmaerkers Bevaring. *Aarsberetning.* 1866. Christiania (Oslo).

—— 1871. Om Affaldsdyngen ved Stenkjaer. *Aarsberetning*, 1871. Christiania (Oslo).

Sacken. E. von 1868. *Das Grabfeld von Hallstatt in Oberösterreich und dessen Alterthümer.* Vienna.

Sarauw. G.F.L. 1903. En stenalders Boplads i Maglemose ved Mullerup, sammenholdt med beslaegtede Fund. *Aarbøger.*

Schenck. A. 1912. *La Suisse préhistorique.* Lausanne.

Schlitz. A. 1901. Steinzeitliche Bestattungsformen in Südwest-Deutschland. *Corr. Bl. d. Dt. Ges. für Anthrop., Ethnol. und Urgesch.*

—— 1902. *Corr. Bl. d. Ges. für Anthrop., Ethnol.....*

—— 1904. Über den Stand der neolithischen Stilfrage in Südwest-Deutschland. *Mitt. d. Anthrop. Ges. in Wien*, XXXIV.

Schwabedissen. H. 1954. Die Federmessergruppen des nordwest-europäischen Flachlandes. *Offa-Bücher* NF 9: 1-2.

Shetelig. H. 1902. Spidser og knive af Skifer. *Kgl. Norske Videnskaselskabets Skrifter*, 1902: 3

Spicyn. A.A. 1903. Mednyj vek v verhnem Povolze. *Zapiski Otdelenija Arheologii Russkogo Arheologiceskogo Obscestva*, V: 1.

Stern. E.P. von 1907. Doistoriceskaja Greceskaja kultura na juge Rossii. *Trudy XIII arheologiceskago sezda b Ekaterinoslave 1905.*

Stjerna. K. 1910. Les groupes de civilisation en Scandinavie à l'époque des sépultures à galerie. *L'Anthropologie*, XXI.

—— 1911. Före hällkisttiden. *Antikvarisk tidskrift*, 19: 2.

Tallgren. A.M. 1911. Die Kupfer- und Bronzezeit in Nord- und Ost-Russland, I: Die ältere Metallzeit in Ostrussland. *SMYA-FFT*, XXV: 1

—— 1914. Den östeuropeiska bronsålderskulturen i Finland. *Finskt Museum.*

—— 1916. Tuntematon vaskikautinen kulturi. *Valvoja.*

—— 1919. L'époque dite d'Ananino. *SMYA-FFT*, XXXI.

—— 1922. Zur Archäologie Eestis. *Acta et commentationes Universitatis Dorpatensis*, B, II: 6.

—— 1926. La Pontide préscytique après l'introduction des métaux. *Eurasia septentrionalis antiqua*, II.

Trigger. B. 1978. *Time and Traditions: essays in archaeological interpretation.* Edinburgh.

Tylor. E.B. 1871. *Primitive Culture.* London. New edition 1903.

—— 1873. *Die Anfänge der Kultur.* Leipzig. (German transl. of above.)

Undset. I. 1881. *Jernalderens begyndelse.* Christiania (Oslo).

—— 1889. Terramaren in Ungarn. *Mitt. anthrop. Ges. in Wien*, XIX.

Zacharuk. J.N. 1976. Arheologiceskaja kultura. *Vostocnaja Evropa v epochu kamnja i bronzy.*

IX
Philippe-Charles Schmerling (1791-1836)

SIGFRIED J. DE LAET

Rijksuniversiteit Ghent, Belgium

Philippe-Charles Schmerling was born in Delft in 1791. His father was a doctor, and he too wanted to enter the medical profession. At the time, however, Holland was under French rule. Napoleon had abolished the universities, but the needs of his armies caused the French administration to create special schools in the chief town of each *département* for the accelerated training of army surgeons. In 1809 and 1810, Schmerling attended lectures at the Leyden school. A year's practical training at The Hague, under the tutorship of Dr de Riemer, followed. The latter had built up an important collection of anatomical specimens, which had won wide enough renown to attract the attention of the great G. Cuvier, who paid a visit to Dr de Riemer in 1811, the year that Schmerling worked there. It is most probable that here lies the clue to Schmerling's later interest in anatomy and palaeontology.

In 1812, at the end of his three years' term of studies, Schmerling attained the rank of 'health officer' (i.e. army surgeon).

At the end of 1813, after the battle of Leipzig, Holland entered into open revolt against Napoleon and the French domination. William of Orange landed in Holland on 30 November, was proclaimed Prince-Sovereign and proceeded to raise an army of conscripts. Schmerling was drafted as a surgeon and garrisoned at Venlo, where he served for three years, without participating in the Waterloo campaign. In 1814 he resigned his commission but stayed on at Venlo, building up a practice as general physician. In 1821, he married Sara-Henriette-Caroline de Douglas, a member of the Scottish nobility.

In 1815, Belgium and Holland merged to form the United Kingdom of the Netherlands. Two years later King William I reinstated the old universities and created a number of new ones. The University of Liège was among the latter. Feeling that his medical training was inadequate, Schmerling moved to Liège at the end of 1821 and attended lectures at the Faculty of Medicine till 1825. That year the public presentation of his thesis *De studii psychologiae in medicine utilitate et necessitate* earned him a doctorate in medicine.

During the years that followed, he continued his career as a general practitioner and made a name himself ministering to the poor. He did not, however, lose his interest in medical research, as is shown by the publication in 1832 of a booklet entitled *Quelques observations sur la teinture de colchique*, a study of the use of colchicum in the treatment of gout and rheumatism.

At the age of thirty-eight, his interests quite suddenly took another turn. In September 1829, he was called out to attend to a quarryman who lived at Chokier, a village some 15 km from Liège. While here, he noticed that the quarryman's children were playing with exceptionally large bones and elicited the information that a large number of similar bones had been discovered in a cavity cut through by the quarrying. The workman himself did not consider this find to be very remarkable, as he thought the bones came from an old and forgotten cemetery. Schmerling asked the man to collect for him all future finds of a similar nature; he acquired the bones that the children were playing with as payment for his medical attendance and began studying them. It did not take him long to reach the conclusion that they belonged to extinct animal species. This discovery started him off on the study of geology and especially of palaeontology.

First of all, he began a systematic quest for caves and holes which might yield fossil bones. The Chokier cave was the very first of a large number in the provinces of Liège and Luxembourg which Schmerling discovered and investigated. In less than four years he succeeded in exploring at least forty. He spared neither time nor money nor energy in collecting and studying the bone-remains of extinct animals. Indeed, Schmerling – who never hesitated to 'creep on all fours' through pipes and galleries to reach new caves – must be regarded as one of the very first speleologists in Belgium.

During those first few years, he spent no less than 20,000 to 30,000 gold francs – a very considerable sum indeed at the time – on this hobby of his. As early as 1833, i.e. less than four years after the discovery of Chokier, he published a first volume of his *Recherches sur les ossements découverts dans les cavernes de la province de Liège*, a volume of 170 pages, measuring 26.6 cm by 20.6 cm, together with an album of measuring 46.6 cm by 30.3 cm, containing 34 beautiful lithographs. Less than a year later, this was followed by the publication of a second volume (196 pages) with an album containing 40 lithographs. The exceptional significance of this pioneering work in the fields of palaeontology, physical anthropology and prehistory will soon become apparent.

Already in 1832, Schmerling had sent to the Royal Academy of Belgium a note on the human fossils which he had discovered, and on 12 October 1833 he also sent the first volume of his *Recherches* to this learned body. On 5 April 1834, the Academy elected him an associate member.

Abroad, Schmerling's work aroused much interest but it often also encountered downright scepticism. In fact, it was only much later, after his death, that the scientific world would fully realize how valuable his work was. Among the foreigners who came to see

Schmerling's collection and the caves he had discovered, were Alexander von Humboldt (who was convinced of the correctness of Schmerling's views) and the famous English geologist Charles Lyell; the latter now at first expressed his scepticism in his *Principles of Geology* (1830-33), but a quarter of a century later he came to Belgium to visit some of Schmerling's caves, himself discovered there a number of fossil bones and as a result changed his mind about Schmerling's work.

In 1835, five years after the independence of Belgium, the State Universities of Liège and Ghent were reinstated and Schmerling, although still a Dutch national, was appointed professor of zoology at the former. One year later, alas, Schmerling, who had been suffering from a heart disease since 1833, died on 6 November. Only a few days before his death, he had been elected a member of the *Koninklijk Nederlandsch Instituut van Wetenschappen, Letteren en Schoone Kunsten in Amsterdam* (as the Royal Dutch Academy was called from 1816 to 1851).

After his death, Schmerling was soon forgotten and the majority of the copies of his *Recherches* remained unsold until they were finally bought by a grocer, who used them to wrap up his merchandise. His collections were bought by the State and given to the University of Liège. The human fossils and most of the artifacts are still there, but the larger part of the palaeontological remains were lost through the neglect of Schmerling's successors.

Before commenting briefly on the value and impact of Schmerling's scientific work, I would like to point out how his career reflects the mentality that prevailed in the scientific world of his day, especially as far as the apparent indifference to political events is concerned. Schmerling worked during the period ranging from 1829 to 1836, and it should be noted that 1830 was the year of the Belgian armed revolt against the Dutch and that it was not until 1839 that a peace treaty between the two countries was signed. The revolutionary movement had been led mainly by liberals from Liège. None of this, however, seems to have troubled Schmerling in any way: although he remained a Dutch national, he did not interrrupt his research. He published his work in French, became a member of the Belgian Royal Academy in 1834 and a professor at the University of Liège in 1835, all this notwithstanding his rather poor knowledge of the French language. Looking at the events from the other side, one would expect the Dutch to consider him a traitor for staying on in Belgium, but he was nevertheless elected a member of the Dutch Academy in 1836. The contemporary attitude of the Dutch and Belgian scientific world, particularly the tendency to consider itself to be *au-dessus de la mêlée*, strikes us these days as quite admirable. Personally, I much regret that such an attitude is unthinkable today.

Let me now give a brief survey of the scientific importance of Schmerling's work in several fields.

Medicine

Although Schmerling's first publications concern the field of medical research and although he took part in scientific controversies, his contribution to medical knowledge can hardly be regarded as of prime importance. His main contributions to science clearly pertain to other fields: geology, palaeontology, physical anthropology and prehistory.

Geology

In his *Antiquity of Man*, published more than a quarter of a century after Schmerling's death, we find Lyell writing:

'... To be let down, as Schmerling was, day after day, by a rope tied to a tree so as to slide to the foot of the first opening of the Engis cave, where the best preserved human skulls were found; and after thus gaining access to the first subterranean gallery, to creep on all fours through a contracted passage leading to larger chambers, there to superintend by torchlight, week after week and year after year, the workmen who were breaking through the stalagmite crust as hard as marble in order to remove piece by piece the underlying bone breccia nearly as hard; to stand for hours with one's feet in the mud and with water dripping from the roof on one's head, in order to mark the position and guard against the loss of each single bone of a skeleton, and at length, after finding leisure, strength and courage for all these operations, to look forward, as the fruit of one's labour, to the publication of unwelcome intelligence, opposed to the prepossessions of the scientific as well as of the unscientific public – when these circumstances are taken into account, we need scarcely wonder, not only that a passing traveller failed to stop and scrutinize the evidence, but that a quarter of a century should have elapsed before even the neighbouring professors of the University of Liège came forth to vindicate the truthfulness of their indefatigable and clear-sighted countryman ...' (Lyell 1863, pp. 68-69)

Among the most important caves studied by Schmerling are those of Chokier, Engis, Engihoul, Fond-de-Forêt and Goffontaine. Some of these are still often mentioned in the geological and archaeological literature. If one may regret that Schmerling paid little or no attention to the stratigraphy of the different layers in the caves – but then stratigraphy itself was a quite unknown concept at the time – one should nevertheless mention the importance of his theory concerning the origins and the formation processes of these caves. Today these theories are somewhat out of date, but in the early nineteenth century they were relatively advanced. Quite revolutionary for his times was the fact that he proceeded to have the breccia with bone remains chemically analysed. Other questions also attracted his attention: Why was there a notable difference in the state of preservation of bones found in the same cave? Why did some caves yield a large quantity of bones while others yielded none?

Palaeontology

This was Schmerling's main field of interest. The study of 18,000 to 20,000 fossil bones allowed him to identify more than 60 extinct animal species, several of which were unknown until he discovered them. To list them briefly: four kinds of bats, one hedgehog, two kinds of shrewmice, one mole, six kinds of bears (a.o. *Ursus spelaeus, Ursus priscus,* as well as two kinds till then unknown: *Ursus giganteus* and *Ursus Leodiensis*), one badger, one glutton, several kinds of polecats, weasels, martens, two kinds of dogs, wolf, fox, hyena, several *Feliadea* (inter *alia Felis antiqua,* and the hitherto unknown, *Felis Engiholiensis, Felis prisca* and *Cattus minuta*), squirrels, rat, dormouse, mouse, hamster, several kinds of field-mice and field-rats, agouti, beaver, hare, rabbit, mammoth, several kinds of boars, rhinoceros, tapir, horse, twelve kinds of ruminants (including three types of reindeer, giant deer, deer, roedeer, antelope, goat, sheep, and three varieties of *Bos*), as well as several kinds of birds, reptiles, molluscs and fish.

Owing to his lack of knowledge of stratigraphy, Schmerling thought that all these animals had lived contemporaneously, and as most of them are extinct today, he believed furthermore that the last natural catastrophe had eradicated only part of the fauna, the species still alive today having survived. This theory is to be considered within the framework of the geological 'catastrophe' approach which was supported, among others, by W. Buckland and G. Cuvier. Whatever the context, the remarkable thing is Schmerling's discovery and identification of several animal species which were till then unknown.

Schmerling's medical training also bore other fruit: he identified several bone diseases, (*inter alia,* rickets or rachitis), traces of which he discovered on bones of cave-bears and other extinct animals. This also led him to contest the prevalent theory concerning the causes of rickets, which was then seen as a typical civilization-disease caused by a diet that included rye-bread, insufficiently baked bread, warm drinks such as coffee and tea, a surfeit of pastry and sweets, etc.

Schmerling's research in the field of palaeontology was important, but entirely in line with the work of some of his contemporaries such as W. Buckland (1784-1856), who was professor of geology at Oxford before becoming Dean of Westminster, and who had himself discovered 21 fossil species in the cave of Kirkdall.

Anthropology

Even more important was Schmerling's discovery of human fossil remains among fossil animal bones. This led him to the conclusion 'que les ossemens humains ont été ensevelis à la même époque et par les mêmes causes que ceux des restes des races éteintes'. Schmerling had found the remains of three individuals (including two skulls) in the cave of Engis and the remains of another three individuals in the cave of Engihoul. At the time of the discovery scientific attention was focussed on the existence of fossil man. In accordance with his 'catastrophe' theory, G. Cuvier had denied the existence of fossil man. Some discoveries, e.g. by Tournal in the Grotte de Bize, Département Aude (1828), by Christol at Pondres, near Nîmes (1829), by Boué in the Rhineland, by Count Razounowsky in Austria, by Count von Sternberg at Costritz, by J. MacEnery in Kent's Cavern at Torquay (1825-29), had pointed to the contemporaneity of man and exinct animal species. The authenticity of some of these discoveries is doubtful, but they had drawn attention to the problem. In general, however, the scientific world remained sceptical, mainly because of the influence of Cuvier's 'catastrophe' theory.

Later on, the two skulls found by Schmerling in the Engis cave proved to be of exceptional importance. Skull No. 1 belgoned to an elderly man and was discovered under a breccia layer containing rhinoceros bones. Skull No. 2 was found at the end of the cave, next to an elephant's tooth; it belonged to a juvenile; when recovered this skull fell apart and Schmerling was unable to restore it. Later excavations demonstrated the existence of at least two archaeological layers, one Mousterian, the other Late Perigordian. Today we know that skull No. 1 belongs to a *homo sapiens sapiens*, although it is still uncertain whether he was of Cro-Magnon or Combe-Capelle type. My colleague, F. Twiesselmann, cautiously uses the term *homo sapiens fossilis*. Long after Schmerling's death it was finally possible to restore the second skull, which was then found to belong to a *homo Neanderthalensis*. In fact, the discovery of skull No. 2 in the Engis cave antedates the find of the famous eponymous Neanderthal skeleton, which provoked such heated controversy, by no less than 17 years.

Schmerling limited his comments to the discussion of skull No. 1 and, noting some differences between it and the present-day European, he looked elsewhere for parallels and thought he had found them among the Ethiopians. As a result, this skull assumed an important place in the anthropological literature of the nineteenth century. It was studied by, among others, Vogt, Prüner, Bey, Virchow, Turner, de Quatrefages, Spring, Busk, Lyell, Huxley and Fraipont. Among the finds of remains of fossil man, made in the period from 1825 to 1830, those of MacEnery and of Schmerling are certainly the most convincing ones, but their importance was recognized only 30 years later.

Prehistoric archaeology

Schmerling not only uncovered animal and human remains, he also discovered several artifacts in ivory, bone and flint. In Chapter X of Volume II of his *Recherches* (pp. 178-79), he briefly describes *Les débris travaillés par la main de l'homme:*

'... Une chose bien singulière parmi tant de singularités, dans les produits des fouilles des cavernes ossifères, c'est la présence de fragmens de silex dont la forme régulière a frappé, au premier abord, mon attention. Dans toutes les cavernes de notre province où j'ai trouvé des ossemens fossiles en abondance, j'ai aussi rencontré une quantité plus ou moins considérable de ces silex.

Ces silex, fig. 10, pl. 36, sont d'une longueur et d'une largeur variables; ils ont une face plane et une autre triangulaire, les faces étant à-peu-près de même dimension; les bord externes sont très-tranchans, mais les extrémités sont obtuses. Ce qui prouve que ces silex ont été long-temps exposés aux influences atmosphériques, avant d'avoir été enfouis dans les cavernes, c'est qu'ils sont tous couverts d'une croûte blanchâtre, qui, dans quelques-uns, que j'ai brisés, ne dépasse pas l'épaisseur d'une ligne, tandis que le centre est d'un gris bleuâtre. La forme de ces silex est tellement régulière, qu'il est impossible de les confondre avec ceux que l'on rencontre dans la craie et dans le terrain tertiaire. Toute réflexion faite, il faut admettre que ces silex ont été taillés par la main de l'homme, et qu'ils ont pu servir pour faire des flèches ou des couteaux.'

Schmerling firmly rejects the opinion of those who, without taking into account the factual evidence, the possibility that such old artifacts could exist, and he demonstrates that those he found could not possibly have been mixed with the animal bones at some later date. The few artifacts reproduced by Schmerling in his album of the *Recherches* are among the earliest illustrated prehistoric objects in the history of archaeological research.

This discussion of prehistoric artifacts should, I must again stress, be seen within the framework of the spirit of Schmerling's times. Palaeolithic artifacts had then been known for some years. In 1797, John Frere had discovered at Hoxne in Suffolk a few Acheulean handaxes, together with fossil animal bones, but his interpretation of these objects as prehistoric weapons had attracted little or no attention. In 1806 Nyerup had published his *Oversyn over foedrelandets mindesmaerker fra oldtiden*, and in 1816 C.J. Thomsen had elaborated his hypothesis concerning the three ages on the occasion of the exhibition of Danish antiquities at the National Museum of Copenhagen, which was inaugurated in 1819. But this work of the Danish scientists remained largely unknown in Western Europe for a long time, and both Frere's and Schmerling's finds were admitted as artifacts only after the recognition in 1859 of those made by Boucher de Perthes in the Somme valley from 1837 on.

My conclusions can be summarized as follows: in the fields of palaeontology, anthropology and archaeology, Schmerling was about a quarter of a century ahead of his time. No wonder that soon after his death he was forgotten and that he was remembered only when his theses had become generally acceptable by the world of learning.

BIBLIOGRAPHY

ANGELROTH, H. 1945 Ph.-Ch. Schmerling. *Bulletin soc. r. belge d'anthrop. et de préhist.* LVI: 44-57.

CELS, A. and V. JACQUES 1896-97 Schmerling. Contribution à l'histoire du préhistorique en Belgique. *Bull. soc. d'anthrop. de Bruxelles* XV: 86-106.

CHARPENTIER-LEJEUNE, M. 1967 L'Université de Liège et les débuts de la paléontologie humaine. *Chron. de l'Univ. de Liège:* 119-27.

DANIEL, GLYN 1950 *A Hundred Years of Archaeology.* London: 34-35.

DANTHINE, H. 1954 Un bâton d'ivoire découvert par Schmerling à Fond-de-Forêt. *Mélanges J. Hamal-Nandrin:* 122-27.

FRAIPONT, CH. 1927 Les découvertes les plus importantes en anthropologie et en préhistoire faites par des Belges depuis Schmerling. *Congrès de l'Inst. intern. d'Anthrop.* 3. Amsterdam.

—— 1936 *Les hommes fossiles d'Engis.* Paris.

FREDÉRICQ, L. 1911-13 Schmerling (Philippe-Charles). *Biographie nationale publiée par l'Académie royale de Belgique*, Vol. XXI: 728-34.

LE ROY, A. 1869 Schmerling (Philippe-Charles). *Liber memorialis. L'université de Liège depuis sa fondation.* Liège: 550-66.

LYELL, C. 1830/33 *Principles of Geology.* London.

—— 1863 *The Antiquity of Man.* London.

MALAISE, C. 1860 Mémoire sur les découvertes paléontologiques faites en Belgique jusqu'à ce jour. *Mémoires de la Société libre d'Emulation de Liège*, n.s. I: 113-81: 146-48

—— 1863 *L'homme fossile.* Brussels and Leipzig.

MORREN, CH. 1838 Notice sur la vie et les travaux de P.C. Schmerling. *Annuaire de l'Acad. royale des Sciences de Bruxelles* 4: 130-50.

TWIESSELMAN, F. 1958 Les Néanderthaliens découverts en Belgique. In *Hundert Jahre Neanderthal, Neanderthal Centenary 1856-1956.* Cologne: 63-71.

X
Ludwig Lindenschmit and the Three Age System

KURT BÖHNER

Römisch-Germanisches Zentralmuseum, Mainz, West Germany

The Three Age System as a typological and chronological basic classification of prehistoric antiquities was not the outcome of theoretical reflection, but resulted from the ordering of numerous prehistoric burial finds in Scandinavian and North German museums (Beltz 1925). Following Jasperson's division into stone, bronze and iron of grave goods found in Oestergaard (1828) near Flensburg, the Copenhagen museum director, C. J. Thomsen, used the same system as a basis for his *Ledetraad til Nordisk Oldkyndighed (A Guide to Northern Antiquities)* 1836/37. J. F. Danneil in Salzwedel published similar findings in 1836 and F. Lisch in Schwerin arrived at a like conclusion from his own excavations. Today we consider it normal to divide the prehistoric period into Stone, Bronze and Iron Age and we ask ourselves how such a knowledgeable scholar as Ludwig Lindenschmit could fight against the system throughout his life with total conviction. Although the question of the correctness of the Three Age System has long been settled, it is still interesting to reflect on the bitter academic disagreement for the sake of the historical aspect of prehistoric research, because it shows the difficulties with which our faculty had to wrestle in its early stages in order to reach generally accepted rules.

With the help of the German Historical and Antiquarian Associations Lindenschmit founded in 1852 the Central Roman Germanic Museum in Mainz. Its task was to combine in its collections true reproductions and drawings of pre- and early historic antiquities which were to enable comparative studies of the antiquities from all over Germany to be carried out. Lindenschmit published his own collection of antiquities arranged in relevant groups in the work *Alterthümer unserer Heidnischen Vorzeit (Antiquities from our pagan prehistory)*, the first volume of which was published in 1858. The model for this publication was the Danish catalogue *Afbildninger fra det kgl. Museum for nordiske Oldsager in Kjöbenhavn* of 1854. As *Antiquities . . .* was initially meant to publish only particular groups of finds, the first volume confined itself to pictorial reproductions of the actual artifacts, their descriptions and also details of where they were found. The system of classification was borrowed from that used by the Copenhagen museum: stone, bronze and iron age. To quote from the preface: '. . . on the whole we keep to the known grouping which shows us three main periods: stone age, bronze age and iron age, as these three different materials were used to make tools and weapons.' We can detect a distinct change in the second volume (1870): in general the admittedly useful lay-out of the work was to remain the same, only in the description of the plates every reference to the Three Age System of the stone, bronze and iron age was abandoned. 'To understand the reason for departing from the Three Age System we need only point to the fact, now widely accepted, that the use of iron tools north of the Alps was never a necessarily general one and that even the more widespread usage of iron could only gradually displace the primitive weapons and tools of stone, bone and hardwood. The value of a systematic grouping of the burial finds according to the substances from which the tools and weapons were made is therefore diminished precisely for its most important purpose, namely the determination of the age of the finds, which in view of the countless mixed practices and transitional stages can only be sought in the style and character of the artifacts and the overall appearance of the old burial grounds' (preface). This passage expresses Lindenschmit's aversion to dividing prehistoric times into stone, bronze and iron ages, and at the same time attests the lifelong battle he waged with all his might against this generally accepted system. Although he seemed to be the loser from the very start of this controversy, we must not forget that the Three Age System was in his day only applicable to the material ordering of the antiquities in the National Museum in Copenhagen and a few North German collections; it could not be directly carried over to the known South German finds of that time. On the other hand Lindenschmit's observations, while preventing him from accepting the Three Age System, were certainly right. Only a more modern generation, represented in particular by O. Montelius and P. Reinecke, was able to reconcile the two viewpoints in such a way as to present a picture of the Three Age System which seems self-evident to us today.

In Denmark as well as in northern Germany, examinations of many closed burial finds have resulted in the knowledge that the tools which came from the 'large stone burial chambers' were almost all made of stone, whilst the 'stone cists, and 'little burial containers covered by stone heaps' from the 'cremation period' held bronze objects. Still other 'burial chambers' and 'grave mounds' were furnished with offerings of iron. On the strength of the regular recurrence of these observations on the finds, the director of the National Museum for Antiquities in Copenhagen, C.J. Thomsen (1788-1865) wrote in the *Guide to Northern Antiquities*, published by the Royal Association for the Study of Nordic Prehistory (Copenhagen), of a stone, a bronze and an iron age, a classification which, as already mentioned, the North

German scholars J. F. Danneil (1788-1868) in Salzwedel and G. Chr. Lisch (1801-1888) in Schwerin found substantiated by the finds in their field of studies. Whereas Thomsen only gave an explanatory description of the antiquities and the type of burial places of the stone, bronze and iron ages in his *Guide*, his successor as director of the National Museum of Copenhagen, J.J.A. Worsaae (1821-1885) tried to use the three ages as evidence of historical facts, which he summed up as follows in his booklet *The National Science of Antiquity in Germany*, published in 1846: 'Therefore it is evident that in the stone age only the coastal regions of Europe were populated by the above-mentioned prehistoric people and that the inland areas only received their inhabitants during the bronze age and from a mixed origin of tribes. It is almost certain that the bronze culture did not relate to one people alone, namely the Celts, but was shared by different tribes at a certain cultural level – Greeks, Scythians, Teutons and Scandinavians, as well as Celts. Reports of the Greeks and Scythians strongly support this hypothesis. Therefore the bronze articles found in South Germany may well be Celtic, but those from the eastern and northern parts of Germany equally well Germanic or Slavic. The correspondence of shapes and decorations can no doubt be accounted for by the fact that they are the simplest and most natural ones. Likewise the culture of the iron age should not be regarded as pertaining to one particular people. It probably originated with the Celts in South Germany, but was most likely taken over by the Germanic, Scandinavian and Slavic tribes later. We can with some degree of certainty regard the iron age in Mecklenburg as having begun with the immigration of Slavic tribes at the end of the fifth century.' (Worsaae 1846). Throughout his life Worsaae stuck to his opinion that the different ages are to be attributed to different tribes. In his *Prehistory of the North* (1878) he still thought it likely that the 'old' and 'young' stone age corresponded with the immigration of two tribes into the North and that the 'bronze culture' was brought to the North from Asia – above all India – by an immigrant tribe. But while this book clearly implies that the iron age in the Mediterranean area had already begun in the ninth-eighth centuries BC and in Central Europe in the fifth-fourth centuries and that it spread from there to the northern regions, in 1846 Worsaae still believed that the iron age had not reached the North until after the beginning of our era following certain changes in Gaul in the second-first centuries BC. His visit to German museums, on which his booklet of 1846 was based, made Worsaae already well aware that the archaeological studies presented greater difficulties there than in the North, because the immigration of a great many more tribes had to be reckoned with than the three, or at the most four, in Scandinavia. Furthermore, it seemed to him that south of Thuringia there were no burial places of the stone age and he assumed that this area was only colonized from the bronze age onwards. Worsaae also discovered that there were not half as many antiquities of the bronze age in Central Germany as there were in the North of Germany and Scandinavia.

In the year 1852 Lindenschmit published the princely Celtic burial of Weisskirchen (Lindenschmit 1852). As at that time he took the bronze jug to be Roman, though recognizing that the ornamentation of the Weisskirchen offerings differed clearly from those in the Frankish grave in Selzen, he believed that the Weisskirchen burial was older than that in Selzen and assigned it to a member of the Alemannic tribe of the fifth century.

When the first volume of *Antiquities* appeared in 1858 it was already clear to him that there was a connection between the bronze jug and the recently published pre-Roman jug from Italy. He therefore declared the jug to be an Etruscan import. This led to his firm conviction that the 'bronze industry' originated in the area around the Mediterranean and derived mainly from the Etruscans who exported goods to the area north of the Alps, where they were copied locally here and there. He backed up this hypothesis by drawing upon numerous ancient writers and their reports on trade connections between North and South. He also attached importance to the fact that the grave in Weisskirchen and other burial finds in South Germany contained both bronze and iron artifacts, which seemed to run counter to the idea of making a clear distinction between the two groups of materials, as the northern finds led one to do. In this context Lindenschmit also called in as witness the Greek poet Homer, who in his verse refers simultaneously to articles of bronze and iron.

In due course these observations came to be supported by reflections of a fundamental nature. At that time the general opinion was that living standards advanced progressively; therefore Lindenschmit did not think it possible that such artistic objects as the 'bronze culture' produced could have sprung out of the 'prehistoric cultural state', so to speak. He was no less concerned over the anomaly, to which Worsaae, as already mentioned, had drawn attention and which was emphasized by Hans Hildebrand in his book *The Heathen Age in Sweden,* that the sequence of Stone, Bronze and Iron Ages resulted from the immigration of various tribes (especially the 'Indogermanic tribes' who were supposed to have brought the art of bronze work with them from the East to the North European area). Was Lindenschmit after all convinced that the Teutons were the original inhabitants of Central Europe? – an hypothesis which his brother Wilhelm had rigorously supported in opposition to the 'Celtic Theorists' in his *The Riddle of Prehistoric Times or did the Germans immigrate?* (1846). After visiting the museums in Copenhagen and Schwerin in 1858 and studying the local antiquities, Lindenschmit had felt strongly that 'a close examination of the completely isolated position of the bronze implements, their foreign character and the contrast which they offer against the evidence of the country's culture in the preceding and succeeding periods' (Lindenschmit 1876) was called for. As he even believed he had discovered similarities between the bronze vessels of the North and those of 'old Italian bronze vessels in the Rhineland', he also maintained that the bronze objects found in the North were imports from the Mediterranean region – especially Etruria. 'The introduction of bronze tools from a southern industry with many associated customs and abuses seems more likely than the transfer and transplantation to the far North of one branch of art and craftsmanship torn out of its natural milieu, the southern culture as a whole' (Lindenschmit 1860).

That Lindenschmit could not yet recognize the different time factors represented by the finds he compared is evident from these words of his: 'The use of the stone weapons reaches into the time of the Roman wars, as is proved by the stone axes and stone arrowheads that were found in the choked well of the Roman fort in Mainz next to the shattered remains of a colossal bronze statue. The Frankish burial grounds are the first to show that bronze is wholly replaced by iron' (Lindenschmit 1876).

In his old age Lindenschmit did accept the succession of the Three Periods to the extent that he believed they occurred during the quarrels between the Romans and Teutons (Lindenschmit 1880-89). 'In this way the order of the cultural development evolved, judging by the monuments, facts and finds. Chronologically, bronze certainly succeeded stone and only after both of these did iron appear in its full scope and importance; but this relationship between the materials is quite different from the previously accepted interpretation and at the same time fully agrees with the historical traditions, which new efforts at clarification either made merely one-sided and restricted use of or thought to do without altogether.' Lindenschmit fought against 'Celtomania' right until the end of his life. Even in his *Handbook of German Antiquity* (Part One, 'The Antiquities of the Merovingian Age' – 1880-1889), written in old age, he mocked Heinrich Schreiber of Freiburg, who had linked the Bronze Age with the Celts, in the following ironical manner: 'On the whole the Teutons would appear to be barbaric intruders upon, and oppressors of, an industrious and civilized population, unresponsive to and unfit for Celtic culture, as later for the Roman. The lower level of their culture, although only recently brought in with them from Asia, is proved by the fact that they were put to work by subject Celts in the fields, the pastures, on the farmyard and in the home. They seem to have barely owned a language, because in the entire country there is no mountain, hill, river or stream, field or valley to which they were able to give a name, so that the Celts had to "loosen their tongues" by informing them of the necessary *copia verborum*. And they must have been frightful people, for, although in a minority, they imbued large numbers of Celts with such respect and awe with their stone hammers, that these buried and hid their bronze swords and daggers which at one time had been the terror of that part of the world' (Lindenschmit 1880-89).

Taking the bitter quarrel over the Three Age System as a whole one might, I suppose, regard it as one of the tragic processes that every science goes through, where scholars earnestly wrestle with problems the preconditions for solving which have not yet been created. Recognition of the Three Age System was certainly assured in the North by many closed burial finds. But the typological relationship between the Nordic forms and the often dissimilar antiquities of South Germany was still unknown, as were the spread and timing of the bronze finds in the North and South. Therefore all the essential preconditions for a fruitful typological and chronological discussion were lacking; which is why they scarcely play a part in the argument on either side. Lindenschmit's comparison of Nordic bronze vessels with 'old Italian bronze vessels in the Rhineland' shows how content he still was with broad concurrences. Of great importance, though, were the completely opposed fundamental theories on both sides: in the North the antiquities were subdivided into three periods, backed by philology and its hypothesis of an Indogermanic immigration into Central Europe – the legacy of various immigrant tribes. The idea of a connection between the immigration from Asia and the beginning of the local bronze age was specially favoured. Assuming, however, that knowledge of bronze and its working was introduced here by the Indogermanic tribes from Asia and especially from India, then a direct connection between the northern and Mediterranean bronze finds is out of the question. Lindenschmit was of the opinion that the Three Age System of the North in no way applied to the southern finds. Nevertheless he seemed convinced of the close connection between the area south and north of the Alps, on the strength of the South German objects imported from the Mediterranean and the reports of many ancient authors. He flatly rejected the Three Age System and thought his approach to be the better one, because he did not believe in the immigration of Teutons from Asia to Central Europe, nor in the theory that artistic development had already reached a peak in a much earlier 'bronze culture'. On following this battle of wills and words one comes to the conclusion that the Three Age System had been archaeologically established in the North, but could not yet be applied to the southern area of Germany. The conflicting opinions of both sides contained some correct observations, but these lacked the common ground that would lead to a profitable dialogue.

It was only possible for the generation after Lindenschmit's to carry out comparative investigations of individual forms, and so arrive at criteria for the typological ordering of the antiquities in the North and South. In the North this step was mainly taken by Oscar Montelius (1843-1921), in the South by Paul Reinecke (1872-1958). Certainly the Three Age System thereby proved to be fundamentally correct for both of them. All the same, Lindenschmit's telling observation that there were substantial differences between North and Central European finds and many indications that the latter had close connections with the Mediterranean culture was of great importance to future research. The work of Montelius and Reinecke has made the differences between the bronze and iron age in North and Central Europe manifestly clear. Not until they related the finds north of the Alps in a typological and chronological way with those of the Mediterranean area was it possible to achieve positive results. Only now has it been recognized that the pre-Roman, Roman and Merovingian times which Lindenschmit and his contemporaries still believed to be unchanging epochs of prehistory, were very differentiated and incorporated a wide-ranging cultural development. This knowledge also throws a new light on the changing cultural relationship between North and South.

BIBLIOGRAPHY

BELTZ. R. 1925 in M. EBERT. *Reallexikon der Vorgeschichte* 2: 457 ff.

LINDENSCHMIT, L. 1852 *Ein deutsches Hügelgrab aus der letzten Zeit des Heidenthums.*

——— 1860 *Die vaterländischen Alterthümer der Fürstlich Hohenzoller'schen Sammlungen zu Sigmaringen:* 169.

——— 1876 'Entgegnung auf die vorstehenden Bemerkungen des Herrn Sophus Müller zu meiner "Beurteilung der nordischen Bronzecultur und des Dreiperiodensystems",' *Archiv für Anthropologie* 9.

——— 1880-89 *Handbuch der deutschen Alterthumskunde*, Part I

WORSAAE, J.J.A. 1846 *Die nationale Alterthumskunde in Deutschland.*

XI

Heinrich Schliemann and Rudolf Virchow: their contributions towards developing historical Archaeology

JOACHIM HERRMANN

Akademie der Wissenschaften der DDR, Berlin, German Democratic Republic

In the development of the science of prehistory and early history in the second half of the nineteenth century the importance of Rudolf Virchow is unchallenged. Several studies, including a recent book by Christian Andree which uses a wide range of sources,[1] bring out essential aspects concerning Rudolf Virchow and Heinrich Schliemann in developing archaeological methodology.

Ernst Meyer, an outstanding expert on Schliemann's correspondence and diaries, has dealt with the relations between Virchow and Schliemann, especially their personal contacts. It was under the very influence of Virchow, he maintains, that the 'amateur' Schliemann became a scientist who was to some extent socially acceptable. 'Starting in 1879, Virchow taught Schliemann scientific thinking.'[2] This statement certainly applies neither in general – after all, Schliemann had obtained his doctor's degree seven years before he became acquainted with Virchow – nor where the Troy excavations and his archaeological studies were concerned. Virchow saw his acquaintance with Schliemann differently. He went to Troy and started co-operating with Schliemann because of the latter's substantial scientific findings and successes from the mid seventies on.[3] Intellectually, they were on much the same level, enabling them to discuss scientific problems.[4] This alone explains why Virchow gave his support to Schliemann in the Berlin Academy.[5] As early as 1881, Virchow wrote:

'Today it is pointless to ask whether Schliemann started from right or false premises when he began his studies. Not only did his success decide in his favour but also his scientific method proved a success.'[6]

It was precisely this method that constituted the basis for the co-operation of these two scholars. How was the development of Schliemann's methods achieved and what were its main characteristics?

Schliemann's success in the field of methodology has as yet hardly been worked out. The picture we have of Schliemann is largely influenced by supporters of classical archaeology, often still working in the Winckelmann tradition. The views expressed by Ernst Curtius about Schliemann are echoed even in contemporary scientific-historical literature. The idea of a dilettante treasure-seeker has been given credence not least by Schliemann's adventurous life which he described in his *Autobiography* in a manner calculated to transfigure his own personality. [7] This *Autobiography* in no way stands up to careful historical analysis, now made possible by the publication of numerous letters. [8]

Schliemann, the son of a country parson, grew up with his six brothers and sisters in poor circumstances in a secluded region of Mecklenburg. Already in the fifties of the nineteenth century he had reached the climax of his career as a successful wholesale merchant; when he was 44 years old he retired from commerce, studied in Paris, took a doctor's degree in Rostock and turned towards scientific work to which he devoted the rest of his life.

Schliemann himself originated the legend according to which the 'dream of Troy' had pursued him since his early childhood and made Trojan research his aim in life. This legend cannot be sustained. An analysis of his correspondence and diaries shows it to have been a *post-eventum* invention. His breaking away from business was due to other motives and different objectives: Schliemann intended to become a landed proprietor and to devote himself to agriculture; he considered leading the life of a man of independent means, and he tried to be active in the field of philology. Serious efforts of this kind undertaken in 1857/58 failed. Rather discouraged, he wrote: 'It is also too late to turn to a scientific career ... because I have been working too long a time as a merchant to hope that I can still achieve something in the scientific field ...' [9]

What proved really decisive was his journey to Greece and Asia Minor from May to July 1868. Only after he had undertaken this journey, was Schliemann convinced that he would find Homer's Troy beneath the hill of Hissarlik, the palace of Odysseus on Ithaca, the castle of Agamemnon in Mycenae; in a word, that his was the task of finding out by archaeological means the historical truth about pre-historic Greece, which had hitherto been surrounded by myths and legends. [10]

Thus it was that in 1868 Schliemann finally found a new field of activity. Not only did he have the necessary financial means for this undertaking but extensive journeys to the most important places of ancient culture in the Mediterranean area, in Asia Minor, India, China and Japan, as well as visits to America, had considerably extended Schliemann's ideas of the culture and history of mankind. Having learned Arabic in 1858 and 1859, he acquired a knowledge of Arab literature which widened his horizons far beyond Greek and Roman antiquity. His studies in Paris enabled him also to probe deeper into history, and acquainted him with several streams of historical understanding. When he began in 1868 to define the future aims of his life and the particular field of his study he was already well versed in cultural history. Where did archaeology stand at that time?

Classical archaeology in the style of Winkelmann hardly concerned itself with archaeological fieldwork. It had dismissed the mythical period of Greek antiquity as an unreal legendary era. Archaeology, or what was considered to be archaeology, was determined by acquiring antiquities in a more or less orderly and expensive way, by collecting and interpreting them in terms of cultural history. It scarcely knew any historical objectives and, consequently, lacked methods designed for studying historical links. This situation was bound to be regarded as a serious impediment by contrast with the rapid advance of the natural sciences and the demands made on history to which the social movements gave rise at that time. In 1859, Darwin formulated his theory of the evolution of species, and ten years later he incorporated man in his theory of natural history. In the same period Boucher de Perthes from Abbeville proved, by determined stratigraphical research work in the Somme valley, the existence of ice-age man and his culture. In Central and Northern Europe first attempts were made to systematize the prehistory of man with the help of the Three Age System. In the Orient, cultures hitherto unknown began to emerge from the darkness of millennia.

With the development of industry, trade and colonialism all over the world, interest in historical matters grew, reaching far beyond the European boundaries. Traditional research into history during the first half of the nineteenth century was not prepared for that; information was mainly available only on a national or at best a European basis and the sources drawn from documents. Nations without any such written history were considered to have no history. 'Prehistory', which was regarded as a necessary and separate requirement of competent bourgeois historiography, became the research field of new scientific disciplines, especially of anthropology, ethnography and historical archaeology. Exploring such depths of history, which stretched back to the remote time of anthropogenesis, implied a dependence on some special natural sciences and upon Darwinism.

Heinrich Schliemann certainly did not see those connections in the late 'sixties. But it can safely be assumed that he became acquainted during his studies at Paris with the intellectual streams of the kind mentioned above.

When defining his scientific objectives Schliemann must, owing to his educational background, inevitably have had his attention drawn to the link between prehistory and written history; where Greece was concerned, this link was sure to arouse public interest.

Such reflections may have occupied Schliemann's mind when, in 1868, he met Calvert, the American consul in the Dardanelles. Being interested in antiquity, Calvert had dealt with the problem of Troy. Schliemann was challenged by the contradictory views on the locality of Troy. Supported by the military authority of Helmuth von Moltke, it was generally thought to be in Bunar-bashi.

Thirty soundings carried out at the site of Bunar-bashi convinced Schliemann that this could never have been the site of Troy. His analysis led him to Hissarlik and he decided to start excavations there. The purpose of his work was, he wrote, to 'shed light on the prehistoric Hellenistic world which was completely in the dark'[11] and 'to reveal the most interesting sides of world history for science'.[12]

These objectives could be realized only if Schliemann used new methods.

Already during the preliminary work for his book *Ithaka, der Peloponnes und Troja* (Ithaca, the Peloponnese and Troy) Schliemann had extensively applied, in 1868, the method of making soundings.[13] As far as I know, Schliemann was the first to adopt this scientific method for archaeological work on such a scale. Later, it was also used at Troy for locating the lower town, as well as for preparatory studies in Tiryns, Mycenae and other places. Thus archaeological research was given a means of opening up a larger area, enabling a first, general assessment of it to be made.

Hitherto, when assessing Schliemann's achievements, this aspect of preparing for larger excavations has been overlooked. Schliemann, it is claimed, did not 'owe his successes to systematic search according to calculations but to lucky and instinctive finding', impelled by enthusiasm.[14] This is a false conclusion and is based, first of all, on the biographers' ignorance of the methodological foundations of archaeological research in Schliemann's day.

No stratigraphical investigation had been carried out at comparable sites before Schliemann. For this reason, no one had any idea about the way in which superimposed cultural strata of different eras might be shown to the researcher. An important principle established and persistently adhered to by Schliemann was the need to dig down to the solid bedrock. He had been perfectly right in recognizing that the Greek strata could be separated from the pre-Greek ones only by this method. That is why he dug a trench, 40 m. wide at the top, through the hill of Troy, deep enough to reach the solid bedrock which test soundings had told him lay 16 m. below the surface.[15]

Today it is an accepted methodological principle that a complicated archaeological series of strata can be clearly analysed only when beginning with the solid bedrock. Schliemann developed this principle in practice and so could solve, for the most part, the complicated stratigraphical problems he was faced with at Troy.

Documentation of finds according to strata and depth is basic to the stratigraphical method. Schliemann took depth into account from the very beginning, a classification of the strata not being possible till they had been identified.

With a view to distinguishing and dating the strata Schliemann searched for a 'guiding fossil', which he found in pottery. In the study of pottery he was a 'cornucopia of archaeological wisdom'.[16]

For the Aegean, however, there was no comparative material available. For this reason, Schliemann undertook, in 1875, educative journeys to Italy, England, France, the Netherlands, Denmark, Sweden and Germany. There he established contact with scholars concerned with prehistoric archaeology, among others Rudolf Virchow. Virchow and he had one aim in common, namely to develop historical archaeology, and they worked together on most friendly terms.

Schliemann was convinced that the historical objective of his studies could be achieved only in co-operation with experts from a wide range of disciplines. From the outset, therefore, his works incorporate studies and analyses done by philologists, orientalists, numismatists, anthropologists, architects, topographers, chemists and spectrographers. [17] What he wanted was to 'surround himself with a General Staff of natural scientists, architects and archaeologists', [18] an intention which he implemented to a degree which was unusual for his time. The recognition that natural scientific studies play an important part in working out the principal features of the most ancient history, was, no doubt, strongly encouraged and stimulated by concrete advice and recommendations from Virchow, though Schliemann had come to this conclusion already before the two men met; it was the basis for his co-operation with Virchow. [19] However, decades were to pass before the recognition that archaeology and the natural sciences should closely co-operate in the field of historical research gradually gained ground.

Thus, step by step, through his immediate archaeological fieldwork and by systematic analysis of his findings, Schliemann laid the methodological foundations for a general picture of history and cultural history; he never presented them in an explicit way but they were nevertheless disseminated by numerous publications, and they stimulated discussions. His work in Troy, Mycenae, Tiryns and Orchomenos furthered the advance of the comparative method in archaeology. In this respect, too, he shared the intentions of Virchow who pursued these, as we know, in a big way. In connection with the efforts devoted to this method Schliemann's attention was directed, in 1875, to the Pommeranian Face-Urn Culture and thus to Virchow. Their discussions about comparative archaeology are reflected in a great many letters exchanged between them. [20]

This fruitful methodological co-operation between Virchow and Schliemann was of immediate advantage to European archaeology through numerous papers and lectures delivered by Virchow, through invitations to Schliemann to take part in meetings of European archaeological societies and, of course, through Schliemann's work. It is worth recalling that Carl Schuchhardt was one of the first to present the work of Heinrich Schliemann and to analyse it in an expert manner. Through Schuchhardt, the methodological findings of Schliemann's excavations were introduced into provincial Roman archaeology and prehistoric archaeology. [21]

BIBLIOGRAPHICAL REFERENCES

1   Christian Andree *Rudolf Virchow als Prähistoriker* (Rudolf Virchow as a prehistorian). Vols 1 and 2, Cologne – Vienna 1976; Berlin 1976.

2   E. Meyer, 'Schliemann und Virchow' (Schliemann and Virchow). In *Gymnasium* 62, 1955: 446.

3   Cf. R. Virchow in: *Zeitschrift für Ethnologie* 11, 1879. Negotiations: 179-80; 204-17; 254-81.

4   H. Schliemann, *Briefwechsel* (Correspondence). Vol. 2, 1876-90, Ed. E Meyer, Berlin 1958, No. 78: 106; No. 81: 108-09; No. 140: 164 ff.

5   ibid. No. 65: 90.

6   Preface to H. Schliemann, *Ilios, Stadt und Land der Trojaner* (Ilium, town and land of the Trojans), Leipzig 1881: IX

7   H. Schliemann, *Selbstbiographie* (Autobiography). Continued until his death by A. Brueckner. Ed. Sophie Schliemann, 6th edn, Leipzig 1944.

8   J. Hermann, *Heinrich Schliemann. Wegbereiter einer neuen Wissenschaft* (Heinrich Schliemann. Pioneer of a new science). Berlin 1974: 11-17.

9   Letter to Bessov, Petersburg, dated 27 December, 1858, from Messina. In: *Briefwechsel* (Correspondence) Vol. 1, 1842-75, Ed. E. Meyer, Berlin, 1953, No. 62: 95 f. Likewise letter dated November 30, 1859, to Giulio Nicati, London (ibid. No. 67: 98 ff).

10 H. Schliemann, *Ithaka, der Peleponnes und Troja. Archaeologische Forschungen* (Ithaca, the Peleponnese and Troy. Archaeological studies). Leipzig 1869.

11 *Briefwechsel* Vol. 1, 1953, loc. cit. 9, No.

131: 165.

12 ibid note 285: 335.

13 Schliemann, *Ithaka . . .*, loc. cit. 10: 28 ff; 62 ff, 152 ff.

14 E. Meyer, Introduction. In: H. Schliemann, *Briefe* (Letters). Ed. E. Meyer, Leipzig 1936: 47. Likewise F. Thierfelder *Heinrich Schliemann.* 1958: 24.

15 *Briefwechsel* (Correspondence) Vol. 1, 1953, loc. cit. 9, No. 195: 220.

16 H. Schliemann, *Ilios. Stadt und Land der Trojaner.* Leipzig 1881: 243.

17 Cf., e.g., *Briefwechsel* (Correspondence) 2, 1958, loc. cit. 4, No. 40: 71; No. 51: 80; No. 52: 80; No. 172: 195.

18 *Briefwechsel* (Correspondence), loc. cit. 14, 1936, No. 203: 288.

19 In 1876, e.g., Schliemann invited Virchow to come to Mycenae to examine the finds in the shaft graves in their anthropological aspects. When Virchow was not able to respond to this invitation, Schliemann emphasized that thus a great many findings were lost. – Letter dated 28 January, 1877, in *Briefe* (Letters) loc. cit. 14, 1936, No. 58: 149.

20 *Briefwechsel* (Correspondence) 1936, loc. cit. 4, No. 81: 108; No. 140: 164; No. 247: 259.
    Briefwechsel (Correspondence) 1936, loc. cit. 14, No. 79: 168 and elsewhere.

21 C. Schuchhardt, *Schliemanns Ausgrabungen in Troja, Tiryns, Mykenae, Orchomenos, Ithaka im Lichte der heutigen Wissenschaft* (Schliemann's excavations in Troy, Tiryns, Mycenae, Orchomenos, Ithaca in the light of contemporary science.) Leipzig 1890 (2nd edn 1891).

XII

Notes on the history of Ibero-American Archaeology

JOSÉ L. LORENZO

Instituto Nacional de Antropología e Historia, Mexico

No systems theory or models of any kind will be applied in this study nor will anything about sampling strategics, holistic philosophy, or dialectical materialism hidden under an archaeological processual cloak be proffered. Simply some facts and a few ideas.

It must be recognized that although a possible proliferation of terms might have application in modern social studies, 'Ibero-America' is actually the only appropriate one for referring to countries that appeared in history, starting with the dawn of the nineteenth century, as part of what were Spanish and Portuguese colonies, inasmuch as the role of the French, British, Dutch, and Danish enclaves in the historical and social processes of that region was insignificant.

The term 'pre-Columbian' should also be defined. It is generally understood to apply to events before the arrival of Columbus – everything prior to 1492. If one considers that in his four voyages between 1492 and 1504, Columbus covered a specific geographical sector limited to the Greater and Lesser Antilles and a few points on the northern coast of South America, then the concept of 'pre-Columbian' is applicable only to the dates and places of such contacts. The use of the term in its broadest sense would mean that the kingdoms of Ahuizotl (1481-1501) and Moctezuma Xocoyotzin (1502-20) in Mexico, and of Tupac Inka Yupanqui (1470-93), Wayna Kapac (1493-1527), and Waskar Inka (1527-32) in Cuzco were partially or totally post-Columbian.

Obviously, it is incongruent to apply the term 'pre-Columbian' as a temporal concept to the American hemisphere as a whole.

Some Mexican authors use the term 'pre-Cortesian' to refer to the entire period preceding the arrival of the Spaniards headed by Cortes. However, this is no less tenable; were one to accept such usage, it would be necessary for the sake of consistency to coin a specific term using the name of whatever conquistador or missionary had set foot on a given territory for the first time.

The most practical solution is the one adopted in Mexico where the term 'pre-Hispanic' is used to connote the epoch prior to the arrival of the Hispanic intruders, who may be either Spaniards or Portuguese, since Hispania was the ancient name for the Iberian Peninsula.

Another point that should be clearly established is that there is a prevailing ideology in every epoch with which both the outgoing and the incoming ideologies, among others, usually co-exist. Concentrating on the dominant line of thought in any one epoch will not enable us to appreciate the role of archaeology as a whole, since to understand it fully we must also take into account the special circumstances surrounding the archaeology with which we are concerned, as well as the place and conditions material to its existence.

Today, the Ibero-American countries may, in a sense, be divided into two main, extreme groups with a natural intermediate zone based upon the number of Indian inhabitants in each. Since this division does, in fact, exist and delineates very significant political processes of a national character, as will be seen later, it is useful for understanding certain developmental processes in archaeology. On the one hand, we have countries like Uruguay and Costa Rica where the Indian has long disappeared from the scene. At the other end of the spectrum are Bolivia, Peru, Ecuador, and Guatemala which have very high percentages of Indian population. Also, there are those countries such as Mexico, where the Indians have lost many of their social characteristics but retain their biological ones and constitute a majority of the population. Finally, countries like Argentina and Chile have remnants of Indian population, geographically and socially on the fringe; and there are still others in which blacks, the descendants of African slaves brought over as plantation and mine hands, now make up a very substantial part of the population, mixed with Caucasians and some Asiatics.

The presence of Indians as an absolute, or near majority has a clear-cut origin, closely linked to the topic to be developed here. The Conquest, or rather, the conquistador, was confronted by two high civilizations, the Meso-American and the Andean, and many other groups scattered throughout the continent which, in the best of cases, were at a level of development that might be termed 'chieftainship,' and a number of what were merely roving bands. The high civilizations practised agriculture and lived in fixed settlements; the others were nomadic hunters and gatherers. Mexico, Guatemala, Honduras, and El Salvador on the one hand, and Ecuador, Bolivia, and Peru on the other, are the countries that arose in the high-civilization areas and in which the Indian presence is felt in varying degrees.

There is such a strong link between archaeology and ethnography in Ibero-America that no archaeologist could ever hope to understand his subject fully or reach any valid conclusions regarding it without a solid grasp of the other discipline.

Let us simply remember that in addition to the chronicles that tell us of the way of life in Tenochtitlan or Cuzco, we also have those that were written by men who lived with the Chibchas, Chorotegas, Arawaks, Tainos, Pericues, and Sirionos. Their descriptions contains sufficient information – the product of first-hand experience – to enable us to interpret reliably aspects of social life at phases that would be difficult to recognize on the basis of purely archaeological materials. The opportunities offered by comparative studies of archaeological contexts and their ethnographical equivalents have not turned to account as they should have been; moreover, it is possible through extensive in-depth study of the chronicles to obtain information covering Old World phases that could not be clarified adequately through archaeology alone.

This long preamble is not just an introduction to the topic but a necessary prologue for understanding the channels through which Ibero-American Archaeology courses. It is, therefore, essential to describe the ideology that was in the ascendancy at the time of the Conquest and in the centuries that followed. What is more, I do not believe it possible to understand anything about the history of Ibero-American or European Archaeology unless we try to follow the thread of the History of Ideas.

Columbus discovered America in the same year that Granada, the last Moorish bastion in Spain, fell. It was only a few years before, that the kingdoms of Castille and Aragon were unified. The struggle against the feudal lords was going on and Spain, which had been fighting the Moors for seven centuries, did not take part in the Crusades (they had them at home) nor did the Renaissance gain a complete ascendancy since scholastic philosophy still held sway there.

In 1493, Pope Alexander VI simply allocated the newly discovered world and all lands to be discovered there in the future to Spain and Portugal in a proportion which, with a few slight adjustments, was ratified by the Treaty of Tordesillas in 1494. All the lands discovered to the east of a line 370 leagues west of the Azores and Cape Verde went to Portugal and everything west of it to Spain.

The monarch who was crowned Charles V, Emperor and King of the Low Countries and Germany became, in 1519, Charles I of the Spains, the Two Sicilies, and the Americas. As of 1580, under Philip II, Spain was united with Portugal and its colonies.

Rinascere, the impulse that characterized the Renaissance and gave it its name, the turning back to Greco-Roman humanism, gave rise to a mode in archaeology. Although the same ideal prevailed in Ibero-America during that epoch, it was not applicable to the high cultures of America since there was absolutely no relation between those who might have put it into effect, namely the Europeans, and the material, which was American.

The Counter-Reformation arose to smother the nascent Renaissance which, although arriving late, was beginning to make itself felt in Spain and Portugal. However, it seems to have subsisted in the American colonies in a watered-down form side by side with the weighty presence of the medieval world.

To discover and to narrate were two of the conquistadores' closely allied principles. In these fields there is no conflict with the authorities and considerable freedom is permitted with respect to what is discovered and what is narrated. The rhetorical style of Humanism is relinquished and replaced by a much more streamlined one.

It was necessary for the consolidation of the colonizing process to obtain information about the newly conquered peoples and so chronicles were written throughout the length and breadth of America during the sixteenth century which are now our basic sources. The first of those known to us was written by Fray Pedro de Pané in 1496 and from then on they continued to be produced well into the eighteenth century as colonization advanced in the territories initially neglected because of the difficulties involved or because the prospects did not seem promising.

The chroniclers used the Indians, their material works and social organization, to reflect their own accomplishment, the Conquest, at the same time that, in certain cases, they presented the conquered population as rational beings and, therefore, deserving of more humane treatment. However, what remains for the archaeologist are descriptions that may to some extent be utilized along the lines in which the Old Testament has been applied to the Middle East, *toute proportion gradée*. There is something more, however.

Printing was introduced into Spain in 1473 and the first book on chivalry, in Catalan and titled *Tirant lo Blanch*, was published in 1490. In 1508, the very popular *Amadis de Gaula* appeared and within a few years, there were more than fifty books on chivalry. Their narratives were quickly dismissed as absurd but the mark they left on most readers is extremely important. Among the tales told, some of the most common are about Amazons, dwarves, enchanted islands, the fountain of youth, the seven mythical cities, and 'El Dorado'. However, the reality described in the chronicles of the Conquest very often appeared more fanciful than the imaginary happenings to be found in books on chivalry. We read in Bernal Diaz del Castillo that the sight of the great city of Mexico, Tenochtitlan, from a distance was comparable to the enchantments described in *Amadis de Gaula*.

Inasmuch as the supporting documentation exists, there can be no doubt that many expeditions were organized to search for the wonders described in those books.

The Indians were aware of the past even before the arrival of the Europeans. This was quite clear with respect to tribal genealogy with which, naturally, an element of legend and myth was bound up, that increased with the passing of time. In almost all of these groups there was a tradition of a very ancient generation of giants, whose bones were found in ravines or excavations. We now know, however, that these belonged to fossil proboscidians, though the earliest conquistadores themselves believed them to be the bones of giants.

The idea of the past – already archaeological at that time – was manifest in at least two places: San Juan Teotihuacan and Cholula. The pre-Hispanic inhabitants of the village of San Juan Teotihuacan were well aware of the many mounds, unquestionably man-made, present in their territory; these they worshipped, holding propitiation ceremonies every twenty days atop the largest – today known as the Pyramid of the Sun – attended by the priests of Mexico-Tenochtitlan and, it is said, by Moctezuma himself.

Nor did the enormous earth mass in Cholula that had been a pyramid, over 100 metres in height and with a base of 300 by 370 metres, go unnoticed. Important propitiatory ceremonies were held there too.

In Peru, this reverence for the past, this historical sense, was present in the Inca cult of the mummies of their dead kings observed by the descendants of each royal house and its servants whose sole functions was to maintain it, at public expense.

Counting devices known as *quipus* were, because of the Conquest, almost all lost, and the *quipucamayoc* – those who knew how to interpret them – disappeared for the same reason. In addition to keeping the census and all the accounts of the Tahuantinsuyo, the *quipus* were used to record historical events and genealogies. Moreover, no priests able to read the Meso-American codices were left. Nevertheless, among the few codices that have come down to us there are some of a historical, genealogical character that can be interpreted as far back as into the ninth century.

Racial, social, linguistic, and cultural differences gave rise to a society in which a small European minority governed as an aristocracy over the indigenous masses. A neo-medieval system thus came into being that survived as an anachronism in which the theology that had split the Old Continent prevailed over history. The Indian majority lost its past and the mestizo elements that appeared in the racial fusion were uncertain of their identity.

Among the notable mestizo and Indian writers who appeared in the wake of the Conquest in both regions of high pre-Hispanic civilization, Meso-America and the Andean zone, two in particular deserve mention: Fernando de Alva Ixtlizxochitl in Mexico and, in Peru, Gomez Suarez de Figueroa, the Inca Garcilaso de la Vega's real name.

Alva Ixtlixochitl (1575-1650) was descended from the royal family of Texcoco; Inca Garcilaso's mother belonged to the royal house of Cuzco and his father was a conquistador. The former spent his entire life in Mexico while the latter lived in Peru for only twenty years of his long life (1539-1617).

Each sought in his own literary style to demonstrate from the vantage point of the Spanish-dominated world they inhabited the beneficence and civilization of the Indian world of the past to which they themselves belonged. To accomplish this, Ixtlixochitl used pre-

Hispanic documents and conversations with elderly Indians as his source material for describing the customs and way of life of his people, whilst the Inca, for his part, compiled and synthesized many chronicles and much oral information with which to provide an organized history of his maternal ancestors. Both sought to show that civilization existed in their worlds before the arrival of the Spaniards, a conclusion to which they pointed with pride.

Their works, together with many others of the period, produced a curious effect in Mexican and Peruvian archaeology respectively. Because numerous documents describing very fully the lives of the peoples during the decades – perhaps a century – before the Conquest were available, archaeology perhaps has been given least attention in these two countries, inasmuch as that which archaeology seeks to reconstruct actually lives in the chronicles. Of course, although this may not be so true from a strict archaeological standpoint, it applies where earlier stages or less well-documented regions are concerned.

In Ixtlixochitl and the Inca, one encounters the problem of race consciousness, the *angst* of the mestizo; and, if we are correct in saying that they were seeking their own national identities, with them it was a question of class nationalism, since they were both primarily noblemen. It is understandable that for Ibero-Americans, archaeology should be inseparable from history – their own history.

Around 1551, Pedro Cieza de León wrote *El Señorio de los Incas,* in which he relates a visit to Sacsayhuaman in Cuzco. This is perhaps the first defence of the pre-Hispanic cultural heritage from the architectural standpoint:

'And, going about taking note, (he writes) I saw alongside this fortress a stone which I measured and it was two hundred and seventy of my palms in circumference and so tall that it would seem to have been born there and all the Indians say that this stone grew tired in that place and that they could no longer move it from there; and, truly, if it were not so clearly evident that it had been dressed, I would not have given credence, no matter how much it was sworn, that the power of men could have put it there, where it will remain to bear witness of what were the inventors of such a great work; the Spaniards, however, have already demolished and left it so, and I would have preferred not to have been witness to the great guilt of those governing who permitted that such a prodigious thing should have been demolished and broken up, without consideration for the times and for what might yet transpire, and it would have been better to have left it standing and to have had a guard placed over it.'

Another paragraph of the same Chapter (LI) contains a defence of Inca edifices: 'It would be only just to preserve what remains of this fortress and that of Guarco in memory of the grandeur of this land and in order to continue having two such fortresses there, ready-made and at such little expense.'

Present in these two paragraphs, unquestionably, is the pride of the conquistador in what cost so much effort to win; by glorifying the work of the Inca, he seeks his own glorification. In addition, however, there is an element of respect mixed with self-interest, in that these fortresses are, or are said to be, still usable. And this defence was not an isolated phenomenon. The Viceroy Francisco de Toledo was against the Spaniards dismantling Sacsayhuaman in order to use its stones for building houses. In 1577, he went even further and forbade the Jesuits to take them for the construction of their monastery and a dwelling. The respect evinced is obvious.

On the other side of the coin are the permits issued by the Crown to private individuals to excavate the tombs of chieftains on condition that one-fifth of the gold and jewels found go to the Crown.

To summarize: although there was nothing in sixteenth-century Ibero-America that resembles archaeology, a series of chronicles were produced that have been of inestimable aid in archaeological interpretation, to say nothing of their unique value as ethnographic material. Let us not forget, furthermore, that the conquistadores and their creole and mestizo descendants could not avoid making use of the articles produced by the Indians, nor do without the roads and causeways built by the same hands, even less, the irrigation systems and drinking water aqueducts; neither could they ignore the active presence all around them of the Indians, despite their decimation by wars and the diseases brought from Europe. That century, of expansion and consolidation of the Conquest, was of great importance moreover for the future in that the creoles and mestizos began to make their presence felt in public life, perhaps not yet wielding great influence, but in growing numbers.

The seventeenth century in Europe was the age of rationalism. Descartes, Spinoza, Leibniz, Locke, and Bacon do not, however, appear to have reached Ibero-America, where the philosophical tide they represented had little chance of penetrating a world completely dominated by the scholasticism characteristic of the Counter-Reformation, which was perhaps even stronger there than in the metropolitan centres. It is true that rationalism in Descartes is anti-historical since he sought the supremacy of science, admitting only that which was absolutely beyond doubt. On the other hand, an Italian rationalist, Vico, denied Cartesianism by affirming that the only possible knowledge is historical, of that which has happened, of what is made by man, since everything else, having been made by God, can only be known by Him. Vico was the first to apply what is today called culture-history.

The seventeenth century was a time of relative tranquillity, of setting down, with the rising importance of the creole and mestizo, who began to take a more active part in the local economy, always in open opposition to the Crown and its representatives by whom they were treated as second-class citizens. 'Castes' then arose, a racial classification system both social and economic.

Demarcation between one century and another, of course, does not show up the course of events – new eras are not ushered in at 12 midnight on 31 December. We use that method, nevertheless, because it helps to designate periods, even though there are specific examples that show how unrealistic this can be.

A case in point is that of Alonso de Ercilla y Zuñiga, who took a very active part in the conquest of Chile and who between 1569 and 1589 published his famous book *La Araucana*, considered one of the greatest works of its kind in the Spanish language. The epic struggle of the Araucanians against the Spaniards, as related by Ercilla, so glorified the conduct of the Indians that it introduced the concept into Europe of the 'noble savage,' later adopted by other authors with much less or no justification at all, but who reflected a contemporary attitude. In the face of such happenings, division into centuries is seen to be unreal.

An event that perhaps fits better into established chronology is the case of a celebration reported to have taken place in the mining town of Pausa, in the province of Parinacocha, Peru, in 1602; on this occasion, among many masked players, there was one group in ancient dress that put on a show representing the splendour and glory of the Inca civilization. But this was by no means an isolated instance. Examples of such reverence for the pre-Hispanic past are to be found throughout Ibero-America.

Chronicles continued to be written during the seventeenth century since there were still territories and peoples to be conquered, although by then spiritual victory had taken precedence over military conquest.

In its early decades, the eighteenth century was not materially different from the preceding one. All in all, there is no doubt that it was the Enlightenment that aroused self-awareness among Americans, which in many instances was channelled into activities that tended to bring out the values present in the hemisphere. At the same time, this created the need for fuller knowledge of their own world. The effective presence of a creole bourgeoisie who were shown the path to independence by the Enlightenment and the revolutions in the English colonies and France, gave rise to discussion on American reality which took the form of study of the Indian past. The civilizing achievements of the native populations were re-evaluated and the works of the past reclaimed as their own.

The influence of Charles III of Spain made itself felt. In addition to being a typical enlightened despot of the time, he had been King of Naples and was therefore conversant with archaeological matters, having got to know Herculaneum and Pompeii, where he ordered excavations to be made. This led to his sending Captain Antonio del Río to the ruins of Palenque in 1786. The ruins of Xochicalco and El

Tajín were visited by José Antonio de Alzate y Ramírez and he wrote about them in the famous *Gaceta de Literatura* in 1791. In 1792, Antonio de León y Gama, an astronomer and physicist of the Real y Pontificia Universidad de México, published an extensively documented study dealing with two monoliths – the great statue of *Coatlicue* and the 'Aztec Calendar', which were discovered while the paving was being repaired in the main plaza of Mexico City – to which he added an analysis of the calendrical system of the ancient Mexicans.

It is of interest that between 1771 and 1779, the Viceroy Bucareli ordered a museum to be established in the University of Mexico for housing Indian antiquities, an idea that undoubtedly came from Charles III who had created museums elsewhere.

The epoch of the naturalists also began at that time with scientists combing the seas, climbing mountains, and crossing deserts in search of information on the physical and biological world. La Condamine was perhaps the best known of them, but there were others of note, the last of whom was probably Alexander von Humboldt.

These scientists were not primarily interested in ruins or remains of the Indian past; nevertheless, since it was impossible to ignore them, their descriptions have inevitably come down to us.

In 1767, Charles III expelled the Jesuits from Spain and the overseas colonies; they had already been ousted from Portugal and its colonies in 1759. This political act had very significant repercussions upon the cultural development of Ibero-America since, as is well known, one of the principal activities of this order lay in the field of what we now call higher education. As far as our particular subject is concerned, they had been gathering information and documents on the Indian past for many years and using the material to build collections and libraries that were veritable museums. Unfortunately, all this material was scattered and disappeared upon their expulsion. To offset this, their place of exile in Bologna, where they had been brought together by the Holy See, saw the emergence of important authors, like Clavijero, who defended pre-Hispanic America against the attacks of de Pauw and Buffon, demonstrating that its civilizations were part of world culture.

The eighteenth century ended with a spate of activity on the part of the creoles and mestizos, which was guided into the appropriate channels when Napoleon invaded Spain, Fernando VII abdicated, and the American colonies began to find their way to independence.

After the armed struggle against Spain, came the task of consolidating the independent governments. Power remained in the hands of the creoles and mestizos and a succession of struggles ensued that left the new-born countries impoverished and in debt. This, of course, resulted in a decline of interest in the Indian past and its study was taken over at that point by the Europeans and North Americans whose countries sought collateral economic benefits in the new republics.

Consuls and businessmen travelled all over Ibero-America in their leisure time – which seems to have been considerable – taking notes, making drawings, and acquiring archaeological pieces either by purchase from the inhabitants or through excavations.

These materials began to arrive at the great museums of the United States and Europe despite the fact that all the young republics of Central and South America possessing remains of high civilizations had passed laws protecting this heritage and even established museums.

Simon Bolivar himself, apparently, issued a decree for the protection of archaeological property, which came into force between 1820 and 1830, the year of his death. In Mexico, legislation was passed in 1827 that prohibited the export of monuments or antiquities.

Shortly before the middle of the nineteenth century, under the spell of romanticism, travellers with independent means and an insatiable thirst for adventure and new horizons arrived on the scene: J. Lloyd Stephens in Mexico and Central America and Sir Clements Markham in Peru are typical.

The romantic vision of archaeological ruins that spread among a certain sector of the Victorian intelligentsia was soon overshadowed by positivism as a scientific approach.

The first application of positivism to archaeological research in Mexico was that of the members of the *Commission Scientifique du Mexique,* a group of scientists who, like those that travelled to Egypt with Napoleon, accompanied Maximilian of Habsburg. The influence that the ideology of the members of this Commission might have had was minimal. As far as most of the country was concerned they were invaders and, despite the fact that they did some interesting work which established significant guidelines, it was impossible to obtain any better results in view of the short duration of the French intervention – from May, 1864 to June, 1867 – and the state of war that existed. However, the positivist philosophy was dominant in Ibero-America during the latter part of the nineteenth century and the first two decades of the twentieth.

The consolidation of power among the Ibero-American bourgeoisies, the relative tranquility of the second part of the nineteenth century, the placing of their natural resources at the disposal of foreign capital for exploitation in association with domestic assets, and the building of railroads and port facilities, all stimulated the formation of an important intellectual stratum. Scientific societies were created, new museums founded and old ones improved. However, few scholars concerned with Ibero-American archaeology undertook excavations and even fewer considered such archaeology, the remains of their past, to be related to their national aspirations. They were for the most part concerned with the 'primitive' but regarded it as something foreign.

And so, from the end of the nineteenth century to the present, within the context of a variety of philosophical orientations oncerning the practice of archaeology, Ibero-America has been invaded by foreign archaeologists, alone or in teams, either insulated from or co-operating with national archaeologists, who have found a wide field in which to obtain artifacts and gain personal renown. For the countries themselves, there remains a certain body of knowledge always col-oured by the nature of those who perform the work, this being another form of colonialism, inasmuch as the country provides the raw ma-terial and receives the manufactured product, but loses out because it does not conform to their ideals, is not truly concerned with the national interest.

Ibero-American archaeologists have a historical and social obli-gation when practising archaeology. This includes not only those who work in the regions where the high cultures flourished and where the Indians are sometimes in a majority but also those of us in the countries where there is no Indian population at all or where it is highly diluted.

Let me cite two extreme examples. On the one hand, there is Mexico with its revolution of 1910 in which the biologically Indian indigenous or rural masses made up the fighting forces and shed their blood. As a consequence, they participated in the country's political life and a process of restitution was initiated which led to a so-called 'Indian policy', with the result that lustre was shed on the values of the native past and the pre-Hispanic phase elevated to a place of honour in national history.

On the other hand, there is Argentina where the Indian population, hunters and gatherers for the most part or incipient farmers, were physically and socially displaced and the nation founded on a mass proletariat from Europe as its base. But, even there, despite the ravings of Ameghino who sought to place the origin of man in the Tertiary strata of the Pampas, a sense of making archaeology part of their history is to be found and is gathering strength.

In some countries, archaeology began to be practised outside of the museums which were mere repositories for archaeological or ethnog-raphical pieces, as well as samples of flora, fauna, minerals, and items of historical interest, all obtained by donation or casual discovery. Trained staffs were small and rarely interested in searching for ad-ditional material, although this was easy to come by. Broadly speak-ing, these museums belong to the government, although nominally serving a university which derives its funds from the same source.

Subsequently, archaeology was taken over *in toto* by the State in some countries on the principle that everything archaeological was national property, as set forth in several Constitutions which preserve the absolutist concept of the Spanish monarchy with respect to the ownership of territory and its fruits. Naturally, in practice, this re-sulted in centralization and absolute legal protection which is, in fact, not so absolute.

In Ibero-America, archaeology is practised by universities and museums that are either attached to them or themselves national institutions, and by government organizations. The universities always have a very limited potential and their activities tend to revolve around projects of a personal, selective, and long-term character. Under local laws, materials may be preserved in museums and university collections or, after being studied, turned over to the government, generally for a national museum. In some cases, if the university has no anthropology department which would normally be in charge of archaeological research, it does have a museum and it is the centre of such activities.

There are also instances in which the national museum, a State organization, practises archaeology, centralizing all such activity, including the granting of excavation permits to foreigners and even the strengthening of laws for the protection of the archaeological inheritance.

Finally, there are national institutes which by law, as in the case of Mexico, have an absolute monopoly of archaeology, operating special research departments and museums of their own. In these cases legislation gives the institution power.

Ibero-America still does not have fiscal systems such as would prompt the setting-up of the kind of foundations that are created by big capital for tax purposes, and actually, all funds come out of the same purse – the State's.

There is no need to discuss archaeological methods here. Suffice it merely to indicate that we are aware of the confusion that reigns between means and ends. Today, as a matter of fact, two antagonistic ideologies exist, perhaps not so much in regard to how the discipline is exercised as with respect to its ultimate aim, although these are two aspects of the same thing. On the one hand, there is the neopositivist current which as applied to the social sciences is, in the light of traditional logic, a source of serious contradiction and tautology since its negation of historicism makes processes unintelligible or relegates them to the background, and this also produces incoherence. It should be noted that most of the neopositivists in the field of archaeology are not really that, since their philosophical involvement does not go beyond the application of certain procedures, thereby reducing ideology to the status of a mere mechanism. The other ideology embraces dialectical materialism as a scientific system of research, seeking in its application a social explanation that is historical in nature and conforms to a non-dogmatic, non-unilinear evolutionism. Certainly, the two positions should not be considered solely from their extreme aspects since there are other intermediate ones with a still viable historical-cultural slant. However, what is not feasible from any standpoint is the reconciliation of neopositivism and dialectical materialism that is sought in certain structuralist approaches.

As we all know, there is a tendency to muddy the simplest concepts through the use – some would say abuse – of cryptic phraseology, of vocabulary reserved for initiates, which continues to burgeon among those we call 'café archaeologists'. This, to be sure, applies equally to either extreme.

Archaeology, to many of us a social science and adjunct of history, is possibly the discipline that comes closest to so-called 'total history', which seeks to absorb all interrelations, all causes and effects. It may very well be that those unable to grasp the need for archaeology as history will simply continue to look on the latter as something that somebody once disdainfully styled *histoire-bataille*. Of course, the blame does not rest with history but with those who do not comprehend what history is.

The aim of this brief paper is not to bring esoterica to light but to suggest an approach that will make full use of the unique opportunity offered by the ancient sources of Ibero-America to lay a foundation for ancient history that will encompass protohistory and prehistory through the written evidence of what the conquistadores, missionaries, and officials of the Crown saw and experienced. Never has such a complete and direct body of evidence been available, provided by eyewitnesses, i.e. those in a position to fill in all the information that archaeology is unable to do through its primary sources, the remains of material culture.

BIBLIOGRAPHY

BERNAL, IGNACIO 1960 Archeology and written sources. *Akten des 34, Amer. Kongr.:* 219-25 Vienna.

BONAVIA, DUCCIO and ROGGER RAVINES 1970 *Arqueologia Peruana: Precursores* Casa de la Cultura del Peru. Lima.

CASTANEDA, FRANCISCO DE 1905 Relación de Tecciztlan y su partido in: *Papeles de la Nueva España*, 7 Vols, 6: 209-36 Francisco del Paso y Troncoso, camp. Est. Tipográfico Sucs. Rivadeneyra Madrid.

CIEZA DE LEÓN, PEDRO 1968 *El Señorio de los Incas.* Biblioteca Peruana, 1st Ser., Vol III: 9-194 Lima.

DANIEL, GLYN 1950 *A Hundred Years of Archaeology.* London.
—— 1967 *The Origins and Growth of Archaeology.* Harmondsworth.

IXTLILXOCHITL, FERNANDO DE ALVA 1952 *Obras Históricas*, 2 Vols. Editorial Nacional, S.A. Mexico.

KON, I.S. 1976 *Neopositivismo y materialismo histórico* Ediciones de Cultura Popular. Mexico.

LEONARD, IRVING A. 1953 *Los libros del Conquis-* *tador.* Fondo de Cultura Económica. Mexico.
—— 1974 *La Epoca Barroca en el México Colonial.* Fondo de Cultura Económica, Col. Popular, 129. Mexico.

LORENZO, JOSE L. 1976a La Arqueología Mexicana y los arqueólogos norteamericanos, *Depto. de Prehistoria, INAH, Cuads, Trabajo No. 14.* Mexico.
—— 1976b *Hacia una arqueología social. Reunión de Teotihuacán, 1975.* Instituto Nacional de Antropología e Historia. Mexico.

PELLETIER, A. and J.-J. COBLOT 1975 *Materialismo Histórico e Historia de la Civilización* Editorial Grijalbo, S.A., Col. Teoría y Práxis. Mexico.

RAVINES, ROGGER (comp.) 1970 *Cien Años de Arqueología en el Peru.* Fuentes e Investigaciones para la Historia del Peru, 3 Instituto de Estudios Peruanos Eds. Petróleos del Peru. Lima.

ROJAS, GABRIEL DE 192 Relación de Cholula *Rev. Mex. Ests. Histors.* 1 (6): 158-69. Mexico.

VAZQUEZ, JOSEFINA ZORAIDA 1978 *Historia de la Historiografía* Ediciones Ateneo. Mexico.

XIII
Sponte nascitur ollae...

ANDRZEJ ABRAMOWICZ

Polish Academy of Sciences, Łódź, Poland

The once widely held and long-lasting belief that pots spontaneously grow in the earth can probably be traced back to Jan Długosz, the eminent Polish historian (1415-1480) who makes two references to this subject in his *Annales seu cronicae incliti Regni Poloniae* (concluded after 1470).[1] The first reference is in Book I where he maintains that in Poland, in the grounds of the village of Nochowo near Śrem and at the village of Kozielsko near Łekno 'pots are born in the womb of the earth, by the art of nature alone, without any human agency ...' Długosz refers to this subject again in Book XI, where he relates how in 1416 King Władysław Jagiełło ordered the fields of Nochowo village to be dug in his presence so that the spontaneous growth of pots in Poland could be confirmed. This operation was prompted by the doubt expressed by Ernest, Prince of Austria, who had sent a special envoy whose mission was to learn the truth on the spot. The excavations were duly carried out, and a number of pots recovered. Several of them were given to the envoy who was to present them to the prince.

Today we know that the site excavated was probably a cremation cemetery of the Lusatian culture from the Bronze or Early Iron Age. It seems rather surprising that Długosz failed to identify the pots as pagan cinerary urns, conversant as he was with the funerary rites of Poland's pagan neighbours, that is the Prussians, Lithuanians and Samogitians. It was in his lifetime that the Lithuanians were converted to Christianity. When describing Lithuanian burial rites Długosz expressed the view that they were imitating the customs practised by the ancient inhabitants of Italy. Still more surprising is the fact that the pots were not recognized by the King, who himself was a recent convert and had doubtless witnessed many a cremation ceremony. It is possible that the King was aware of the nature of the Nochowo find but preferred to keep this knowledge to himself, since in 1416 he was violently attacked by the Teutonic Knights as a false Christian. In view of this it might have been awkward for him to appear as an expert on pagan subjects.

The idea of the growing pots became immensely popular among both Polish and foreign scholars. Those who wrote on this topic included Matthew of Miechów (1519)[2] and Martin Kromer (1577).[3]

Sebastian Münster, a German geographer, who learned about this phenomenon from Matthew of Miechów, reported it in his *Cosmographiae Universalis*, which was published in 1544 and ran to several editions.[4] The pots were mentioned in 1565 by the papal nuncio, Fulvio Ruggieri,[5] and later by a Frenchman, Jacob Esprinchard who in 1597 travelled in Silesia and Little Poland.[6] This notion spread into Germany and Bohemia,[7] reaching as far as Switzerland and Italy and finding apparent corroboration in constant new discoveries. In my view, the reason why the idea endured for so long was less because it reflected popular belief, than because it became part of the scientific system of that period. In Długosz's account philosophical terminology was already in evidence and subsequently the naturalists repeatedly introduced *ollae fictiles* into their classification systems as separate kinds of fossil. It is characteristic that J. Kentmann includes them as *vasa fictilia* in his work *Nomenclaturae rerum fossilium* (Tiguri, 1565)[8] and even the famous Swiss naturalist, Conrad Gesner, seems to have distinguished between *ollae nativae* and *urnae fictiles*, the latter being recognized as graves from pagan times (Conradi Gesneri, *De rerum fossilium ...* Tiguri, 1565).[9] Therefore the discoveries of cremation graves which were interpreted correctly did not conflict with the belief in pots growing in the earth. The existence of both categories seemed equally acceptable. The confusion and uncertainty of this period are manifested by Ulysse Aldrovandi who knew something about fossil pots but mentioned them in the chapter 'De ostracite' on crustaceans.[10] In Silesia the recovered pots were correctly identified at a relatively early date. In 1544 George Uber, an inhabitant of Wroctaw, describes in a letter in Latin addressed to Andrew Aurifaber urns found at Masłów near Trzebnica, rightly assuming the place to be a pagan cemetery.[11] Another noteworthy Silesian was Caspar Schwenckfelt who in his work *Stirpium et Fossilium Silesiae Catalogus* (Lipsiae 1600) countered the views held by uneducated people who believed in the spontaneous growth of pots or regarded them as being used by dwarfs, by setting against them the opinion of learned men who rightly guessed that the pots were pagan burials.[12] In the natural sciences, the correct interpretation of pots as ancient urns was advanced by the Polish scholar of Scottish origin, John Johnston (1603-1675). He expressed this view in his *Thaumatographia naturalis* published in Amsterdam in 1632, adding that he saw urns of this kind in the library in Toruń.[13] Incidentally, this is the first mention in Poland of urns kept in a library where some sort of a cabinet of curiosities must have existed. In later editions of his *Thaumatographia* (1661 and 1664) Johnston mentioned further urns which he saw in London in the collection of the Earl of Arundel. However, among naturalists the belief in the spontaneous growth of pots persisted. By way of example may be mentioned Ehrenfried Hagendorn, a German physician and naturalist from Lusatia who wrote in 1672 that nature should not be denied the ability to fabricate pots of this kind (Credo tamen, naturae in ejusmodi fabricandi ollulis possibilitatem non esse detrahendam). [14]

Hagendorn was still cited in the first half of the eighteenth century by the well-known Polish naturalist, Gabriel Rzączyński, who in his two works: *Historia naturalis curiosa Regni Poloniae, Magni Ducatus Litvaniae ...* (Sandomirae 1721) and *Auctuarium Historiae naturalis ...* (Gedani, 1745) separately described *ollae fossiles seu nativae* and *urnae fictiles sepulchrales*. [15] Though well aware of the fact that several scientists refuted the possibility of the spontaneous growth of pots, he nevertheless endorsed Hagendorn's opinion. This, however, did not prevent him from citing – in another chapter – a long list of sites which yielded urns with cremated bones and about whose sepulchral character he had no doubts. In 1778 Rzączyński was severely criticized by a French scholar and writer Jean-Baptiste Dubois who wrote: 'La crédulité est une belle chose, surtout en Physique; le globe s'embellit à ses yeux, les merveilles se multiplient, et elle met sur le compte de la Nature ce que la Nature n'a jamais produit'. [16]

The problem of the spontaneously grown pots has not yet been gone into fully though the literature on this subject is fairly abundant. [17] Interesting possibilities may open up when a parallel is drawn between this notion and the interpretation of flint tools as thunderbolts, since in both cases an attempt has been made to explain these phenomena in the light of natural science.

It would be equally illuminating to compare the question of the spontaneously grown pots with that of the spontaneous generation discussed by naturalists, namely the idea current in Antiquity and in the Middle Ages – and in the case of microbes persisting until Pasteur's time – that living beings can be born from minerals or from decomposing organic substances.

BIBLIOGRAPHICAL REFERENCES

1   JOANNIS DŁUGOSSI *Annales seu cronicae incliti Regni Poloniae*, Libri I – VIII, Varsaviae 1964-75; JOANNIS DŁUGOSSII SEU LONGINI canonici cracoviensis *Historiae Poloniae librii XII*, Cracoviae 1873-78.

2   *Chronica Polonorum*, Cracoviae 1521, p. V.

3   *Polonia sive de situ, populis, moribus, magistratibus et republica regni Polonici libri duo*, Coloniae 1577, p.26.

4   *Cosmographiae Universalis lib. VI*, 1550, p.888.

5   *Relacje nuncjuszów apostolskich innych osób o Polsce od roku 1548 do 1690*, vol. I, Berlin – Poznań 1864, p.118.

6   B. GEREMEK. Relacja Jakuba Esprincharda z podróży przez Śląsk i Mało polske/Relation d'un voyage à travers la Silésie et la Petite Pologne par Jacques Esprinchard/, *Kwartalnik Historii Kultury Materialnej*, VII: 1959, p.452.

7   JOHANN MATHESIUS. *Sarepta oder Bergpostill Sampt der Johimsthalischen kurzen Chroniken*, Nürnberg 1562, carta 278a; BOHUSLAV BALBIN. *Miscellanea Historica Regni Bohemiae*, Decadis I. Liber I, qui historiam naturalem complecitur, cap. XLIX, Pragae 1679; J.H. SEYFRID. *Neu aufgelegt und vermehrte Medulla mirabilium naturae*, Nürnberg 1694, p.463; *Centuria herbarum mirabilium...Durch* JOHANNEM OLORINUM... Magdeburg 1616, p.103.

8   IO. KENTMANI. Dresdensis Medici, *Nomenclaturae rerum fossilium*...Tiguri 1565, fol. 9.

9   CONRADI GESNERI. *De rerum fossilium, lapidum et gemmarum maximè, figuris et similitudinibus liber*...Tiguri 1565, fol. 88.

10 VLYSSIS ALDROVANDI. *Museum metallicum in libros IIII distributum* ... Bononia 1648, p.596.

11 H. SEGER. Maslographia 1711-1911, 'Schlesiens Vorzeit in Bild und Schrift', N.F. 7: 1912, pp.1-16.

12 *Stirpium et Fossilium Silesiae Catalogus...per* CASPARUM SCHWENCKFELT. Lipsiae 1600, p.406.

13 JON. JONSTONI *Thaumatographia naturalis, in decem clases distincta* ... Amsterdami 1632, p.139.

14 D. EHRENFRIED HAGENDORN. De ollis fictilibus in argillae fodinis inventis, *Miscelanea curiosa medico-physica academiae curiosorum sive Ephemeridum medico-physicarum germanicarum* Annus Tertius, Anni scilicet *MDCLXXII*, Lipsiae et Francofurti 1673, p.247.

15 *Historia naturalis curiosa Regni Poloniae, Magni Ducatus Litvaniae, annexarumque provinciarum, in tractatus XX divisa ... Opera* P. GABRIELIS RZĄCZYŃSKI ... *Sandomiriae* 1721, pp.6, 13-15. *Auctuarium historiae naturalis Regni Poloniae Magnique Ducatus Lithvaniae Annexarumque Provinciarum in puncta XII ... Opus posthumum* P. GABRIELIS RZĄCZYŃSKI ... Gedani 1745, pp.14, 22-24.

16 *Essai sur l'histoire littéraire de Pologne par M.D.* ... (DUBOIS) Berlin MDCCLXXVIII, p.416.

17 J. KOSTRZEWSKI. *Dzieje polskich badań prehistorycznych*, Poznań 1947, pp.2-3; S. NOSEK. *Zarys historii badań archeologicznych w Małopolsce*, Wrocław – Warszawa – Kraków 1967, p.2; L. FRANZ. 'Selbstgewachsene' Altertümer, *Wiener Prähistorische Zeitschrift*, 18: 1931, pp.10-21; L. FRANZ. Wenn Altertümer wachsen, *Germanoslavica*, 4: 1936, pp.26-42; K.H. JACOB-FRIESEN. *Graundfragen der Urgeschichtsforschung*, Hannover 1928, pp.102-106; P.H. STEMMERMANN. *Die Anfänge der deutschen Vorgeschichtsforschung. Deutschlands Bodenaltertümer in der Anschauung des 16. u. 17. Jahrhunderts*, Heidelberg 1934; H. GUMMEL. *Forschungsgeschichte in Deutschland*, Berlin 1938.

XIV
The history of Archaeology in Czechoslovakia
K. SKLENÁŘ
Národní Museum, Prague, Czechoslovakia

On reading through existing general surveys of the history of European archaeology, it soon becomes evident that they have concentrated upon several 'classical' countries – England, France, Denmark,
or Germany; some other countries with a relatively rich archaeological
tradition remain outside the field of vision of these surveys. The
reasons for this are (1) a traditional conception and elaboration of the
history of archaeology, (2) the language barrier and (3) insufficient
interest on the part of many countries in learning about and propaga-
ting their own traditions.

Czechoslovakia provides a good example. To a certain extent, it is
its own fault, because interest in the history of archaeology was almost
minimal there until quite recently although Czechoslovakia – and
especially its western third, Bohemia – has an old and rich tradition of
research.

It would be incorrect to convey the impression that the development
of Czech archaeology was on a par, for instance, with advances in
England or Germany. Two factors in particular had a considerable
influence on Czech archaeology at the outset. The first was a lack of
arresting ancient surface monuments, like the remains of Roman
buildings on the territory of the one-time Roman provinces or the
megalithic monuments of western and northern Europe.

The second factor is more political in character. In the sixteenth
century the Bohemian Kingdom became part of the Habsburg Empire, but after the defeat of the Czech uprising of 1618-21 it lost its
relative independence. Its economy was ruined by the ensuing Thirty
Years War, the land was impoverished, the Czech nobility, as the
leading political stratum of the nation, was all but liquidated, and the
educated people went into Protestant exile to Germany, Holland,
England, and Sweden, to avoid the political and cultural pressures of
the Catholic Counter-reformation. In the seventeenth and eighteenth
centuries – at a time when Western Europe was gathering strength and
the foundations were laid for European archaeology – the Czech
nation, within the framework of the relatively backward Habsburg
Empire, went through a period of unprecedented adversity.

The endeavours of the Vienna court to Germanize Bohemia and Moravia in the eighteenth century, however, caused a reaction and resistance in the form of the so-called 'national revival', which had much in common with the economic rise of the Czech middle classes. It was at this point that Czech archaeology, as one of the instruments of the national consciousness, made its first advances.

If we glance back today at its development it looks like a spiral oscillating between two basic approaches to the source material – archaeological and historical. It can be formulated as a simplified table, by dividing this development into three basic periods, each of which consists of two phases:

PERIOD:	I. antiquarian		II. archaeological		III. (pre) historical	
PHASE:	1	2	3	4	5	6
	primary analysis	romantic synthesis	archaeo-logical analysis	archaeo-logical synthesis	prehis-torical analysis	prehis-torical synthesis
DATE:		1836	1868	1899	1910	?

The first phase – *primary analysis* – is a period of recognition of the sources. The relatively unobtrusive character of archaeological landmarks on Czechoslovak territory was responsible for the fact that Czech chroniclers and historians of the sixteenth and seventeenth centuries did not know them. Only one author, Václav Hájek of Libočany, mentions in his *Czech Chronicle* (Prague, 1541) the extensive Celtic oppidum of Závist near Prague. The first mention of ancient vessels discovered in Bohemia is contained in a book of sermons (*Sarepta oder Bergpostill*, Nürnberg, 1562), by the German humanist Johann Mathesius, a Lutheran pastor in northwestern Bohemia.

In Moravia, Bishop Jan of Doubravka (Joannes Dubravius) wrote in 1552 about the discoveries of amber at the Celtic oppidum of Staré Hradisko, and in 1571 another bishop, Jan Blahoslav, reported finds of bones in the Palaeolithic locality of Předmostí. Staré Hradisko as the find-place of prehistoric amber is also plotted on the map of Moravia made in 1627 by the great Moravian scholar Jan Amos Komenský (Comenius).

Otherwise, interest in the nation's beginnings was concentrated on questions of a historical-philological nature (e.g. disputes at Prague University at the beginning of the seventeenth century on the origin of the Slavs) or the problem of the so-called 'old Czech tales' handed down in Czech literature from early medieval times onwards as tales from 'pagan' times which preceded written history. (Linked to these are the first known planned digs in Bohemia in the seventeenth century, directed to the search for the grave of 'first father' Čech [Czech]-Bohemus.)

A basic change came about after the middle of the eighteenth century in the period of the Enlightenment, Germanization and National Revival. By the aristocracy and scholars in Bohemia of that century, patriotism was understood chiefly as a relationship to the country; nationalism grew stronger from the beginning of the following century as the ideology of the petit bourgeoisie (lower middle class), which became the leading element in the birth of a modern Czech nation and from which came a new generation of educated people.

Bohemia and Moravia headed in many respects the intellectual life of the Habsburg monarchy. The first scientific association in this empire was established in Olomouc (Moravia) in 1746. The first outstanding academy-type institution was the Royal Bohemian Society of Sciences in Prague, which also dealt with archaeology; it developed gradually from 1774 on. The study of and writing on archaeology was stimulated by several outstanding finds, e.g. the greatest known find to date of Celtic gold coins near Podmokly, Bohemia, in 1771, or the Bronze Age urnfields destroyed during the construction of the Hradec Králové fortress between 1768 and 1778.

The first phase of development is characterized by several personalities. Johann Mathesius, in the sixteenth century, writes about finds as proof of God's power, Bohuslav Balbín in the seventeenth treats them as rarities. In the eighteenth century, Karel J. Biener of Bienenberg (1731-1798), the first great figure of Czech archaeology, regarded them as interesting illustrations of ancient historical reports. In 1773 he published the first list of prehistoric finds in Bohemia; he tried to explain them by using only a combination of reports of Roman authors and medieval and more modern chroniclers. Nevertheless, he actually laid the foundation for collecting information and for attempts to provide historical explanations of 'pagan antiquities'.

The most honourable place in this list belongs to the 'father of Czech prehistory', Abbé Josef Dobrovský (1753-1829). This foremost scholar of the Czech Enlightenment, one of the founders of Slavonic studies, went further than Bienenberg in his study on the burial rites of the old Slavs (1786) in which he tried to put the finds in a historical setting; more importantly, as one of the first ever, he insisted on the methodological principle of priority of prehistoric archaeological sources over written sources (he called the finds 'speaking proof' from which it is necessary to construct a picture of prehistoric times). Among his other works of note is the report on investigations carried out at the Iron Age barrows near Lochovice, Bohemia (1802-3), which was the first regular (deliberately undertaken and 'professionally' conducted, documented and published) archaeological excavation in Czechoslovakia (published in 1803).

The second phase – *romantic synthesis* – is a period when the Enlightenment sobriety was replaced by the nationalistic enthusiasm of the new generation; a typical feature of this period was the 'discovery' in 1817 and 1818 of allegedly ancient Slavonic heroic and lyrical songs (the so-called *Manuscripts of Dvůr Králové and Zelená Hora*), very reminiscent, for instance, of Ossian. These poems, which in a basically romantic manner answered the needs of the nation at that time for a depiction of its earliest, glorious past, even became a basic source for Czech prehistory by describing Slavonic beginnings. The manuscripts had also a positive significance, if only because they inspired a great interest in prehistoric monuments, although the glorious period of the Middle Ages remained the major ideological weapon of the National Revival. Archaeological finds were still few and not eloquent enough to satisfy the challenging social demand – and this, in turn, was reflected in the slow rise of interest in archaeology.

This second phase is represented by the three different types of researchers active at that time. Matyás Kalina of Jäthenstein (1772-1848) was educated by the Enlightenment but strongly influenced by the romantic vision of the remote past. This rich Prague lawyer had a good grasp of Middle European literature, had his own collection and worked in the field. At a time when need for synthetic works led to the creation of romantic ideas about the oldest period of Slavonic and Czech history in such outstanding writings as *Slovanské starožitnosti* (Slavonic Antiquities) by Pavel Josef Šafařík (this book, which appeared in 1837, was the foundation stone of European studies on Slavonic origins and beginnings) and the first volume of *Dějiny národu českého* (History of the Czech Nation) by Frantisek Palacký, 1836, Kalina supplemented these historical and philological works with a book on the archaeological aspects of the question, a study aptly named *Böhmens heidnische Opferplätze, Gräber und Alterthümer* (Pagan Sacrificial Places, Graves, and Antiquities in Bohemia, Prague 1836). This catalogue of archaeological finds, accompanied by one of the earliest archaeologically substantiated pictures of the prehistory of Bohemia (and also by the oldest archaeological map of the country), already included 107 localities. Independently of Thomsen's contemporary publication, Kalina speaks – though not yet quite explicitly – of the sequence stone-bronze-iron and tries to classify the graves chronologically according to the absence or presence of iron.

The excavations sponsored by Kalina were carried out mainly by another outstanding archaeologist – Václav Krolmus (1790-1861), pastor at Kalina's estate. The two men worked together in close collaboration. Krolmus was a pure romantic in his theories; but as the most experienced Czech field archaeologist – actually the first paid Czech professional, working between 1846 and 1859 for the National Museum in Prague – he laid the foundations for the prehistoric collection of this museum. (The National Museum was founded as early as 1818 and its scientific journal, which first appeared in 1827 continues to this day, though interest in archaeology was rather weak there before 1840.) An interesting speciality of Krolmus's fieldwork was the systematic observation of new road and railway constructions.

The most outstanding personality of the romantic phase was Jan Erazim Vocel (1802-1871). This educated, stimulating and organizationally talented man founded archaeology in Bohemia as a scientific discipline. In 1843 he formulated the programme of the new 'national Czecho-Slavonic archaeology'; in the same year he created the first archaeological institution (Archaeological Committee of the National Museum in Prague) and guided its activities until his death in 1871. (Also in 1843 a Keeper was assigned to the Museum's archaeological collections, in the person of Josef Vojtech Hellich, a painter whose manuscript on Czech archaeology, written at that time, was the first explicit application of the Three Age System in Czechoslovakia.)

At the National Museum archaeological finds were first exhibited in 1824, but in the 'fifties the first special permanent exhibition of Czech archaeology was built up by Vocel. Following several unsuccessful attempts, Vocel also introduced a periodical for his committee under the title *Památky archaeologické* (Archaeological Monuments), which began to come out in 1854 and continues to appear to this day. In 1850 Vocel had been appointed professor of prehistory and historic archaeology at the Charles University in Prague. It appears to have been the second oldest professorship of this type in the world (Reuvens in Holland, 1818, was the first). Also a chair of Slavonic antiquities was set up at Vienna University for Jan Kollár, the Slovak poet and romantic antiquarian, as early as 1849, but its importance was minimal (Kollár was interested only in allegedly old Slavonic 'idols' and 'runes').

Vocel had wide European connections, especially with Denmark: Thomsen and Worsaae visited him in Prague and the royal archaeologist Frederik VII decorated him with the cross of Danebrog.

Vocel's writings characterize the entire period of the second phase. First to appear were the outlining work *Grundzüge der böhmischen Alterthumskunde* (Principles of Bohemian Archaeology), and the popular handbook *O starožitnostech českých* (On Bohemian Antiquities). Both were published in Prague in 1845. In the 'fifties Vocel fully recognized the meaning and advantages of the comparative method and in 1869 he formulated his 'regressive method' on this principle, a principle which Montelius put into practice later in order to work out his ethnohistorical conclusions and on which Kossinna's 'retrospective method' is based. (Vocel's work was published by the Royal Bohemian Society of Science in Prague 1869 in German under the title *Die Bedeutung der Stein- und Bronzealterthümer für die Urgeschichte der Slaven*.) Vocel also fully understood the importance of find associations and find horizons.

Vocel's life-work *Pravěk země České* (Prehistory of Bohemia) (Prague 1866-68) is the first scientifically written survey of this theme, based on archaeological, historical and philological sources – the best example of the romantic synthesis which already shows some connections with the next period of positivism; this work contains the elements of the Three Age System, but the terms Celtic, German and Slavonic are stressed much more. An interesting feature are the intensive and rather successful attempts to utilize the chemical analysis of bronze antiquities for a relative chronology. From the end of the 'forties Vocel engaged in an intensive search for an exact chronological scheme in collaboration with several chemists of Prague University and his pioneer work was later recognized by Rudolf Virchow.

The third phase – *archaeological analysis* – meant a return to source material, a period of positivism, a shift of interest from ethnohistorical theories to the description and classification of finds. It is on the whole quite typical that this period of minute work in Bohemia is not linked to any personality of Vocel's stature, although Josef Smolík (1832-1915), who in the eighteen-seventies and eighties led Czech archaeology, did a great deal together with his colleagues in the fields of morphology, typology, and terminology. Among researchers active at that time we should note Ludvík Šnajdr, who in 1858 – before Virchow – had recognized Slavonic pottery (the so-called *burgwall* type) and later fought for recognition of the existence of the Neolithic period in Bohemia, in opposition to Smolík. Šnajdr contributed also to the recognition of the Celtic (La Tène) culture in Bohemia in connection with the most famous discovery of the nineteenth century in this country – the Celtic oppidum of Stradonice near Beroun, Middle Bohemia.

The situation developed somewhat differently in Moravia where until this time one can hardly speak about archaeological research. The Brno museum was of the same age as the National Museum in Prague, but it played no important role. On the other hand, this is the time when the caves of the Moravian Karst were first investigated; whereas Bohemian archaeology was directed to later prehistory, in Moravia it was the Palaeolithic archaeology of Czechoslovakia that first received attention, and several researchers became prominent – particularly Jindřich Wankel, known internationally also for his discovery of the Hallstatt Age prince's grave in the Býčí Skála cave. Wankel was the leading spirit of a research group associated with the new museum in Olomouc (founded 1883), which became the first centre of archaeological work in Moravia.

In Bohemia, in the eighteen-nineties there was a big organizational advance: new institutions, associations and museums came into being, along with new periodicals. Two main groups of archaeologists holding different views were formed, and new people came forward to head these groups. The 'Museum school' was led by Professor Josef Ladislav Píč (1847-1911), historian and archaeologist, Smolík's successor and the first head of the independent Department of Prehistory in the National Museum in Prague (1893). Czech archaeology under his leadership turned once again to broader historical problems: just as Smolík had rejected the ethnohistorical approach of Vocel, so Píč scorned the descriptive archaeology of Smolík's time and tried to discover the people and history behind the material. He set himself the task of writing, from this viewpoint, the prehistory of Bohemia, and together with a group of friends – mainly amateur field archaeologists – he organized extensive excavations.

The 'University school' was represented more by theory. The outstanding scholar Lubor Niederle (1865-1944), from 1898 professor of prehistory at Prague University and the author of the substantial work *Lidstvo v době předhistorické* (Mankind in the Prehistoric Period) (Prague, 1893), approached archaeology more from the position of the cultural anthropologist, and later he concentrated on the historical beginnings of Slavs. His collaborator Karel Buchtela (1864-1946), on the other hand, was fully engaged in elaborating Bohemia's archaeological sources from the morphological, stylistic, chronological and genetic aspects.

The fourth phase – *archaeological synthesis* – represents the final encounter of both these groups in the first decade of this century. In the critical struggle, during the publication of Píč's multi-volume lifework *Starožitnosti země České* (Antiquities of Bohemia) (Prague, 1899-1909), both sides formulated their positions in programmatic digests: Píc's *Prehled české archaeologie* (Outline of Bohemian Archaeology) (Prague, 1908), Niederle and Buchtela's *Rukověť české archaeologie* (Handbook of Bohemian Archaeology, Prague, 1910).

Píč burdened his argument, on the one hand with a rejection of the Neolithic, on the other hand with incorrect ethnological reconstructions based on a coincidence of funeral rites. His conception of the Slavonic period was not very strongly influenced by his faith in the false Manuscripts of Dvůr Králové and Zelená Hora; the bitter dispute regarding the genuineness of these manuscripts was nevertheless the main reason why Píč committed suicide, after which the University school had the main say in Czech archaeology. Its chronological and genetic patterns of prehistoric cultures became the basis for a modern system of Bohemian prehistory. The unity of views was reflected also in the first independent congress of Czech archaeologists (Prague, 1912), but the First World War interrupted all activities in this field.

Moravia was not too affected by the in-fighting that went on over Bohemian prehistory. The main emphasis was laid on field investigations and the acquisition of archaeological material. Moravian archaeologists – mostly amateurs and collectors – were grouped in the Moravian Archaeological Club (founded in 1906) around Innocenc Ladislav Červinka (1869-1952) and his periodical *Pravěk* (Prehistoric Times). We cannot speak about this period, however, without mentioning Jaroslav Palliardi (1861-1922), who in his South Moravian excavations was the first to establish the basic Neolithic and Eneolithic chronology in Moravia and in the adjacent Danube area. We should also mention here that the year 1911 saw – with the unearthing of the church foundations in Modrá – the beginning of the famous discoveries of the Great Moravian Empire (ninth century AD).

The fifth phase – *prehistoric analysis* – did not in fact begin until after the First World War, although its foundations were laid by the *Handbook* of 1910. In this period the continuing analysis of increasing amount of source material was directed not just to building a cultural-chronological system of prehistory, but even more to obtaining information about economic and social development. The necessary organizational prerequisities were ensured chiefly by the emergence of an independent Czechoslovak Republic (1918): in 1919 the State Archaeological Institute was established, a centre of scientific research and fieldwork. It was headed by Lubor Niederle, who around this time published several volumes of his life's work *Slovanské starožitnosti* (Slavonic Antiquities) (Prague 1902-34), still one of the basic works of Slavonic archaeology. The institute, later headed by K. Buchtela and from 1939 by Jaroslav Böhm (1901-1962), was in 1952 incorporated into the newly founded Czechoslovak Academy of Science, where it remains today, with research centres, in Prague and Brno.

The National Museum in Prague has remained the centre of Czech museum work, and in Moravia this function has been taken over by the Moravian Museum in Brno. Slovakian museum work was organized mainly after liberation in 1918 and today its centre is the Slovak National Museum in Bratislava.

The training of new specialists considerably increased after 1918, when, in addition to the department of prehistory at Prague University, similar departments were set up in Brno (first Professor Emanuel Šimek, 1883-1963), and in Bratislava. Professors of the Charles University in Prague were usually the main representatives of Czech archaeology: in succession to Niederle this post was held by Albín Stocký (1876-1934), Josef Schránil (1893-1940) and, after the Second World War, Jan Filip (1900-).

Initially the situation in Slovakia was difficult because Slovak archaeology before 1918 had been practically non-existent. The first generation was trained by Professor Jan Eisner (1885-1967) at Bratislava University between the two World Wars. In 1942 the State Archaeological Institute also appeared in Slovakia with Vojtech Budinský-Krička as the first director; later (1953) it became part of the Slovak Academy of Science.

A joint organizational base became available to persons working in this field with the creation in 1919 of the Society of Czechoslovak Prehistorians. In 1956 it was reorganized as the Czechoslovak Archaeological Society of the Czechoslovak Academy of Science.

A brief outline of the fifth phase can, of course, only offer the salient facts and it is clear that it is more in the nature of information rather than any kind of assessment. To complete the picture of the time, however, it is necessary to add that although the rise of independent Czechoslovakia opened up new possibilities for archaeology, the social and financial backing for the needs of research remained at a low level so that archaeology between the wars, having only a very small number of professionals, did not extend beyond the frame of older traditions. It was not until after the Second World War that a rapid development of science took place, the social significance of which is now fully recognized by the socialist state.

But despite all progress made to date, the fact is that the science of prehistory remains in its fifth phase: archaeological research and the process of prehistoric analysis has by no means acquired enough information yet to carry out a consistent prehistoric (or, more accurately, historic) synthesis as the sixth phase of its development. Just when this will come about, remains to be seen: let us hope, however, that when it does come, the contribution of Czechoslovak archaeology will correspond to the working opportunities it presently enjoys.

BIBLIOGRAPHY

A brief selection of works on the history of archaeology in Czechoslovakia, written in a world language or containing a fairly lengthy summary.

General:

SKLENÁŘ K. 1969 Nástin vývoje prehistorického bádání v Čechách do roku 1919 /An Outline of the Development of Prehistoric Research in Bohemia until 1919 – in Czech, with German summary/. Zprávy ČSSA /Bulletin of the Czechoslovak Archaeol. Assoc./ XI: 1-91.

STOCKÝ A. 1924 Le développement de la science préhistorique tchéque. *Anthropologie (Prague)* II, Suppl.: 45-57.

SKUTIL J. 1953 Les débuts de la préhistoire nationale en Tchécoslovaquie. *Bulletin de la Soc. préhist. française* 50: 112-23.

VIGNATIOVÁ J. 1975 Přehled vývoje archeologického bádání na Moravě do začátku XX.stol./Development of Archaeology in Moravia up to the Beginning of 20th Century – in Czech, with German summary/. *Zprávy ČSSA*, XVII: 93-125.

VÝVOJ archeologie v Čechách a na Moravě 1919-1968 /Development of Archaeology in Bohemia and Moravia 1919-1968 – in Czech, with English summary/. *Archeologické studijní materiály* 10/1, 1972 and 10/2, 1975.

Personalities – Institutions:

FILIP J. 1966, 1969 *Enzyklopädisches Handbuch zur Ur- und Frühgeschichte Europas,* I-II. Prague.

NEUSTUPNÝ J. 1968 150th Anniversary of the National Museum in Prague, Czechoslovakia. *Current Anthropology,* 9: 221-224.

SKLENÁŘ K. 1970 Archeologické spisy Josefa Dobrovského a jejich prameny /Archaeological Works of Josef Dobrovský and Their Sources – in Czech, with German summary/. Sborník Národního muzea v Praze /Proceedings of the National Museum in Prague/ A-XXIV: 245-295.

—— 1976 Počátky české archeologie v díle Matyáše Kaliny z Jäthensteinu /The Place of Matthias Kalina of Jäthenstein in the History of Bohemian Archaeology – in Czech, with English summary/. *Sborník Nár. muzea v Praze,* A-XXX: 1-136.

XV
New Zealand Prehistory before 1950

PETER GATHERCOLE

University Museum of Archaeology and Anthropology, University of Cambridge, England

In his book *The Polynesians: Prehistory of an island people*, Bellwood has remarked that 'the period after the Second World War has seen a great increase in the pace of Polynesian research, mainly through the introduction of archaeology and modern linguistic techniques. The older sources such as traditions, comparative ethnology and craniology have now almost entirely given way to these new techniques, and the rate of progress in understanding the Polynesian past has been remarkable' (Bellwood 1978: 18-19). In this paper I shall examine the relevance of Bellwood's remarks to the development of the study of the prehistory of one Polynesian people, the Maoris of New Zealand. Certainly there has been, since 1945, a remarkable growth in archaeology in New Zealand. But important archaeological excavations did occur there in the nineteenth century, and the prehistory of the Maoris was much discussed by interested writers both inside and outside the country. This promising start, however, did not lead immediately or inevitably to the recognition of archaeology as a university subject, and its status within museums was for a long time ambiguous. The point is well illustrated by the fact that although extensive excavations took place as early as the 1870s, no full-time lecturer in prehistoric archaeology was appointed to any of the four university colleges then in existence, until 1954. In that year Jack Golson was appointed to the Department of Anthropology at Auckland University College. To emphasize the significance of this gap, it is worth mentioning that his duties included teaching prehistory as such, not simply that of the Maori or of the South Pacific generally.

This long interval between the initial practice of the subject and its eventual academic recognition might be attributed solely to the fact that New Zealand was a 'new' colonial country, whose settlers had more important subjects in mind when establishing their university, museums and learned societies. This may be so, but the fact remains that 'the whence of the Maori', as a well-known New Zealand historian has recently emphasized (Sorrenson 1977), was a question of wide and persistent interest in the Colony in the nineteenth and early twentieth centuries. Delay in academic recognition, therefore, may have had something to do with the nature of New Zealand society itself. I am concerned as much with this question as with the narrower one of the vicissitudes experienced by archaeology between about 1870 and 1950.

Archaeology began in New Zealand as one way of determining the cultural status of the Moa-hunters. The term was coined by Julius von Haast to describe the people whose material traces had been discovered as early as 1843 in association with bones of the extinct moa. The archaeological evidence comprised mainly stone tools, ovens and middens, the latter often being rich in faunal remains. The controversy that raged in the *Transactions of the New Zealand Institute* between 1871 and 1879 on the age of the Moa-hunter camps, and on the relationship of these ancient hunters to the Maoris, has been extensively discussed by New Zealand scholars (e.g. Duff 1950; Law 1972; Green 1972), and it is unnecessary for me to go over the same ground again. My interest is primarily in the context of the controversy, i.e. in what it did to influence contemporary attitudes towards archaeology, and towards its relationship to other intellectual disciplines, notably ethnology.

The antiquity of the Moa-hunters was established by the fact that, in six recorded instances up to 1870, and numerously in the next decade, there was clear evidence of the association of man-made tools with bones of the extinct moa (Law 1972: 5). Were these first inhabitants Polynesian ancestors of the Maoris, or were they 'autochthones' who arrived at a much earlier time and had no clear links with the Polynesians? Initially von Haast took an extreme position, much influenced by the writings of Lyell and Lubbock on the antiquity of man in Europe. As Green has said: 'Among the ideas he acquired from these sources, the most important for our purposes are (1) the great antiquity of the Moa-hunters, based on their association with an extinct post-Pliocene fauna, (2) a Palaeolithic status based on their use only of crudely chipped stone implements, (3) an association with a wild rather than domestic form of dog, and (4) quite separate origins and perhaps even different races to account for replacement of a Palaeolithic people by a Neolithic group. On all these points he was to be challenged by the evidence of the next eight years...' (Green 1972: 16). Von Haast later modified his view, placing the Moa-hunters within a New Zealand Quaternary period, which could mean 'on analogy with complexes of comparable age in Europe, such as the Danish Peat and Shell Mound People, or even the Swiss Lake Dwellers, that Moa-hunter sites might contain evidence of either domesticated animals or agriculture' (Green 1972: 18). The logic of this argument was that the Moa-hunters need not have been far removed culturally from the Maoris.

As Green and Law have each noted, discussion on the Moa-hunters was couched in language derived from European science and owed much of its form to the nature of archaeological enquiry then prevailing in Europe. This was no doubt inevitable, given the strong influence of European science in New Zealand at the time. This influence was all the more pervasive, and the adoption of European terminology so comprehensive, because it was impossible to explain these archaeological discoveries by reference to ethnology. Mention of the moa in Maori ethnological sources is generally without any form of authenticity, clearly inspired either by the archaeological discoveries themselves or by the willingness of informants to tell their enquirers what they wished to hear (Duff 1950: 290ff). The cultural status of the Moahunters was not determined with any clarity until the 1930s, by which time more sites of greater range in form and content were known. Information available in the 1870s was inadequate and posed questions which could not be answered at that time (Duff 1950: 254ff).

One might have assumed, however, that as archaeology had found ethnology wanting during this controversy, and in the process had forged links with geology, it would have developed on its own. This did not happen. Instead of a growth in archaeological research, there was an overall decline in interest, notably concerning the cultural affinities of the Moa-hunters.

Part of the answer to the question posed at the beginning of this paper is therefore clear. Archaeology began in nineteenth-century New Zealand because certain questions were asked about Maori origins which were prompted by geological and ethnological enquiries. In any case, archaeology was not seen as an independent subject but as a technique useful for clarifying and perhaps answering certain questions. It did not immediately take scholastic root and begin to define and examine pre-European prehistory, nor did it acquire university or museum status. Although amateur excavations continued in various parts of the country, undertaken by certain local groups from time to time, archaeology remained an undeveloped subject.

The main reason for this state of affairs was the successful transplantation of various branches of anthropology to New Zealand, notably ethnology. Since the time of Captain Cook's visits (1769-77), New Zealand has never lacked the interest of Western scholars. It was, and to a degree still is, a new world awaiting description and analysis. After 1840, when it became a Crown Colony, the country attracted many administrators, traders, missionaries and soldiers, and a few professional scientists, who often developed an interest in the ethnology of the native inhabitants. This was, of course, a common experience in colonial societies; the word ethnology admirably subsumed contemporary interest in the origins, customs and beliefs of peoples then being brought under colonial rule in many parts of the world. The intriguing aspect of the Maori case, however, is that the enthusiasm of a number of colonists was so strong and many-sided that an enormous body of anthropological information was rapidly acquired, far more than for any other Polynesian island or group. The range of this information is well indicated in Sorrenson's recent paper (Sorrenson 1977). It included, aside from ethnology, physical anthropology, mythology, folklore and philology. There was much interest in the question of origins, hypothetical or otherwise, but descriptive ethnography was also important. Sorrenson has discussed many of the important writers. They included such men as the missionary Richard Taylor, Governor Sir George Grey, the army surgeon A. S. Thomson, the lawyer John White, and S. Percy Smith, W.E. Gudgeon and Elsdon Best, who were government or military men of various sorts. Not all the material they obtained was published, but enough appeared for it to be generally agreed by about 1880 that Maori ethnology was well known and that it could be regarded as *an independent body of knowledge*, capable of answering most questions about the past. By this process it became part of the accepted world view of the informed New Zealander. The place of archaeology within this phenomenology remained a minor one.

I wish to isolate two stages in the process of bringing Maori ethnology into the colonial consciousness. The first began in 1868 with the foundation of the New Zealand Institute. Among the subjects considered appropriately *practical* for inclusion in its range of interests was ethnology. Following this acceptance into the organized scientific world of the Colony, papers on ethnological subjects were to appear in the Institute's *Transactions* and so receive wide international distribution.

The second stage began in 1892, when twelve men, including Smith, Best, Gudgeon and W.H. Skinner, a surveyor in the Province of Taranaki, gathered in Wellington to found the Polynesian Society. Smith was appointed editor of its *Journal*, a position he was to hold for thirty years.

Much happened to the Maoris between 1868 and 1892, especially with regard to their economic and political power. The second Maori War and the guerilla fighting which followed it ended eventually in the victory of the Colonial government. The basic issue was one of land ownership, but this had profound social, economic and psychological implications. Ever since 1840, there had been widespread concern about the future of the Maoris, not least by themselves, often expressed over their declining numbers. Their estimated population decreased from 100,000 at the time of Cook to 42,100 in 1896, after which it began to recover (Borrie 1959: 249-50). But to many observers the Maoris seemed to be declining in a cultural, if not in a racial, sense. One of the stimuli for the establishment of the Polynesian Society was the need felt to record their ethnology and make it known, before this became little more than an academic and historical pursuit.

However, much ethnological interest towards the end of the nineteenth century was highly abstract, different in scope and style from that of earlier writers. William Colenso, writing in 1865, could be scornful of an uncritical acceptance of traditions. But, as Sorrenson has shown, this attitude did not persist (Sorrenson 1977: 467-70). It is not an exaggeration to say that, around 1890, Maori ethnology became a sort of intellectual plaything among the colonial intelligentsia. Great interest was still being shown in origins, notably by Percy Smith. In 1898-9 he published an interpretation of Polynesian origins called *Hawaiki: the Whence of the Maori*, which claimed, mainly on traditional evidence, that the Polynesians originated ultimately in India. In 1913 and 1915 he followed this with a more explicit account of Maori origins, *The Lore of the Whare Wananga*, based on the accounts of two *tohunga*, Te Matarohanga and Nepia Pohuhu, which set out a more precise history and chronology of Maori settlement. Smith put together the slightly differing tribal accounts of their migrations to New Zealand to make them uniform. Kupe, a traditional ancestor of some tribes, was said to have arrived about AD 950; Toi, another ancestor, about AD 1150, and these were followed in about AD 1350 by a Great Fleet of canoes, transporting the groups from whom the major tribes are descended. Best, and ultimately Smith, accepted the idea that at least some of the first settlers were of Melanesian origin, although their relationship to Kupe and his companions was not clear. It is important to notice that in his paper 'Maori and Maruiwi' (1916), Best identified the North Island Maruiwi with the South Island Maohunters.

Smith and Best accepted *The Lore of the Whare Wananga* without serious criticism and elevated traditions collected in the second half of the nineteenth century into statements of historical facts, without considering possibilities of adulteration or distortion.

This scheme of origins received widespread acceptance by both white and Maori New Zealanders, and still has very considerable popularity. It was neat and definite. It used dates, and spoke of migrations and conquests. Granted earlier writers had also done this, but none so specifically or with such an aura of Maori traditional scholarship at their command. One could almost say that, between them, Smith and Best had Europeanized the 'whence of the Maori'. Indeed, the parallels between the coming of the Maori and that of the European to New Zealand could be construed as remarkably close. Each group had come from far across the seas, and assumed control of the country by virtue of their cultural superiority. Each left their homelands and risked all in order to find new living room, after enduring hardships during the lengthy sea-borne journeys. Each established coastal settlements in a new, unknown land and spread inland, naming features in ways historically familiar to them. Thus, in white eyes, Maoris became latter-day colonists in their own land. If they were a dying race then *The Lore of the Whare Wananga* formed a graceful and wistful epitaph to their settlement of New Zealand, appropriately rescued from oblivion in the nick of time by colonial scholarship.

Later scholars have been very critical of this version of Maori prehistory, though it is worth noting that detailed and thorough reappraisal of these traditions has occurred only recently (Simmons 1976). This has been due partly to the inherent complexity of the subject matter, but there has also been a reluctance to offend Maori sensibilities. Related to these points is the position which ethnology had long enjoyed within the wider structure of New Zealand scientific life. The last point has been latent in my discussion so far, but now needs to be made explicit.

The New Zealand Institute possessed a federal structure. Although modelled to some extent on the British Royal Society (it became the Royal Society of New Zealand in 1933), it was from the start based on autonomous local societies with a membership predominantly of interested amateurs. As Professor Fleming said in his anniversary address in 1967: 'The colonist communities were planned as a cross-section of British society, including educated men who brought an interest in learning, scholarship and enquiry. The separate colonies were distant from each other, communication remained poor, and each had to be self-sufficient' (Fleming 1968: 99). In the nascent urban settlements established in the 1840s and 1850s, there were men who saw the need for topographical, geological, botanical and zoological exploration, and the rapid publication of the results of these enquiries. The first local scientific society which really established itself was the Philosophical Institute of Canterbury, inaugurated in Christchurch in 1862. This and other similar bodies in Auckland, Wellington and Westland were federated in 1867 to form the Institute, set up by Act of the General Assembly. The Otago Institute was admitted in 1869. The New Zealand Institute was established in Wellington, with a library and a Colonial Museum. James Hector, who had been appointed Director of a nationwide Geological Survey in 1865, with its headquarters at the Colonial Meseum, became its Manager.

The other major provinces, Auckland, Canterbury and Otago, were not slow to establish their own museums, which soon became internationally recognized as centres of scientific research. Indeed, von Haast was Director of the Canterbury Museum when he investigated the problem of the Moa-hunters, and the first three curators of the Otago Museum, between 1873 and 1937, were all Fellows of the Royal Society.

The directors of these institutions, however, were natural scientists, who, like von Haast, might have had a serious interest in ethnology and prehistory, but did not consider it necessary to appoint ethnologists to their permanent staffs. Despite the existence of archaeological and ethnological material in their collections, no full-time ethnologist was appointed to a New Zealand museum until 1910, when Elsdon Best, then aged 54, went to the Dominion Museum, Wellington. Indeed, another reason for the establishment of the Polynesian Society in 1892, according to comments made to me by H.D. Skinner, the son of W.H. Skinner, was to try to remedy this lack of interest in ethnology by museums. It took time.

Best's appointment was very beneficial in that he immediately began to publish a long series of detailed monographs in the Museum's *Bulletin* and elsewhere, based on many years' fieldwork. On the other hand, his move to the Dominion Museum emphasized an endemic characteristic in New Zealand scientific and intellectual life. This had always been lively, and not generally remote and 'provincial' as often suggested by visitors. But it *was* provincial in the sense that it continued to be based on the provinces set up after 1840 as one of the instruments of government. Thus many institutions were replicated several times over. This often had very beneficial effects (and still does), but it could also foster isolation and unnecessary rivalries, or enable a powerful group to assume 'national' leadership of a subject without the continual stimulus of outside criticism. It was as difficult to maintain a balance between the provinces in intellectual as in economic and political matters.

The position was noticeably unbalanced in ethnology in the years leading up to the First World War. Smith and Best had very considerable influence in the policies of the Polynesian Society, centred in Wellington. Little archaeology was done except by a few enthusiasts investigating coastal midden sites. One of these enthusiasts was H. D. Skinner, who had explored sites in Taranaki and Nelson as a boy, and in 1910 transferred from Victoria University College, Wellington to Otago University, Dunedin, in order to complete his degree (Freeman 1959; Gathercole, in Skinner 1974). Fascinated by anthropology since boyhood, Skinner took advantage of his discharge from the New Zealand Expeditionary Force in 1915, after being wounded in the Gallipoli campaign, to study at Cambridge under A.C. Haddon. He returned to New Zealand in November 1918, with the opportunity of an appointment as Assistant Ethnologist at the Dominion Museum.

Skinner was well aware of the intense regionalism of New Zealand society. He was also extremely sceptical of the use of traditional evidence in ways propounded by Smith and Best. In Wellington he was destined to be responsible for his work to Best, a man much his senior in age and status but lacking formal academic qualifications. Suddenly Skinner was offered a post at the Otago Museum, a place he knew and liked. He had realized for some time that he would have to challenge the use of traditional evidence as a way of interpreting Maori prehistory, and he was clear that he could do this most effectively away from Wellington. Dunedin had other advantages, too. He could get to many Moa-hunter sites with ease, and even across to the Chatham Islands, whose original inhabitants, the Moriori, had possessed a culture related to that of the Moa-hunters. His dissertation at Cambridge had been on this topic.

In 1923 and 1924 Skinner, who was by then teaching a one-year course in anthropology at Otago, published two papers on the 'Archaeology of Canterbury' in the *Records of the Canterbury Museum*. Thus began his lengthy demonstration 'that Moa-hunter and Moriori were Polynesian in origin on the basis of archaeology, ethnography, physical anthropology, tradition and language' (Green 1972: 19). But Skinner was by predilection and training a comparative ethnologist specializing in the study of material culture, not an archaeologist, however much current attitudes brought them together. At Cambridge his instruction in archaeology had concentrated on the results of Old World discoveries, not on fieldwork methods, an area of research not then much developed. From Haddon and from the American school he had learnt the concept of culture areas, and his paper 'Culture Areas in New Zealand' (1921) was a fine example of the method. But it was never adequately amplified, area by area, in an ethnological sense, in his later published work. He concentrated instead on the study of material culture, and tended to see archaeology primarily as a way of obtaining assemblages of prehistoric artifacts which would both augment and provide contrasting information to ethnological assemblages. The limitations of this approach are obvious to archaeologists today. Skinner himself was well aware of the need to extend archaeological research, and in 1929 D. Teviotdale was appointed as field archaeologist at the Otago Museum, the first appointment of its kind in New Zealand. Skinner also strongly sup orted the work of Lockerbie in Otago, and Duff in Canterbury and Marlborough from the 1930s, which greatly extended knowledge of the Moa-hunters. In later life, when I knew him, Skinner would comment wryly that he knew nothing about stratification, implying that the work then under way, principally by Trotter and Lockerbie in the South Island and by Golson, Green and numerous others in the North Island, was of an order which he had not perceived in earlier decades; also that such work would not have been practicable in the 1920s and 1930s, because resources were then lacking, and, given his ethnological interests, other tactical objectives were more important.

Skinner, however, fully appreciated two points which were very significant for the future. Firstly his defeat of the Smith-Best thesis, notably its Melanesian-Maruiwi aspect, by the use of the evidence of material culture, freed discussion of Maori origins from highly subjective and sometimes racial overtones about Melanesians (and even Aryans). He found it hard to accept my argument that taxonomic studies of artifacts could also be subjective. But this did not materially affect the fact that his work had shifted the area of discussion from one where conclusions were very difficult to substantiate to one where archaeology could increasingly provide confirmatory evidence. The way became clear for the study of Maori and other Polynesian prehistory to be undertaken more on its own terms.

Secondly, Skinner had been well schooled by Haddon, and saw that if archaeology was to grow, it required acceptance within the university system as part of anthropology, however specific to itself its techniques might become. He had foreshadowed this in principle in his call for the establishment of anthropology as a university subject, which appeared as a paper, significantly not in the *Journal of the Polynesian Society* but in the first issue of the *New Zealand Journal of Science and Technology* (Skinner *et al.* 1918). His experience at Otago University between 1920 and 1954, when he retired from teaching, only confirmed this view.

For a number of reasons, however, Skinner decided that his main responsibility was to Otago Museum, of which he became Director in 1938. Although his academic colleagues at Otago University were certainly prepared to accept the teaching of archaeology within his one-year course in anthropology, any extension of that was unlikely, in the prevailing academic climate. There seemed more likelihood of archaeology becoming better established, once the Second World War was over, at one of the university colleges in the North Island, where anthropology could be seen as increasingly relevant to a population which included growing numbers of Maoris and immigrants from other Pacific islands.

By 1950 archaeology had become structurally unbalanced by its history and by intellectual attitudes, both of which had increasingly inhibited its growth. The emphasis in research was still on the study of the Moa-hunters, as was evident from the publication in that year by Roger Duff of the first edition of *The Moa-Hunter Period of Maori Culture.* In the North Island very little research had been undertaken at sites of any period, except by a handful of enthusiasts. It was clear that those interested in archaeology throughout the country needed to be drawn into a national body so that activities by institutions and individuals could be co-ordinated, and government support for such matters as greatly im roved site protection obtained. The first change occurred in 1951 when R.O. Piddington became the first Professor of Anthropology at Auckland University College. He had been one of Malinowski's pupils, and was a perceptive critic of ethnology. The shadows cast by Smith and Best had been long-lived. It required Piddington's appreciation that prehistoric archaeology should be taught within his new department before its structural position could be significantly improved. Teaching began in 1954. The New Zealand Archaeological Association was established in the following year.

Thereafter the study of prehistory was in a better position to free itself from its long association with a concept of Maori ethnology which had both obscured what that prehistory might be, and how archaeological research might be conducted in order to create it.

ACKNOWLEDGMENTS

I would like to thank Professor G.E. Daniel for his forbearance in encouraging the publication of this paper. Thanks are also due to F.W. Shawcross and Dr G. Blake Palmer, who in 1959 first indicated to me the need to study the history of New Zealand prehistory.

BIBLIOGRAPHY

BELLWOOD, P. 1978 *The Polynesians: Prehistory of an island people*. London.

BEST, E. 1916 'Maori and Maruiwi' *Transactions of the New Zealand Institute*, 48: 435-47.

BORRIE, W.D. 1959 'The Maori Population: A Microcosm of a New World', in J.D. Freeman and W.R. Geddes (eds), *Anthropology in the South Seas*, 247-62. New Plymouth.

DUFF, R. 1950 *The Moa-Hunter Period of Maori Culture* (1st edn). Wellington. Printer.

FLEMING, C.A. 1968 'The Royal Society of New Zealand – A Century of Scientific Endeavour', *Transactions of the Royal Society of New Zealand (General)*, 2: 99-144.

FREEMAN, J.D. 1959 'Henry Devenish Skinner: A Memoir', in Freeman and Geddes (see above, under Borrie), 9-27.

GREEN, R.C. 1972 'Moa-hunters, agriculture and changing analogies in New Zealand Prehistory', *New Zealand Archaeological Association Newsletter*, 15: 16-39.

LAW, G. 1972 'Sources of Moas and Moa Hunters', *New Zealand Archaeological Association Newsletter*, 15: 4-15.

SIMMONS, D.R. 1976 *The Great New Zealand Myth: A study of the discovery and origin traditions of the Maori*. Wellington.

SKINNER, H.D. 1921 'Culture Areas in New Zealand', *Journal of the Polynesian Society*, 30: 70-78.

—— 1923 'Archaeology of Canterbury, 1: Moa-bone Point Cave', *Canterbury Museum Records*, 2: 93-104.

—— 1924 'Archaeology of Canterbury, 2: Monck's Cave', *Canterbury Museum Records*, 2: 151-62.

—— 1974 *Comparatively Speaking: Studies in Pacific Material Culture 1921-1972*. Dunedin.

SKINNER, H.D. *et al.* 1918 'Anthropology as a University subject', *New Zealand Journal of Science and Technology*, 1: 257-64.

SMITH, S.P. 1898, 1899 'Hawaiki: the Whence of the Maori', *Journal of the Polynesian Society*, 7: 137-77, 185-223; 8: 1-48.

—— 1913, 1915 *The Lore of the Whare Wananga*. Wellington: Polynesian Society.

SORRENSON, M.P.K. 1977 'The Whence of the Maori: Some Nineteenth Century Exercises in Scientific Method', *Journal of the Polynesian Society*, 86: 449-78

XVI

Indian Archaeology: the first phase, 1784-1861

DILIP K. CHAKRABARTI

University of Delhi, India

Archaeology in India may be said to have begun with the establishment of the Asiatic Society (of Bengal) in Calcutta on January 15,
1784. Its founder, Sir William Jones (1746-1794) had attained considerable fame as a writer and Oriental scholar before coming as a
Supreme Court judge to Calcutta in 1783 (Arberry, 1946). The
professed purpose of the Society was to 'inquire into the history and
antiquities, the arts, sciences and literature of Asia'. An annual publication was proposed and published as *Asiatic Researches*, first in 1788. A
museum was founded in 1814 (Mitra, 1885). Till the organization of
the official Archaeological Survey of India under Alexander Cunningham in 1861 archaeological research in India depended on individual efforts. The purpose of the present paper is to outline these
efforts with emphasis on their interrelationship and theoretical
orientations.

I. *The Asiatic Society in Calcutta*

It was opportune, for two reasons, to found a Society, apparently
modelled on the Royal Society, in 1784 in Calcutta. First, it was
increasingly clear that the original British role of trader in India would
be replaced by that of a territorial ruler. In a sense the time was ripe to
initiate a systematic exploration of the country from various points of
view. In 1793 James Rennel (1793) could write: 'Whatever charges
may be imputable to the Managers for the Company (East India
Company), the neglect of useful science, however, is not among the
number.' About a hundred years later Lord Ripon (1885) could point
out with pride that within less than thirty years of the Battle of Plassey
(1757) which ushered in the British ascendancy in India 'Englishmen
were looking forward with most prophetic eyes to the future which lay
before them, and 'sought to obtain a real and substantial comprehension of the feelings and genius of the people among whom their lot
was to be cast'. It has been suggested that William Jones owed the idea
of the Asiatic Society (of Bengal) to the Society of Arts in Britain.
William Shipley, the founder of the Society of Arts, was related to
Lady Jones and the correspondence between him and Jones 'was, to a

great extent, on a subject which deeply interested Sir William Jones, viz. how far the products of India could be turned to account, for it was with that intent that the Bengal Asiatic Society was founded' (Gibbs, 1885-86: 566). It becomes apparent, if this statement is true, that Jones himself visualized a much wider role for the East India Company.

Secondly, in about this time Western scholarship was more than eager to know about India. For instance, the establishment of the Asiatic Society in Calcutta and the publication of *Asiatic Researches* were greeted effusively by Thomas Maurice (1800: 12-14). The roots of this scholarly interest in India, however, lay deeper than individual instances of effusiveness. To begin with, it must be emphasized that India was never a totally unknown country in the West. The Western contact with India began with the Classical world and continued uninterrupted, albeit dimly, right through the Middle Ages to the period of European advance in the East (cf. Lach, 1968). Writing in 1800 Thomas Maurice (1800: 75-86) could cite not merely D'Anville's *Antiquité Géographique de l'Inde* published in 1775 and some other books of that period but also a Latin folio called *Masseii Historia Indica* dated 1589. Besides, a good amount of travel literature on India was available in Europe in the eighteenth century. The point is that in the eighteenth century the mysteries of India came to be a matter of considerable theoretical interest to Western philosophical thinking. As Poliakov (1971: 183-88) has shown, in their attempt to free themselves of Judaeo-Christian thought many authors turned to India for the origin of culture and religion. The tendency seems to have been quite marked among the French Encyclopaedists. Diderot wrote: 'sciences may be more ancient in India than in Egypt' (Poliakov, 1971: 185). In a letter to the astronomer Jean Bailly, Voltaire almost clinched the issue:

'Finally, Sir, I am convinced that everything has come down to us from the banks of the Ganges, astronomy, astrology, metempsychosis, etc. ...' (Poliakov, 1971: 185).

This mythical image of India also exerted considerable influence on German Romanticism (Wilson, 1964). Even apart from this philosophical element, it may be pointed out that in the second half of the eighteenth century India lay ready for effective European dominance and it is perhaps quite natural that European scholarship would wait eagerly for information and discoveries from India.

II. *Theoretical Roots in the Beginning*

There were two theoretical roots in the beginning and these may be made clear with reference to three authors – James Rennel, William Jones and Thomas Maurice. The first theoretical tradition was that of scientific explorers, particularly surveyors, whose sole aim was not to theorize but to know the country and plot places according to their latitudes and longitudes. James Rennel, F.R.S., 'late Major of Engineers and Surveyor General', as the title page of the third edition of his major work (Rennel, 1793), *Memoir of a map of Hindoostan; or the Mogul Empire* calls him, is a good instance of this tradition. He was knowledgeable enough to state: 'the principal monuments of Hindoo superstition are found in the Peninsula'. In various places of his book there are references to, and brief discussions on, sites: the identification of ancient Pataliputra (Palibothra of the Classical writers) with modern Patna along with a discussion on the confluence of the Son and the Ganges; identification of Ujjayini or Ougein (as he writes) with Ozene of the Periplus and Ptolemy; the 'pagodas' of Ellora (the sculptures of which he thought to be 'early Hindoo' in origin); a mention of the 'site of the very ancient city of Husteenapour', etc. On the site of Gaur in Bengal he (Rennel, 1793: 55-56) offered precise measurements: 'taking the extent of the ruins of Gour at the most reasonable calculation, it is not less than 15 miles in length (extending along the old bank of the Ganges), and from 2 to 3 in breadth'. What is distinctive about these references and discussions by Rennel is that he hardly allows himself to be drawn into speculative exercises. On the ancient monuments he made virtually a single speculative statement: '... to judge from their ancient monuments, they [the Indians] had not carried the imitative arts to anything like the degree of perfection attained by the Greeks and Romans or even by the Egyptians' (Rennel, 1793: xxi-xxii).

Many of the ideas of Sir William Jones have been discussed by his biographers (cf. Cannon, 1964; Mukherjee, 1968). His contribution to Sanskrit studies is well-known, but what is not so well known and appreciated is his basic approach to the study of Indian history and human history in general. The most important source in this connection is the ten 'discourses' he delivered on various topics between 1784 and 1793 (published between 1788 and 1793) before the Asiatic Society as its president. The point to be appreciated first is that in the period when Jones delivered his 'discourses' the Biblical theory of creation was in vogue. There was no doubt about the unitary origin of man from a common ancestor. In this way all branches of human families were linked and likely to show survivals in various spheres of life, which would suggest this common ancestry and spread from a common area. One of the main issues before Jones was to understand these traces of survivals in the Indian context and to demonstrate how ancient India and Indians were linked to the other older human groups in the world. The theme is recurrent in virtually all his 'discourses', and one may easily demonstrate this by referring to a few of them. In the 9th 'discourse' delivered on February 23, 1792, he wrote:

Three sons of the just and virtuous man, whose lineage was preserved from the general inundation, travelled, we are told, as they began to multiply, in three large divisions variously subdivided: the children of Yafet seem, from the traces of Sclavonian names, and the mention of their being enlarged, to have spread themselves far and wide, and to have produced the race, which for want of a correct appellation, we call Tartarian: the colonies formed by the sons of Ham and Shem appear to have been nearly simultaneous; and among those of the latter branch, we find so many names incontestably preserved at this hour in Arabia, that we cannot hesitate in pronouncing them the same people whom hitherto we have denominated Arabs; while the former branch, the most powerful and adventurous of whom were the progeny of Cush, Misr and Rama (names remaining unchanged in Sanscrit, and highly venerated by the Hindus) were in all probability the race I call Indian . . .' (Jones, 1792: 485-86).

The point of original dispersal was considered to be Iran:

'. . . it is no longer probable only, but absolutely certain, that the whole race of man proceeded from Iran as from a centre, whence they migrated at first in three great colonies; and that those three branches grew from a common flock, which had been miraculously preserved in a general convulsion and inundation of this globe' (Jones, 1792: 487).

In the light of this basic premise regarding 'the origin and families of nations' the basic historical issue was to trace similarities between the language, belief and practices of different groups and to determine the common centre and perhaps the routes of dispersal. If Iran was considered the common centre by Jones it was not always thought so by others of his period, but the validity of the basic approach, in the days before evolutionary thinking, was never doubted.

It may be mentioned that Jones' idea of the affinity of Sanskrit with several other ancient languages of the world and his postulate of a common source-language neatly fit in this thought-pattern. In the third 'discourse' delivered on February 2, 1786 he argued that the speakers of Sanskrit

'had an immemorial affinity with the old Persians, Ethiopians and Egyptians, the Phoenicians, Greeks and Tuscans; the Scythians or Goths, and Celts; the Chinese, Japanese and Peruvians; whence, as no reason appears for believing that they were a colony from any one of those nations, or any of those nations from them, we may fairly conclude that they all proceeded from some central country . . .' (Jones, 1788: 430-31).

It has been necessary to emphasize these basic historical linguistic ideas of Jones because these were shared by many of his contemporaries. For instance, Thomas Maurice wrote a 7-volume study of *Indian Antiquities* in which antiquities hardly figured but there were discussions on such issues as the Indian origin of the Druids. Even this supposed Indian connection of the Druids was not an isolated idea. It has been pointed out that the idea originated with Reuben Burrow, an experienced marine surveyor and mathematician, who argued that the position of the Equator was once further north, resulting in a better climate in 'Tartary', Siberia and 'lesser Bukharia', then 'part of the seat of Moses'. The area was inhabited by the Hindus and from there the Hindu religion 'probably spread over the whole earth': in England 'stonehenge is evidently one of the temples of Boodh' (Chakrabarti, 1976). This kind of emphasis on the little known and exotic areas in the midst of central Asia and beyond as at least one of the primary centres of origin of civilization goes, however, beyond Burrow. A general focus on high mountains in this context seems to have been common in the second half of the eighteenth century. Jean Bailly, an astronomer, even suggested Greenland and later on thought more of the Gangetic valley (Poliakov, 1971: 185).

It is in the light of these theories and opinions that some patently wild (from the modern point of view) writings in *Asiatic Researches* make-sense. Francis Wilford, a military engineer, sought to trace the origin of the Nile, among other things, from the Hindu sacred books (Wilford, 1792, 1795). Although Cunningham (1871) wrote patronizingly of Wilford and his theories, one should point out that John Hanning Speke, the discoverer of the source of the Nile, took Wilford seriously enough to incorporate Wilford's conjectural map in his work (1863) on the Nile. The point is that these early writings have to be understood in the background of their theoretical framework which fits in the pre-evolutionary concept of the origin of civilization. This is a point which has not been adequately realized in the context of Indian archaeology.

At this point it may be mentioned that Sir William Jones has been credited with the identification of Classical Palibothra with ancient Pataliputra or modern Patna and thus laying down the foundation of Indian historical geography and archaeology. The point was initially made by Cunningham (1871) and has been repeated by Ray (1953). Jones mentioned this identification in his 10th 'discourse' delivered on February 28, 1793 (Jones, 1795: 10-11). Rennel (1793) discusses this in the third edition of his *Memoir of a Map of Hindoostan* in 1793. Rennel also identified Classical Ozene with ancient Ujjayini in the same work (the first and second editions of this book by Rennel, published in 1788 and 1791 respectively, have not been available to the present author). Besides, Francis Wilford attempted to identify ancient Tagara or modern Ter as early as 1787 (Wilford, 1788). In no case can Jones be credited with laying down the foundation of Indian historical geography and archaeology.

III.   Archaeology till 1830

The first European notice of ancient Indian monuments dates back to the sixteenth and seventeenth centuries. A Portuguese, Garcia de Orta, refers to the rock-out caves of Kanheri, Mandapeshwar and Elephanta, all near Bombay, in his *Coloquios dos Simples e Drogas da*

India, published in Goa in 1563 (Sen, 1949: 343). These caves were visited by the Italian traveller Dr John Francis Gemelli Careri (1695) among others. Careri, in fact, devoted a whole chapter of his work (Sen, 1949) to the description of Kanheri:

'The Pagod or Temple of the Canarin, whereof I intended to give an exact and true account, is one of the greatest wonders in Asia; as well because it is look'd upon as the work of Alexander the Great, as for its extraordinary and incomparable workmanship, which certainly could be undertaken by none but Alexander' (Sen, 1949: 171).

This interpretation notwithstanding, Careri's description of Kanheri is objective and generally accurate.

In 1666 M. de Thevenot, a French traveller, visited Ellora and described it in considerable detail: At Surat I was told great matters of the Pagods of Elora, and therefore I had a mind to see them . . . ' (Sen, 1949: 104). An interesting point to note is that as early as 1666 the rock-cut caves of Ellora were known among the European residents of Surat. Not in all cases, however, were the discussions so detailed and painstaking. Among the casual references one may mention Thomas Coryat's reference in the same period to a 'brasse pillar' in Delhi, supposedly built by Alexander the Great after his victory over 'Porus' (Foster, 1921: 248). This in all probability is the Asokan ironstone pillar. The famous Sun temple of Konarak and the Jagannath (better known in the West as Juggernaut) temple in Puri were important landmarks on the Orissan coast and known as the Black Pagoda and the White Pagoda respectively to the European sailors of the seventeenth century (Mitra, 1968: 3). These references leave no doubt that towards the close of the eighteenth century when proper antiquarian investigations began, monuments and the general archaeological potentialities of India were far from being totally unknown. There is a logical continuity between the isolated seventeenth-century references and investigations taken up consciously at the behest of the Asiatic Society in Calcutta in 1784.

Up to the thirties of the nineteenth century one is hard put to find writings which would be considered strictly archaeological today. There are about three reports on field-discoveries, some descriptions of ancient monuments and occasional notices of sites and monuments in primarily non-archaeological surveys.

The first report on field-discoveries is on the accidental find of some Roman coins near Nellore north of Madras and in the form of a letter from Alexander Davidson (1790), then Governor of the Madras Presidency, to the Asiatic Society in Calcutta. A peasant's plough was 'obstructed by some brick-work: he dug, and discovered the remains of a small Hindu temple, under which a little pot was found with Roman coins and medals of the second century'. Many of these were melted but some reached Davidson. He observed that most of them were in a mint-condition and could hardly have been in circulation, being used either as bullion or as ornaments. The second field-report of this kind was from Jonathan Duncan in Benares and related to the find of 'a stone and marble vessel . . . the one within the other . . . in digging for stones from the subterranean materials of some extensive and ancient buildings in the vicinity of a temple called Sarnauth' (Duncan, 1798). Some human bones were found in the inner vessel, and Duncan realized, from the discovery of a Buddha statue 'found in the same place under ground', that the bones belonged to 'one of the worshippers of Buddha, a set of Indian heretics . . .'. The third field-report of this period concerned the discovery of iron implements, in some megaliths in Malabar (Babington, 1823).

The descriptions of ancient monuments were more frequent. For instance, in the first volume of *Asiatic Researches* William Chambers (1788) wrote on Mahabalipuram and J.H. Harrington (1788) described a cave near Gaya. J. Goldingham (1795, 1798) wrote on Elephanta and Mahabalipuram. C.W. Malet (1799) discussed the caves of Ellora. In 1825 A. Stirling (1825) brought out, perhaps for the first time, the prolific occurrence of temples and other monuments in Orissa. There are many other reports from different parts of India, but they are mostly of a minor kind. The most significant description of an ancient monument in this period was an account of his visit to Ajanta in February 1824 by Lieutenant James Edward Alexander of the 16th Lancers. No European seems to have visited the Ajanta caves before him, but Alexander's account is significant not merely because of this but also because of its rich evocative quality. The rock-cut caves of Ellora were well known by then, but he clearly showed his preference:

'The retired and umbrageous situation of the Adjunta caves, completely secluded from the busy haunts of men, and enclosed with overhanging hills and woods, with a clear stream rushing past them over its rocky bed, evinced a far better and purer taste in those by whom they were excavated, than can be conceded to those who constructed the caverned temples of Ellora, in the face of a low and barren ridge' (Alexander, 1830).

Among the survey reports of this period, undertaken for non-archaeological reasons but containing some useful notices of ancient sites and monuments, two happen to be outstanding. In 1800, only one year after the Battle of Seringapatam which brought Mysore within the fold of British influence, Francis Buchanan was deputed to make an agricultural survey of Mysore. The report was published in 1807 in three volumes (Buchanan, 1807). In 1807 itself he was asked to conduct a statistical survey of the Bengal Presidency, which he did for seven years. The report was submitted in 1816 but published much later, over a length of time and in different parts (cf. Jackson, 1926). In 1830 (Buchanan, 1830) he published a brief account of Bodhgaya. Wherever possible, Buchanan gave objective descriptions of ancient sites, and many of his notices are still useful because many of the details no longer survive in the field.

The second of these surveys was by Colin Mackenzie, done principally in India south of Hyderabad. A military engineer said to be a specialist in the siege of forts, he organized the Survey of India as its first Director General. His own basic survey work was done in the south from about 1783 onwards. The reports were submitted but they have never been published. His collection and documentation of archaeological materials from the south have not been published either, and one knows of him in this field only through what his contemporaries or late contemporaries wrote of his work or collection. It is best to cite Cunningham (1871) on this point:

'His collection of manuscripts and inscriptions is unrivalled for its extent and importance. His drawings of antiquities fill 10 large folio volumes ... To his drawings we partly owe Fergusson's *Tree and Serpent Worship*, and to his collection of manuscripts and inscriptions we are indebted for the greater part of what we at present know of the early history of the southern part of the Peninsula.'

A short sketch of his work may be found in his letter to Sir Alexander Johnston, dated Madras, 1817 (Mackenzie, 1834).

In 1830 Captain Robert Melville Grindlay (1830) published his observations on the sculptures of Ellora. This paper is significant because this seems to be the first publication to try to appreciate Indian sculpture, although according to the yardstick of the Greek Classical excellence.

Without presuming to ascribe to Hindu sculpture the classical purity and elegant proportions of the Grecian chisel, it may not be too much to assert that it displays considerable grandeur of design and intenseness of expression. The muscular powers being less developed in an Indian climate, the Hindu sculptor appears to have resorted to exaggeration to give that energy, which his imagination suggested, but of which he saw no living models; hence all the points of beauty in the human form are overcharged, and the limbs are multiplied to express various attributes and supernatural powers.'

It was also in 1830 that Lieutenant-Colonel James Tod (1830) tried to explain the origin of Indian rock-cut caves:

'We have a right to assume that the cave-worship of the Hindus had the same origin as among the ancient Persians, the Egyptians, and the Greeks, and that these caves were consecrated to rites whose bases were astronomical; and it is fair to infer that this worship originated amongst the Hindus, not confined to India proper, but from remote Scythia, embracing the caves of Bamian, of Jalindra, of Gaya, of Gwalior, of Dhumrar, of Ellora, and of Elephanta.'

One may also mention in passing the report on Chattisgarh by R. Jenkins (1825) and that on Bundelkhand by J. Franklin (1826). These and other reports of this kind contain only marginal information on

the local antiquities but also imply that Indian antiquities were acknowledged items of different regional investigations of this period. In
many cases they contain information which has subsequently been
neglected or lost.

IV.   *Archaeology between 1830 and 1861*

From about 1830 one notes an increase in the number of specifically
archaeological writings. Apart from descriptions of, and observations
on, monuments there is an increasing tendency to report and speculate
on individual sites. There were also some excavations in different parts
of the country. In a sense this was due to the enthusiasm of James
Prinsep (1799-1840) who was the Secretary of the Asiatic Society in
Calcutta in 1832-38. Prinsep came to India as an assistant to the Assay
Master of the Calcutta Mint in 1819. In 1833 he became its Assay
Master but for several years in between he was the Assay Master of the
mint in Benares. Prinsep's attitude to field-studies is apparent from
what he wrote in 1838:

'What the learned world demand of us in India is to be quite certain of our
data, to place the monumental record before them exactly as it now exists,
and to interpret it faithfully and literally' (Prinsep, 1838: 227).

Writing in 1871 Alexander Cunningham (1871) who was closely
associated with him, emphasized that the great point in his character
was his ardent enthusiasm, which 'charmed and melted all who came
in contact with him'. Prinsep's personal influence in making Indian
archaeological work more data-oriented cannot be denied, but his
more significant influence lay in elucidating the historical framework
of ancient India. It may be emphasized that the first major interest in
Indian studies lay not in field-archaeology but in editing ancient texts
and deciphering ancient inscriptions. Only the textual and inscriptional studies could lead to an understandable and dependable framework of ancient Indian chronology. The point was clearly brought out
by H.T. Colebrooke in 1807:

'In the scarcity of authentic materials for the ancient, and even for the
modern, history of the Hindu race, importance is justly attached to all
genuine monuments, and especially inscriptions on stone and metal, which
are occasionally discovered through various accidents. If these be carefully
preserved and diligently examined, and the facts ascertained from them be
judiciously employed towards elucidating the scattered information, which
can be yet collected from the remains of Indian literature, a satisfactory
progress may be finally made investigating the history of the Hindus'
(Colebrooke, 1807).

The process of deciphering the inscriptions began with Charles
Wilkins who with his knowledge of late mediaeval Bengali and *Nagari*
scripts acquired through a study of manuscripts first read a ninth-

century copper-plate inscription from Bihar and then a ninth/tenth century pillar inscription from Bengal (Wilkins, 1788a, 1788b). The issue then became one of proceeding from the known to the unknown, and the process culminated in Prinsep's reading of the Mauryan inscriptions of the third century BC. by 1838 (Prinsep, 1838). Prinsep also significantly contributed to the reading of the contemporary *Kharosthi* script, principally confined to the northwest. Sircar (1976) has pointed out that the south Indian inscriptions, too, were deciphered at about this time. The reading of the inscriptions led to two major things in historical studies. First, it was now possible to establish correlations between inscriptional data and the textual informations which had been steadily piling up since the establishment of the Asiatic Society. Secondly, the new-found ability to read early inscribed coins resulted in a systematic interest in numismatics. Till the inscriptions were read and the coins understood there could not be a serious interest in field-archaeology in India, a country with prominent historical remains. It is hardly surprising that from about 1830 onwards the number of Indian archaeological writings was on the increase.

The lines of archaeological enquiry between 1830 and 1861 were basically in the following directions: the opening of 'topes' or Buddhist *stupas* in the northwest and the resultant increase in interest in the northwestern antiquities, principally Indo-Greek and other contemporary coins; a gradually increasing number of notices of ancient sites throughout the country; occasional excavations in north India; a significant amount of 'barrow-hunting' in the south, and finally a greater realization of the need of a systematic survey.

The principal impetus to the opening of 'topes' in the northwest was provided by a general in Ranjit Singh's army, M. le Chevalier Ventura. He opened the Manikyala *stupa* in Panjab in 1830. His methods and the result can be best appreciated in Prinsep's report on his work (Prinsep, 1834a):

'The excavation was commenced on the 27th April, 1830, at the very bottom of the cupola on the south side, where having met with nothing but loose materials, the work was of necessity discontinued. On the 28th April, the cap of the cupola was laid open, and there at the depth of three feet, six medals (or coins) were discovered. On the 1st May, at the depth of twelve feet, a square mass of masonry was found, exactly in the centre of the mound, and regularly built of quarried stones, in very good preservation. On piercing ten feet into this, a medal was found in the middle of a clod of earth. On the 6th, a silver coin and six copper coins were met with at the depth of twenty feet. ... On the 8th May, the workmen came upon a box of iron [probably copper] which was broken by a stroke of the pick-axe. There was in this box a second smaller box of pure gold... On the 12th May, the perforation had reached thirty-six feet, when another coin presented itself. On the 22nd May, as it was imagined that nothing more would be found in the centre of the cupola, on account of the termination of the square building, an opening was made on the northern side, of the height of six feet and twelve broad. The excavations were pushed forward at both points. On the 25th May, a depth of 45 feet had been attained, when on lifting up a large quarried stone, another similarly squared stone was found underneath, having in its centre a round hole; in the middle of this hole lay deposited a copper box, somewhat similar in form to the gold one just described...' (Prinsep 1834a: 315)

The finds from this stupa which belonged to the early centuries AD were described by Prinsep in detail (Prinsep, 1834b, 1834c, 1834d). A. Court, an engineer in Ranjit Singh's army, gave further information on this stupa and thought it a 'royal tomb' (Court, 1834).

Lieutenant Alexander Burnes of the Bombay Army, seeking 'the topes and Grecian remains in the Panjab', found himself referred from place to place 'like one in search of the philosopher's stone' (Burnes, 1833). He also thought that these *stupas* were royal tombs, 'either the sepulchres of the Bactrian Dynasty or their Indo-Scythic successors'. However, in his note on Burnes' collection of ancient coins Prinsep pointed out that these remains were Buddhist monuments. The search led to Afghanistan where J.G. Gerard (1834) and Charles Masson (1834, 1842) left their marks. The search for coins and other antiquities obviously reached a high pitch, and nowhere is it more apparent than in a letter from Masson to Gerard (Masson, 1834), dated Tattung, March 22, 1834: 'My search for coins at this place has been very unsuccessful; I look forward, however, to a glorious stock from Kabul this year, and only hope that my competitors may not raise the market too high for me.'

One of the most evocative descriptions of 'stupa-hunting' has been given by Major Herbert B. Edwardes of the 1st Bengal European Fusilier Regiment (Edwardes, 1851, vol. I: 336-37) in connection with his notice of the mound of Akra in the southwestern corner of the valley of Bannu. Akra was, in fact, a cluster of mounds and the following report relates to the investigation of one of the outlying ones:

'During the first Bunnoo expedition, in 1847, we were encamped here; and General Cortlandt's sappers dug some way into this outward mound, and came, at a considerable depth, to a small circular chamber, made of large and beautifully-burnt bricks, in which there were some human bones, but nothing to give any clue to their history.

'Rain fell very heavily about the same time, and laid bare a very large quantity of copper coins, which the soldiers amused themselves by picking up, and brought to General Cortlandt and myself. They were generally dreadfully battered and effaced, but on most of them a few Greek and Bactrian letters were very plainly traceable. Some were very perfect indeed, and the raised figures on others, although nearly rubbed level with the surface, could be recognized as corresponding with many better specimens which General Cortlandt had collected in Huzaruh, the Salt Range, and other parts of the Punjab, all over which the Macedonian footsteps are more thickly and ineffaceably trodden in than is, I believe, generally known in England.'

In 1834 P.T. Cautley, an irrigation engineer, was the first to appreciate the broad stratigraphy of an ancient site, Behat, near Saharanpur in the *Doab*, 17 ft below the present surface of the country and upwards of 25 ft below that of the modern town of Behat. Both in this and a subsequent publication he attached considerable significance to the understanding of the location of the site in relation to its contemporary landform. What lends Cautley's work (Cautley, 1834a, 1834b) further significance is Prinsep's dating of the site in the early centuries AD on the basis of the numismatic evidence (Prinsep, 1834e).

Reports on ancient sites came pouring in now, and it is impossible to refer to all of them. In all cases they either drew attention to a monument or suggested the archaeological potential of a site. Edward Conolly (1837), for instance, observed 'upon the past and present conditions of Oujein or Ujjayini'. He points out that the beggars of the town used to collect miscellaneous antiquities ('glass', stone and wooden beads, small jewels of little value, seals ... and a few women's ornaments') and try to sell them to the passing Europeans. Excavations of any kind were rare in north India and conformed to the following notice by Markham Kittoe:

'I have been for the past week engaged at Poonah and Koorkihar; at the former place I excavated round the Buddha temple, took a correct drawing of the very elaborate north doorway and of several idols, a sketch of the entire building and a ground plan. This occupied three days, together with sundry excursions in search of sculptures, etc. I was four days at Koorkihar, and have dug out and collected ten cart loads of idols, all Buddhist' (Kittoe, 1848).

In about the same period A.F. Bellasis (1856a, 1856b) excavated the early historic site of Brahminabad in Sind: 'We had not commenced many minutes before we came upon the edge of a wall: clearing it, we soon came upon a cross wall, and then upon another, until a house with a variety of rooms began fast to take shape, and disclose its proportions' (Bellasis, 1856a). Incidentally, Bellasis provides a graphic description of this ancient site and his general concern with a horizontal exposure antedates in a way John Marshall's much later work in India. An important early writing on Sind is by H.B.E. Frere (1854) who gives information on the megaliths of that region. In the context of Rajasthan, James Tod (1829, 1832) must be mentioned but he never got beyond the description of monuments. The proper architectural study of Indian monuments was, however, initiated by James Fergusson in his *Rock-cut Temples of India* (Fergusson, 1845). An Indigo-planter, Fergusson retired from business to study ancient Indian architecture and toured India between 1835 and 1845 to visit monuments. His basic achievement was the application of the concept of typological evolution in the context of Indian architecture. Fergusson was not an archaeologist in our sense, but to him should go the credit of systematizing the study of ancient Indian monuments

(Allchin, 1961). The work on the *stupas* in the northwest and Afghanistan was comprehensively discussed by H.H. Wilson, mainly on the basis of Charles Masson's work, in 1841 (Wilson, 1841).

It seems that the 'barrow-hunting' in the south became a pleasant pastime in the cool of the Nilgiris. Captain Henry Harkness's description in 1832 (Harkness, 1832) leaves no doubt on this point. This perhaps is the earliest description of this kind in India:

'It was now the month of March; the frost and extreme cold had been succeeded by a milder degree of temperature, and we proposed to pass a few days in our tents, proceeding in the first instance to Caroni, a hill about three or four miles south of Oatacamund. On this hill were some stone circles . . . We opened a central circle, and on clearing away the inner surface . . . came to a pavement, consisting of large flags, which being removed, we found another pavement of smaller stones, but of the same rude description. Below these was a layer of brownish black mould, about two feet in depth, intermixed with pieces of broken earthen pots, bits of charcoal, broken fragments of earthen images of the buffaloe, and with other soil of a blacker and finer kind than that which formed the principal component of the whole. Immediately below the black mould, about three feet from the natural surface, we came to a stratum of strong argillaceous soil, corresponding with what is usually found at the same depth in most parts of the hills . . . Not quite satisfied with our first experiment, we removed with our little working party to a much higher hill . . .' (Harkness, 1832: 35-36).

Captain Meadows Taylor's subsequent work at Jiwarji in the Deccan is in the same tradition but described in detail with a section:

'The second cairn examined had a double ring of stones measuring 16 ft. in diameter, with 4 ft. on each side, total 24 ft. The excavation was begun at the upright stones above the ground in the southwest side, and a little below them were two large pieces of trap-rock. The loose stones continued to a depth of three ft., after which morum [gravel] and earth to a depth of five ft. 2 ins., making in all eight ft. In the centre of the excavation the remains of a human body were found . . . on the west and east sides of the body were the usual small earthen pots etc . . . . With these were the remains of three spearheads of iron much decayed, but still distinguishable in form' (Taylor, 1851: 189).

Away from the barrow-digging in the south, Alexander Cunningham, basically a military surveyor and engineer (Imam, 1963, 1966) who was a close associate of James Prinsep, was thinking of a systematic archaeological survey at the government initiative. His primary work did not begin till the establishment of the Archaeological Survey of India in 1861 under his own charge, but it is clear from two of his pre-1861 publications that his whole approach to Indian field-archaeology was formulated in this period. The first of these publications was in 1843 when he reported on the identification of the ancient site of Sankisa. His main basis was the Chinese pilgrim travel accounts of Fa-Hien and Hiuen-Tsang, although in the case of Sankisa it was Fa-Hien who mattered. He believed in traversing the routes of these Chinese pilgrims who visited India in the fourth and seventh centuries AD respectively, and so identifying all the ancient sites mentioned by them. The Chinese accounts were detailed and would help in building up a reliable historical geography of India. In 1848 Cunningham wrote of the need for a systematic archaeological investigation in which the elucidation of historical geography on the basis of the Chinese pilgrim accounts would be an important part. 'As Pliny in his Eastern Geography follows the route of Alexander, so an enquirier into Indian archaeology should tread in the footsteps of the Chinese pilgrims Hwan Thsang and Fa-Hian' (Cunningham, 1848). Interestingly enough, Cunningham (1843) thought that 'the cave-temples of Ajanta and Ellora possess invaluable treasures hidden in the small stupas which most of them have in the interior. To open these, and to search out all the Buddhistical ruins in India, would be the works of the greatest interest and importance.' With Cunningham and the beginning of his government-sponsored archaeological survey in 1861 ends the first phase of Indian archaeology when archaeology in India was exclusively a matter of individual efforts.

V.   Summary

Some seventeenth-century European travellers in India wrote on Indian monuments, but the foundation of Indian archaeology was laid only with the establishment of the Asiatic Society in Calcutta in 1784. The Society derived impetus both from the growing British ascendancy and the contemporary western scholarly interest in India as a possible source of culture and civilization. There were two theoretical roots in the beginning. On the one hand were surveyors and explorers like James Rennel interested only in plotting sites and accurate field-observations and on the other were scholars like William Jones whose basic problem was to link the history of India to the other early centres of civilization in the light of the Biblical theory of creation. There was not much archaeology till about 1830, just a few notices of field-discoveries, monuments and sites. It was only with the decipherment of early scripts and the consequent clear understanding of the historical framework that the search for sites and antiquities could take a more clear shape. There was a significant increase in the number of discoveries all over India from about 1830. The Buddhist sites and antiquities in the northwest were discovered and appreciated for the first time, along with an interest in the Mediterranean contact of this region. There were occasional excavations of the stupas in the north, but the opening up of the megaliths seems to be more frequent in the south. By 1850 the need for a systematic survey was felt and the Government of India decision to establish an Archaeological Survey in 1861 was in response to this need. It must be emphasized that by the time the Archaeological Survey of India was established the basic

nature of the monuments and historical sites in India was well understood. F.R. Allchin (1961) in his brief survey of the ideas of history in
Indian archaeological writing comes to the same conclusion. He also
argues that the archaeology of Indian civilization reached a definite
pattern by 1850 and that this pattern was embodied in Cunningham's
later work in the Archaeological Survey of India. The growth of
prehistory had to wait till the first discovery of palaeoliths in Madras
by Robert Bruce Foote in 1863, although one finds T.J. Newbold
writing on the ash-mounds (neolithic) in the south as early as 1836
(Newbold, 1836, 1843). From about 1850, if not earlier, 'worked
flints', copper implements, etc. were being reported from various parts
of the country. No less a person than J. Evans discussed some 'worked
flints' from around Jubbalpore in central India as early as 1853
(Dasgupta, 1931), but the significance of these discoveries could not
obviously be understood till 1859.

BIBLIOGRAPHY

Abbreviations

AR   Asiatic Researches
JASB   Journal of the Asiatic Society of Bengal
JBRAS   Journal of the Bombay Branch of the Royal Asiatic Society
JRAS   Journal of the Royal Asiatic Society
JSA   Journal of the Society of Arts
TLSB   Transactions of the Literary Society of Bombay
TRAS   Transactions of the Royal Asiatic Society

ALEXANDER, J.E. 1830 Notice of a visit to the cavern temples of Adjunta in the East Indies, *TRAS* 2: 362-70.

ALLCHIN, F.R. 1961 Ideas of history in Indian archaeological writing: a preliminary study, in C.H. Philips (ed.) *Historians of India, Pakistan and Ceylon* 241-59, London.

ARBERRY, A.J. 1946 *Asiatic Jones*. London.

BABINGTON, J. 1823 Description of the Pandoo Coolies in Malabar, *TLSB*, : 324-30.

BELLASIS, A.F. 1856a An account of the ancient and ruined city of Brahminabad in Sind, *JBRAS* 5: 413-25.

—— 1856b Further observations on the ruined city of Brahminabad in Sind, *JBRAS* 5: 467-77.

BUCHANAN, F. 1807 *A Journey from Madras*. 3 vols. London.

—— 1830 Description of the ruins of Buddha Gaya, *TRAS* 2: 40-51.

BURNES, A. 1833 On the 'topes' and Grecian remains in the Punjab, *JASB* 2: 308-10.

CANNON, G. 1964 *Oriental Jones* New Delhi.

CAUTLEY, P.T. 1834a Discovery of an ancient town near Behut, in the Doab, *JASB* 3: 43-44.

—— 1834b Further account of the remains of an ancient town, discovered at Behut, near Saharanpur, *JASB* 3: 221-27.

CHAKRABARTI, D.K. 1976 India and the Druids *Antiquity* 50: 66-67.

CHAMBERS, W. 1788 Some account of the sculptures and ruins at Mahabalipuram, a place a few miles north of Sadras, and known to seamen by the name of Seven Pagodas, *AR* 1: 145-70.

COLEBROOKE, H.T. 1807 On ancient monuments containing Sanskrit inscriptions, *AR* 9: 398-445.

CONOLLY, E. 1837 Observations upon the past and present condition of Oujein or Ujjayini, *JASB* 6: 813-56.

COURT, A. 1834 Further information on the topes of Manikyala, being the translation of an extract from a manuscript memoir on ancient Taxila, *JASB* 3: 556-62.

CUNNINGHAM, A. 1843 An account of the discovery of the ruins of the Buddhist city of Samkassa, *JRAS* 5: 241-47.

—— 1848 Proposed archaeological investigation, *JASB* 17: 535-36.

—— 1871 Introduction, *Archaeological Survey of*

India. Four Reports Made during the Years 1862-63-64-65 (Simla).

DASGUPTA, H.C. 1931 Bibliography of Indian prehistoric antiquities, *JASB* 27: 1-96.

DAVIDSON, A. 1790 On some Roman coins found at Nelore, *AR* 2: 331.

DUNCAN, J. 1798 An account of the discovery of two urns in the vicinity of Benares, *AR* 5: 131-32.

EDWARDES, H.B. 1851 *A Year on the Punjab Frontier in 1848-49.* Vol. 1 London.

FERGUSSON, J. 1845 *Rock-Cut Temples of India* London.

FOSTER, W. (ed.) 1921 *Early Travels in India, 1583-1619* London.

FRANKLIN, J. 1826 Memoir on Bundelkhand, *TRAS* 1: 259-81.

FRERE, H.B.E. 1854 Descriptive notices of antiquities in Sind, *JBRAS* 5: 349-62.

GERARD, J.G. 1834 Memoir on the topes and antiquities of Afghanistan. *JASB* 3: 321-29.

GIBBS, J. 1885-86 The history of archaeology in India, *JSA* 34: 555-68.

GOLDINGHAM, J. 1795 Some account of the cave in the island of Elephanta, *AR* 4: 409-17.

—— 1798 Some account of the sculptures at Mahabalipooram; usually called the Seven Pagodas, *AR* 5: 69-80.

GRINDLAY, R.M. 1830 Observations on the sculptures in the cave temples of Ellora, *TRAS* 2: 487-90.

HARKNESS, H. 1832 *A Description of a Singular Aboriginal Race Inhabiting the Summit of the Neilgherry Hills, or the Blue Mountains of Coimbatour, in the Southern Peninsula of India.* London.

HARRINGTON, J. 1788 A description of a cave near Gaya, *AR* 1: 276-78.

IMAM, A. 1963 Sir Alexander Cunningham (1814-1893): the first phase of Indian archaeology, *JRAS* 105: 194-207.

—— 1966 *Sir Alexander Cunningham and the Beginnings of Indian Archaeology.* Dacca.

JACKSON, V.H. 1926 *Journal of Francis Buchanan (afterwards Hamilton), Kept during the Survey of the Districts of Patna and Gaya in 1811-1812.* Patna.

JENKINS, R. 1825 Account of ancient Hindu remains in Chattisgher, *AR* 15: 499-515.

JONES, W. 1788 The third anniversary discourse, *AR* 1: 415-31.

—— 1792 On the origin and families of nations, *AR* 3: 479-92.

KITTOE, M. 1848 Extract of a letter from Captain Kittoe, *JASB* 17: 234-36.

LACH, D.F. 1968 *India in the Eyes of Europe, the Sixteenth Century.* Chicago.

MACKENZIE, C. 1834 Biographical sketch, *JRAS* 1: 333-64.

MALET, C.W. 1799 Description of the caves or

excavations, on the mountain, about a mile to the eastward of the town of Ellora, *AR* 6: 389-423.

MASSON, C. 1834 Extracts from Mr Masson's letter to Dr J.G. Gerard, on the excavation of topes, dated Tattung, 22 March, 1834, *JASB* 3: 329-32.

—— 1842 *Narrative of Various Journeys in Baluchistan, Afghanistan and the Punjab Including a Residence in Those Countries from 1826 to 1838,* Vol. 1: London.

MAURICE, T. 1800 *Indian Antiquities,* Vol. 1. London.

MITRA, R.L. 1885 History of the Society, in *Centenary Review of the Asiatic Society of Bengal:* 1-81 (Calcutta).

MUKHERJEE, S.N. 1968 *Sir William Jones: a Study in Eighteenth Century British Attitudes to India:* Cambridge.

NEWBOLD, T.J. 1836 Note on the occurrence of volcanic scoria in the southern peninsula, *JASB* 5: 670-71.

—— 1843 On some ancient mounds of scorious ashes in southern India, *JRAS* 7: 129-36.

POLIAKOV, L. 1974 *The Aryan Myth, a History of Racist and Nationalist Ideas in Europe.* London.

PRINSEP, J. 1834a On the coins and relics discovered by M. le Chevalier Ventura, General in the service of Maha Raja Runjeet Singh, in the tope of Manikyala, *JASB* 3: 313-20.

—— 1834b Continuation of observations on the coins and relics, discovered by General Ventura, in the tope of Manikyala, *JASB* 3: 436-56.

—— 1834c Note on the coins discovered by M. Court, *JASB* 3: 562-67.

—— 1834d Note on the brown liquid, contained in the cylinders from Manikyala, *JASB* 3: 567-76.

—— 1834e Note on the coins found by Captain Cautley at Behut, *JASB* 3: 227-28.

—— 1838 On the edicts of Piyadasi or Asoka, the Buddhist monarch of India, preserved on the Girnar rock in the Gujarat peninsula, and on the Dhauli rock in Cuttack; with the discovery of Ptolemy's name therein, *JASB* 7: 219-82.

RAY, S. 1953 Indian archaeology from Jones to Marshall (1784-1902), *Ancient India* 9: 4-28.

RENNEL, J. 1793 *Memoir of a Map of Hindoostan; or the Mogul Empire (3rd edn).* London.

RIPON, LORD. 1885 Speech, in *Centenary Review of the Asiatic Society of Bengal from 1784 to 1883:* 8-11 Calcutta.

SEN, S. 1949 *Indian Travels of Thevenot and Careri.* New Delhi.

SIRCAR, D.C. 1976 Epigraphical studies in India: some observations, *Studies in Indian Epigraphy* 3: 9-25.

SPEKE, J.H. 1863 *Journal of the Discovery of the Source of the Nile*. London.

STIRLING, A. 1825 *An account, geographical, statistical and Historical of Orissa Proper, or Cuttack*, *AR* 15: 163-338.

TAYLOR, M. 1856 Ancient remains at the village of Jiwarji near Farozabad on the Bhima, *JBRAS*, 3: 179-93.

TOD, J. 1829 *Annals and Antiquities of Rajasthan*, Vol. 1. London.

—— 1830 Remarks on certain sculptures in the cave temples of Ellora, *TRAS* 2: 328-39.

—— 1832 *Annals and Antiquities of Rajasthan*, Vol. 2. London.

WILFORD, F. 1788 Remarks on the city of Tagara, *AR* 1: 369-75.

—— 1792 On Egypt and other countries adjacent to the Cali river, or Nile of Ethiopia from the ancient books of the Hindus, *AR* 3: 295-468.

—— 1795 A dissertation on Semiramis, the origin of Mecca etc. from the Hindu sacred books, *AR* 4: 363-84.

WILKINS, C. 1788a A royal grant of land, engraved on a copper plate, bearing date twenty-three years before Christ, and discovered among the ruins at Mongueer, *AR* 1: 123-30.

—— 1788b An inscription on a pillar near Buddal, *AR* 1: 131-44.

WILSON, A.L. 1964 *A Mythical Image : the ideal of India in German Romanticism*.

WILSON, H.H. 1841 *Ariana Antiqua*. London.

XVII
Summary and conclusions
STUART PIGGOTT
Professor Emeritus of Archaeology at the University of Edinburgh, Scotland

When trying to form some personal conclusions on the main themes expressed in the papers presented here there came to my mind two great scholars, neither of them archaeologists, whose thinking has profoundly influenced my own attitude to the history of archaeology. The first is the late Basil Willey, a profound and perceptive student of English literature, and the second that distinguished art historian, Sir Ernst Gombrich. Both, in their respective fields, were concerned with related problems in the history of ideas that are shared by us in the study of the history of archaeology, which may be summed up in two words, explanations and requirements, demanded and satisfied in ways which changed as the contemporary temper of thought and emotion sought new objectives or found old concepts unsatisfactory.

Willey (writing now nearly half a century ago) was concerned with understanding a phase of thought that is in fact closely connected with the beginnings of archaeology in Western Europe, the new scientific approach which in England is associated with the name of Francis Bacon, the phenomenon of the Intellectual Revolution in the later seventeenth century and the founding of the Royal Society. The traditional medieval world-picture of Aristotle and the Schoolmen was failing to give intellectual satisfaction and emotional assurance, and a new 'truth' and a new 'explanation' were sought. 'An explanation "explains" best', wrote Willey, 'when it meets some need of our nature, some deep-seated demand for assurance. "Explanation" may perhaps be roughly defined as a re-statement of something – event, theory, doctrine, etc. – in terms of the current interests and assumptions. It satisfies, as explanation, because it appeals to that particular set of assumptions, as superseding those of a past age or of a former state of mind.' (*The Seventeenth Century Background* (1934), Chap. I). What Willey said of the seventeenth century can equally be applied to any period, and in archaeology for instance we have only to look back a decade or two to see how the emergence of the 'New Archaeology' in America was the outcome of exactly such a process of re-statement 'in terms of the current interests and assumptions' of the 1960s. Indeed, farther back in the history of our subject, the same need of a new 'explanation' for the past led to the enthusiastic welcome of Romanticism and Druids once the appeal of the empirical and scientific approach was waning in the eighteenth century.

To this useful concept of changing 'truths' and 'explanations' demanded in archaeology and prehistory, we can now usefully add Gombrich's perception of 'requirement' – in this instance in the field of pictorial art but of wider application. He pointed out that any pictorial representation 'is not a faithful record of a visual experience but the faithful construction of a pictorial model. Neither the subjectivity of vision nor the sway of conventions need lead us to deny that such a model can be constructed to any required degree of accuracy. What is decisive here is clearly the word "required". The form of a representation cannot be divorced from its purpose and the requirements of the society in which the given visual language gains currency.' (*Art and Illusion* (1960), 90). And so in the history of archaeology: the 'requirements' of the earlier nineteenth century were not those of Pitt-Rivers; those of the earlier twentieth century did not include Thiessen polygons. As Jacquetta Hawkes said of Stonehenge, every age gets the archaeology it deserves – or desires.

It is with the English philosopher-archaeologist R.G. Collingwood that we associate the ideas not only of an excavation properly proceeding on the principle of question and answer, of problems posed and techniques devised and applied in the hope of their elucidation, but behind this the concept of there being an unattainable past-in-itself and a series of pasts-as-known, the knowledge depending on the questioner and the intellectual framework in which his objectives are conceived. To this several of us have in recent years added a third past, the past-as-wished-for; the Stonehenge desired. I am happy to put on record (I think for the first time in print) that we owe this felicitous phrase to Glyn Daniel, who first used it in an informal public lecture in the late 1950s, since when it has gained deserved (if unacknowledged) currency. It is of course in this insidious emotional, rather than intellectual concept that the past is not only manipulated, but manufactured, when the forgeries of which he has written in his chapter, such as the Piltdown Skull, are produced, and in which at the present day we have the ready acceptance by the credulous of the psychologically reassuring myths of charlatans.

If we review the contributions to the history of archaeology set out in this book in terms of a chronicle of changing requirements, explanations and views of the past attainable within the climate of thought of the times, we see not only an internal consistency, but avoid the latent historical fallacy of looking at the past from our own viewpoint and judging it accordingly. Of course Thomsen or Montelius did not see the evidence of bronze implements as we see it today; Schliemann did not dig Troy as Sir Mortimer Wheeler might have done. But to quote

Collingwood again, if we do make comparisons of this sort we should remember that 'Bach was not trying to write like Beethoven and failing; Athens was not a relatively unsuccessful attempt to produce Rome' (*The Idea of History* (1946), 329).

When the miraculous was acceptable as an explanation for antiquities, as for so much else, the accommodatingly fertile soil of Poland burgeoned with self-generated pots 'by the art of nature alone', as Abramowicz shows: with natural processes not themselves understood this was reasonable enough in the fifteenth century. In seventeenth-century England barbed-and-tanged flint arrowheads were widely thought to be natural rather than artificially 'formed stones' within a misunderstood taxonomy, and Ole Worm in Denmark had difficulty in making up his mind; but as the chapters by Rodden, Gräslund and the late Ole Klindt-Jensen demonstrate, the status of stone tools once established by ethnographic comparison, the way was open to the construction of theoretical classificatory systems wherein antiquities of other inorganic substances could be arranged. Some sort of a 'three ages' system defined technologically in terms of the materials used for edge-tools had often been envisaged from classical times onwards, but Thomsen was the first to actually demonstrate an originally theoretical model by the use of associated finds. It was original, though within the current views of an archaeological development as a uniform pattern consonant with geological thinking, and possible in a geographical area where internal development from prehistory into the Middle Ages was uninterrupted by the Romans, and where in Copenhagen there was a museum of outstanding completeness. In a nineteenth century increasingly affected by often misunderstood and simplistic versions of biological evolutionary theory such an ordering of archaeological material found welcome acceptance, and it has been suggested that Sir William Wilde's arrangement and cataloguing of antiquities in the museum of the Royal Irish Academy in 1857-61 on an 'Animal, Vegetable, Mineral' system inspired General Pitt-Rivers's interest in archaeological typology (M.W. Thompson, *General Pitt-Rivers* (1977), 113). On the other hand, the name of Sir William's famous son Oscar (shared, through Napoleon and Bernadotte, with the Swedish Royal House, Montelius and the elder Almgren) reminds us not only of the Romantic 'requirement' in eighteenth-century archaeology, but of the past-as-wished-for that produced not only the forgery of Macpherson's Ossian poems (with Oscar as a hero), but as Sklenář records here, the comparable invented 'ancient Slav' poems of the early nineteenth century in Central Europe.

The growth of nation states and the re-alignment of political boundaries in the last century gave an emotional assurance to a search for one's prehistoric ancestors, and with this an optimistic belief in what seemed the great potential of skull measurements: the ethnic explanatory model. Looking at Schliemann and Virchow in the Germany of their time, Herrmann stresses that one of the former's problems at Troy was that, unlike the known prehistoric settlements of middle Europe it was not flat, but disconcertingly three-dimensional, and so demanding new techniques of attack. In parenthesis, I wonder whether the late development of 'post-hole archaeology' and the investigation of prehistoric settlement in Britain may have been partly the result of there being in the field too many demonstrably three-dimensional monuments like barrows or hill-forts, encouraging sectional excavation, together with an insular failure to appreciate and apply the techniques for recovering lost wooden structures worked out on the Roman *limes* by German archaeologists at the beginning of this century. On the Continent, prehistoric sites were soon to be examined in like manner by many excavators, including Gerhard Bersu, who then personally demonstrated his skill at Little Woodbury in the late 1930s.

Again as part of a changing climate of thought and emotion, settlement archaeology has taken on an added dimension, not only seen as valuable and necessary in itself, but acquiring a new respectability in a world distrustful and ashamed of the aristocratic and autocratic aspects of antiquity, and reassured and made at ease with the basic subsistence-economics of mankind at large. The whirligig of time brings in its revenges in other ways too in the history of archaeology, as the theoretical schemes of social evolution, the 'conjectural history' of the eighteenth-century British and French philosophers, are again finding a favoured place in thought about the past. To make a final quotation from Basil Willey, this time on John Locke, the influential philosopher (or archaeologist) must 'be in the position to supply his generation with precisely the doctrine most congenial to them'. We can only hope no future historian of archaeology will go on to say that any of us share, as Willey said of the men of the eighteenth-century Enlightenment, 'the sense of being at last in possession of the truth, which gladdened this enviable age'.

Index of names